SILENT VOYAGE

AUTHOR MARIA DE VILLIERS

ISBN 978-0-620-62832-7

Publisher: J. F de Villiers

Post Office, Morgan Bay, 5292, South Africa

Stillevaarder@yahoo.com

jfdevil37@gmail.com

mariacatharina.devilliers@gmail.com

https://www.facebook.com/IslandTimeSailientDeafSailing?fref=ts

Frontice Page: Charl de Villiers

Printers: Copy World: East London

CONTENTS

THE HALF-LIVED LIFE

From Moby Dick

For as this appalling ocean surrounds the verdant land, so in the soul of man there lies one insular Tahiti, full of peace and joy, but encompassed by all of the horrors of the half-lived life.

Herman Melville

While preparing for the SA Dart Sailing championships my brother, Gerrie, burst a brain aneurism and died five days later.

Early in January 2003, my family and I flew from Texas and for the first time in eleven years I set foot upon South African soil. In the midst of a violent lightning and thunder storm, that ominously stayed overhead, we drove the five hours from Johannesburg to the family farm Linton, in the far north of South Africa. In revisiting this place of joy and agony a dormant abscess inside my soul, which I had so carefully hidden from the prying eyes of the outside world, started festering afresh.

After all those years Gerrie's death brought me back to South Africa where the many unresolved issues, which I had thought were put behind me, painfully resurfaced: The suicide of my beloved mother, which is something one never gets over, and the unaccommodating country which I loved and hated simultaneously.

The next morning the tormenting guilt of being in Gerrie's presence, but only at his funeral, pained me immensely. When my father and my brothers and I carried Gerrie's casket to the freshly dug grave next to our mother's, the hurt became unbearable.

The day after the funeral I paid a brief visit to "Overvlakte" on the banks of the Limpopo, the place that I had once called "my farm". Visiting all the familiar sites was heart-breaking especially seeing that the beautiful piece of land where Gerrie and I had dreamt of becoming successful farmers had been developed into a fully operational citrus farm. But before taking leave, remembering Gerrie's and my childhood ambition to solo circumnavigate, I vowed that our sailing dream of days gone by wasn't also going to be ruined.

For so many years I had been cherishing the thought of a solo circumnavigation but sadly it kept fading away into the shadows of all my other responsibilities and, until then, it would probably have petered out into oblivion. But there, at Overvlakte, I had pledged that I was not going to live a half-lived life or die before at least attempting it. Gerrie's untimely death had reignited the passion that he and I had so keenly shared and I solemnly undertook that, in so doing, I will also pay tribute to him.

Departing from South Africa I had new hope and it included reuniting our splintered family and to finally heal myself from everything that had gone before.

Upon my return to Texas, I discussed the idea of a solo circumnavigation with my wife Beverly, daughter Sharleen and son, Gideon. There were huge family and financial implications but, after some serious debate, they gave me their full support.

However, when I started to discuss the possibilities of this mission with a wider circle of acquaintances, I was surprised to discover that certain people totally rejected it. Some even told me straight that they thought it would be irresponsible to attempt a solo circumnavigation. In fact, one of my critics even sent an email, warning that it would be outright hedonistic.

With all the conflicting views and the huge implications, self-doubts started to surface. To gain more information about the seas and to understand the objections being flung at me, I decided to do more thorough research. I reread all my sailing books as well as many others that I could lay my hands on, such as those written by Robin Knox-Johnson, Bernard Moitessier and Sir Francis Chichester. And I devoured every piece of sailing information on the internet.

As a child it was the movie "The Dove" that had initially fuelled my desire to sail solo around the world and, in researching the possibility of such a journey, I rewatched the video many times. Later, I continued to do an in-depth analysis of the book, paragraph by paragraph, almost like in Bible study.

I was still in two minds whether the trip was mission impossible when, during April 2003, I ruptured my right leg's hamstring, playing rugby in soggy conditions for the Victoria Rugby Club and got booked off from work.

At the time of Gerrie's funeral there hadn't been time to visit my dad's place in Morgan Bay, near the wild coast of South Africa, and I decided to utilise my sick leave to revisit South Africa and to solicit his views.

From the onset my dad encouraged me to pursue my dream and not be side-tracked by the numerous obstacles. In the evenings around the barbeque fire we seriously debated all the problems, other essential preparations and the possible routes.

Based on the non-stop circumnavigation of Sir Robin Knox-Johnson, my mind was set to "run the easting down": An expression for the fast passages achieved in the "Roaring Forties", which in turn is a term for the strong westerly winds found between the 40th to 49th degrees latitudes in the Southern Hemisphere. To speed up travel times, round-the-world racing sailors generally take advantage of this route. And, due to time and budget constraints, I was adamant to take the faster route around Cape Horn.

However, in spite of his initial enthusiasm, Dad had very strong views about the safety of this route. Needless to say, heated debates ensued. He maintained that the southerly route came packaged with dangerous storms, stirring up fifty-foot waves which could easily cause a sailboat to pitch-pole (trip forward, like in a summersault).

No matter how hard I had tried to convince Dad nothing, absolutely "nothing", could sway him and in the end he only gave his blessing on condition that I wouldn't take the "seemingly dangerous" southern route around Cape Horn: A decision I would later bitterly regret.

A SEA HORSE

Cherish your visions and your dreams as they are the children of your soul, the blueprints of your ultimate achievements.

Napoleon Hill

After a wholesome week of recuperation at Morgan Bay, a place that I fondly remember from my youth and where I had once lived for only a short while, I returned to America with my mind set to make the voyage happen.

However, there was just one tiny snag! I had a burning desire to solo circumnavigate but didn't have the right yacht to attempt it with. I started to search and kept my ear to the ground (pun intended). When I spotted a "For Sale" sign on a 1977, trashed-out Tartan 37, called Island Time (IT for short), docked right under my nose at the Serendipity Marina, I figured the gods must have smiled upon me.

And for a second time I experienced

"love at first sight"…

I started schooling at Kuilsriver Primary in January 1967. Neatly dressed in a uniform and blazer I was extremely chuffed with the prospect of at last joining the league of the educated.

Unlike the other weepy kids around me, I couldn't wait for Mom to leave. She probably sensed my excitement and hastily waved goodbye.

The teacher seated us, like they usually do when it's the first school day for grade one's and let us play with modelling clay. Suddenly Irma and Ingrid, twin sisters, sandwiched me and started to simultaneously kiss me, one on the left and the other on the right cheek. My heart made summersaults and I thoroughly enjoyed the innocent kissing.

But when the other children stared and giggled behind their hands, pointing at us, my cheeks started to burn, not only from the fervent kissing but also from the continuous blushing. However, the girls seemed to be spurred on by the childish giggles and enthusiastically advanced their kissing onslaught.

It became a bit much and I didn't know how to handle the situation, so I intensely stared at the teacher for help. Spotting my dilemma she, with the tip of her tongue in the corner of her mouth, winked at me and gave me a thumbs-up. She then instructed the girls to stop, which they reluctantly did but, when the teacher wasn't watching, followed it up right through the school day.

So, not only had my schooling commenced but I also experienced love at first sight and it was my first lesson in kissing girls. And with the twins, it was a double whammy! Afterwards we became good friends and just to feed their kissing frenzy, I often excitedly pedalled my bicycle all the way to their place and back.

We sadly lost touch. In later years, I briefly met Ingrid at Varsity but by that time both of us had our own lives to live and were no longer interested in the kissing games of yesteryear.

And similar to my first experience of love at first sight, I knew that I had fallen in love and prayed that IT wouldn't somehow slip through my fingers.

I had just read Sharon Ragle's book: "The Oceans are Waiting - Around the World on the Yacht Tigger", when I learned that they were docked at the marina. Sharon and Dave had completed a circumnavigation a few years earlier on their Tartan 37, the sister ship to Island Time. I was excited to meet the author and hoped to get their views about such a voyage, so I went round to introduce myself.

After the necessary platitudes I told them about my dream and the reason for wanting to do it. Later they came with me to check out IT's features and alerted me to some obvious flaws. However their opinion was unanimous and

I remember their words very well: "IT will be able to withstand a circumnavigation and surf the waves together with the dolphins".

Their comment was a huge encouragement and became almost a spiritual reassurance to me. At the time I was just a naïve bloke with a dream and didn't know that their prediction would literally come true.

After the initial negotiations with the seller, IT got hauled out and docked at Laddy Matusek's rustic boatyard. I got hold of a ship surveyor to inspect her and he discovered a number of glitches. There was a long list of required repairs but generally IT was only in need of some serious Tender Loving Care. I had already fallen in love with her and to me there was no problem with the caring part. In a huge leap of faith I took out a loan to buy Island Time and started to tackle the problems, one by one.

The weather had dictated that I should be ready for departure by early March 2004 but, no matter how hard I worked during my spare time, I soon realised that it would take a miracle to fix her on time. Thus, in August 2003, I exchanged my full-time job for a part-time one.

Being on a tight budget I used my newly acquired skills as a stainless steel and aluminium welder to overhaul all the metalwork. And my experience as a fitter cum fabricator stood me in good stead to fix whatever I could, which also saved a lot of money and limited costly outsourced repairs to the bare minimum.

I was already emotionally and financially heavily committed when, on the 9th of September 2003, I received the devastating news that my planned journey might be in serious jeopardy. There was an incident on the news about the U.S. Coast Guard that had banned Steve Turner, a fifty-two year old deaf sailor, from taking his boat out to sea because "he couldn't keep a hearing watch". As I read the subscripts on the TV, I could see my life's dream going up in flames. Nevertheless, Steve didn't accept the Coast Guard's ban and decided to take the matter to court.

I anxiously followed the lobbying around the case. With that dark cloud hanging over my dream, threatening to crush it, I nevertheless decided not to put my preparations on hold and continued with the repairs.

But, even working part-time, it was soon clear that there was no way that I would be able to complete the required list of repairs to be ready for a March departure. So I took yet another difficult decision and in a giant leap of faith I quit my part-time job to work full-time on IT.

When the court judgement finally came that the U.S. Coast Guard was ordered to jettison its longstanding policy that deaf boaters who operate without a hearing person on board are in violation of regulations, I smiled from ear to ear. Thanks to Steve Turner's perseverance my dream was rescued.

However, I did take note of the concerns raised by the U.S. Coast Guard and to compensate for my own deafness I acquired the necessary assistive devices.

Knowing that the Coast Guard could no longer stand in my way I slaved away to put my family's mind at ease that I would attempt my dream on a seaworthy vessel, fitted out with all the mandatory safety equipment.

In a self-congratulatory mood I mentally patted myself on the back that I was going to make it. However, just when I thought the coast was clear, another catastrophe showed its ugly face.

What the Coast Guard couldn't achieve, I almost did to myself! After their announcement I was confident enough to take IT out to sea but, not even a mile from the marina, I misjudged the shallow waters of Matagorda Bay and ran aground.

Back at the harbour a quick check revealed that the retractable centreboard (sitting in a pocket in the hull and could lengthen the depth of the keel, extremely valuable when going upwind) had been damaged beyond repair. It was not just a misfortune but a major disaster because there was simply no leeway in my budget to replace it with a new one. I was beside myself with anger and at no one but myself. I screamed, ranted and raved!

In a very miserable mood I dragged myself over to the Ragels to break the news: After all the effort and nail-biting months of awaiting the Coast Guard's decision, I would not be sailing. Sharon listened to my squealing and then patiently calmed me down.

With a mischievous grin she told me that six years earlier, after completing their circumnavigation, they had a similar mishap backing out of a slip at Kemah, a Gulf Coast sailing mecca, not far from Serendipity Marina. Their centreboard, identical to IT's, broke loose and fell into the thick mud of the marina. After that calamity they decided to fill the centreboard trunk and to simply sail without it. She offered to accompany me the next day to show me the exact spot where it had been buried and if I could salvage that centreboard, it was there for the taking.

On a cold-grey Texas morning, emulating my mood, we travelled to Kemah. I must admit to my mind they were overly optimistic and it was possibly a futile exercise: Never mind actually finding the centreboard but it was probably completely corroded. However I didn't want to be rude and turn down their kind offer, so I kept my reservations to myself.

We walked to the dock and Sharon pointed directly to the spot where it had fallen. With the long pole we have brought along, I probed the water. I stabbed the mud several times at the appointed spot but no luck and I was about to give up when I hit something hard. By poking around repeatedly, I determined the object could indeed be the centreboard stuck in about seven feet of water and another three of mud.

In that stinging cold dawn I put on my wetsuit, aqualung and diving mask. I tied a strong rope around my waist and strapped on weights to pull me down. I stepped off the dock and splashed into the muddy water, letting the cold seep under the wetsuit. I soon realised that in that thick, soupy water the diving mask was of no use, except to keep my eyes clean. I groped through the mud and felt around the object's shape. Sure enough, it was the centre-board. I found the shaft bushing and tied the rope around it.

After surfacing, I took off the diving gear and stood on the dock with my end of the line wrapped around my waist. I heaved and tugged like a Sumo wrestler until I felt the centre-board broke the suction of its muddy hibernation. We hauled the three hundred pounds of lead and fiberglass onto the pier. After hosing it down, my careful inspection revealed that it was unscathed.

Like a phoenix she had arose, not from ashes but from mud. I was extremely grateful that it had preserved itself for me and I jumped, laughed and practically danced a jig with Sharon and Dave. But at the time, I didn't know that the phoenix and I would still wrestle in the near future.

Thanks to the Ragles, I was back on track. In a strange way forces in the universe had combined for us to meet and I am forever grateful for their sound advice, pointing me in the right direction. They became not only my sailing mentors but also assisted, before and during the trip, with my emotional preparation.

In getting fit for my upcoming departure I climbed the mast, practicing the ascent and descent until I could qualify as a trapeze artist. But what I couldn't rehearse, or predict, was how my badly burned skin would react to the weather conditions and the salt water. It would only be during the journey that I would find that out.

Finally, by the middle of February 2004, the overhauling of IT was complete. My dad flew from South Africa to Texas, checking for himself that the boat was ready and that all was well. He also wrenched a few more assurances from me not to break any safety rules, as well as presenting me with a long list of do's and don'ts. During his visit, in twenty-five knot winds, we did a five-hour shake-down sail in Matagorda Bay. While I demonstrated to him that I was quite capable to manage IT on my own, a small pod of dolphins happily played around us.

Dad made sure that I was equipped to bridge any eventuality where my disability could hamper my performance and bought me a brand new laptop. He sat for hours trying to marry it to the satellite phone and eventually discovered that Outlook Express 7, pre-installed on the laptop, was incompatible with the satellite phone. We then paid a visit to Dixie Computers and, after listening to my plight, Mr Pearce donated two second hand and refurbished Dell laptops that had Outlook Express 6 pre-installed. Thanks to Mr Pearce my dad managed to get the computers and the satellite phone to talk to each other, which finally sorted out my communication deficit.

As the March deadline drew to a close, it was time for the surveyor's certificate of approval and he came around for a final inspection. When I showed him the numerous repairs and upgrades, he gave IT a clean bill of health. And in sailing lingo, he wished me "fair winds and a following sea."

The beast was transformed into a beauty. With all the hard work that she had required, and all those hours working to transform her, a special bond had developed between us. She had her own character and I no longer thought of her as just another yacht but as a kind of sea-horse with her own personality. She became my trusted sailing partner and, although I would later discover a more spiteful side, I totally adored her.

After six months, two months part-time and four months full-time, the groundwork was successfully completed. It was countdown and I had to wait one more week before I could depart.

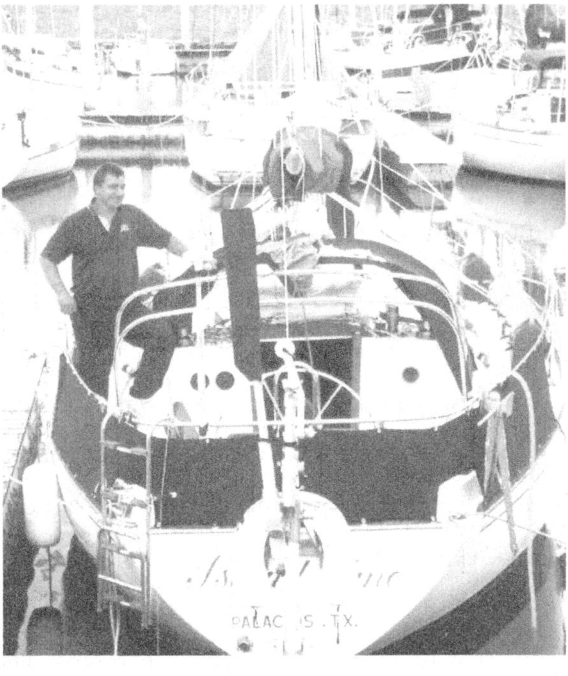

THE BURNING THING

Thought is the wind, knowledge the sail, and mankind the vessel.

Augustus Hare

In the build up towards my departure I had very little time to think about anything else but the preparations and repairs. However, you would be surprized how much one thinks when you live in a world that is totally soundless and painfully mute. In this solely, silent world one frequently finds that the only genuine torturing or comforting companions are your thoughts.

And during the week before my departure old memories of the painful events which had steered me to that point in my life, where I found myself to be a foreigner in a strange country, with only one burning thing left inside me, agonizingly resurfaced.

When the ship surveyor finally left, my dad went to town looking for a spare cable for the computer and I stayed behind, alone on IT. The forecast came through on the weather fax, predicting that during the next week the weather would be favourable and therefore, touch wood, my departure would be imminent.

The preceding weeks of worry had taken its toll and I was in a pensive mood. Although, for many years I had skilfully suppressed the story, it nevertheless mischievously sneaked back into my mind. Looking at the weather forecast I remembered what my dad had told me about another forecast but that one had been an

ominous prediction…

Our family, together with other families, had been invited to spend Easter with friends on the Island at the Great Brak River in the Western Cape Province of South Africa.

On the evening of the 12th of April 1968, also my late mother's 28th birthday, my dad had told me that I, seven years old, and the other kids were happily playing outside. Our hosts informed them that they had also invited an elderly neighbour for sun downers and she could predict the future. All you have to do was pour her a few double brandies but my father, being highly sceptical, just laughed and said that it was all bullshit.

When the "clairvoyant" ultimately arrived, she was duly fed a few strong ones, and after our hosts requested her to tell them something about their friends, pointing to my parents, she looked straight at my father, ignoring my mother and directly addressed him: "You have three boys!" But my father shook his head and quickly corrected her: "We have four boys, all of them playing outside". Then she paused, leaned towards him and almost whispered a question: "Is one of them badly burned or deaf?"

My father said that he became irritated because he could see that her question had upset my mother. So he took my mom's hand and again corrected the women: "No you are wrong!" He put his arm consolingly around my mother's shoulder and placing an emphasis on the "we", he said: "We, my wife and I, have four perfectly healthy boys!"

Dad said that the woman downed the rest of her brandy, got up, shook her head and without greeting anybody marched out of the house.

I suppose there are more things in heaven and earth of which we are unaware of. Or was it just a lucky guess? Her prediction was right: Nine months later I got badly burnt and subsequently became deaf. At the time she had not said anything about my mother but by ignoring her implied something and twenty-one years later my mother died. Thirty-four years later Gerrie passed away and that left my dad with three sons, one of them badly burnt and deaf.

And I realised that I would have to do some heavy weathering and it would be better to be in the weather than guessing whether the weather be fine or not.

My dad was not yet back from the shop and having unveiled the "prediction", I couldn't stop the memories of what had followed. At first I blocked out the total recall of the burning accident by focussing on a white light deep inside my head, but it slipped back or perhaps I allowed it and was ready for it. And it burst through my mind's door

with a bang…

We had just relocated from Kuilsriver to Durbanville and moved into a big house on a one hectare spread with lots of bushes, trees and an enormously picturesque garden. It was still school holiday and I, eight years old, invited some of my schoolmates for a Monday night sleepover. We camped out in our huge boy's dormitory which could easily sleep up to nine guys.

Early Tuesday morning, the 9th of January 1969 and a drizzly, unseasonable summer's morning in Cape Town, we were already playing a serious game of cowboys and crooks. We even got dressed like cowboys with hats, black western belts, gun holsters and cap-loaded toy guns. The day was filled with the happy sounds of nine carefree boys, their ages ranging between seven and eleven. But my two younger brothers, Francois and Christo, were not allowed to come close to us big boys. They were time and again, without the slightest sentimentality, chased away when trying to inquisitively peep into the action.

Bang! Bang! You're dead! Our game rules were equally serious: When somebody got "shot" he must spin around, collapse on the spot with both arms and legs spread-eagled, lie absolutely motionless on his stomach and play completely dead. Miraculously, on the count of thirty, one was allowed to leap up in the air and become fully alive again. But, after an hour and many times "dead", our energies were sapped and we became very hungry.

As if we were really camping out, Mom had specially bought us eighteen lamb chops to barbeque. Since most of us had already been "Voortrekkers", the Afrikaans version of Boy Scouts, we were very familiar with making campfires and the boys eagerly scattered around, collecting grass and twigs to neatly stack in a pyramidal shape onto the ground of our make-

believe battlefield. We lit the grass with matches but the fire quickly died down, seemingly the morning's drizzle had made it too soggy and wet to catch alight.

But the hunger pains were badly gnawing and one of my friends impatiently proposed that we should try some methylated spirits. I knew the stuff well: When entertaining guests at a fondue party my mom had poured it onto cotton wool and placed it in the burner under the pot. And Gerrie claimed that he knew where the bottle of spirits had been hidden.

Worried about our starving friends, the two of us wasted no time and sprinted towards the house. With our index fingers to our mouths, signalling silence to each other, we cautiously sneaked through the kitchen door and into the pantry. I effortlessly lifted Gerrie up so that he could grab the bottle of spirits, which had been hidden on the top shelf, out of sight and reach of inquisitive young children.

Once he got hold of the bottle, one of those thick one litre glass bottles three quarters filled with purple liquid (unbeknown to him or any of us to be highly flammable), I took it from him and tucked it tightly under my shirt. We again managed to tiptoe unnoticed out of the house and raced back to our friends. Mom, sitting in the lounge with Auntie Gwen, who had come over to welcome her new neighbours, was totally oblivious to our mischief.

Toni, my eleven year old cousin, also the eldest in the group, took the bottle from me and poured some of the liquid onto the twig pyramid, put it down and threw a match on the twigs. At last, with a swoosh sound the twigs caught fire. We hastily gathered some more twigs, stacked them onto the smouldering heap but after a few minutes the same thing happened, the flames died down, again.

Sensing the disappointment of the hungry group Toni again picked up the bottle and said: "I am going to pour on some more". As Toni emptied the bottle of spirits I backed off. Suddenly the flames shot back into the bottle and then out, launching a flame projectile and I was caught right in the middle of its firing line.

For a split second I saw it coming and my first instinct was using my right hand to protect my face. Like a napalm bomb a giant inferno engulfed me, sucking and squeezing precious air out of my lungs. Fortunately the bottle didn't explode! Toni with the bottle in his hand didn't even sustain a scratch.

Fleetingly with a thundering blast that joyful morning was transformed into my worst nightmare and completely altered the course of my life. The by-standing boys started to scream hysterically and, with their frantic cries echoing in my brain, I started to madly roll on the ground, but it didn't help to get rid of the flames. So, I jumped up and, in an effort to get away from the flames, feverishly ran around in circles to free myself from the sizzling infidel that was holding me in its fiery grip. At that point I was a ball of fire and being cooked alive.

My brave six year old cousin Deon, almost two years my junior, saw that the running around actually made things worse and, after a number of attempts, with sheer teeth grinding willpower he managed to tackle me down. He slapped at the flames and got them extinguished but, unfortunately, in this courageous attempt sustained some minor burns on his hands and forearms.

Getting up, I desperately tore at my smouldering clothes and watched in disbelief as my polyester shirt disintegrated. Looking down, I saw that my cotton rugby shorts were smoking and hastily pulled it down, tossing it aside. And then I saw that my polyester underpants had totally evaporated.

Gerrie, with a shocked face and hands over his ears, started to scream uncontrollably: "My brother, my brother, my brother!" I ordered him to shut up and to get Mom. He darted like a scared rabbit towards the house, but disobeyed my command, and in the distance I could still hear his hysterical screams, all the way to the house: "My brother, my brother, my brother…"

Completely naked and in shock, with Deon beside me, I slowly swaggered in the general direction of the house. There was absolutely no pain or at least at that stage, I didn't sense any. Swaying like a zombie, I saw Mom and when she saw me her face distorted with horror. She freaked out and cried: "My child, my child, my child, God please help me!"

In a state of sheer panic Mom ran to the house, grabbed a soft blanket, ran back to me, wrapped it caringly around me, picked me up like a baby and sprinted towards Auntie Gwen's powerful 3.5 litre Mercedes, which had been parked in our driveway.

In a pathetic heap, laying on the backseat with my head on Mom's lap, all I said repeatedly was that I was so deeply sorry. While Auntie Gwen sped her powerful Benz to the hospital Mom put up a brave face, told me in a gentle voice to hush and that everything was going to be alright.

Meanwhile Auntie Gwen ran red lights and stop signs, all the time honking and flashing the car's headlights. A cocky traffic cop on a motorcycle soon tried to pull her over but he had no chance. Through the open window she shouted on the top of her voice, gave him a finger and yelled about the emergency. Fortunately he got the message and with sirens on full blast, took off and cleared the road for us. It felt to me that at some places we were going at 100 miles per hour.

Eighteen minutes later, arriving at the Karl Bremer Hospital, Mom tenderly picked me up and ran for the emergency unit where the nurses quickly took over. They put me on a stretcher and wheeled me into a very dark hospital room which felt cold, extremely weird and, shivering like a leaf, an acute fear attacked me.

Everything felt unreal, as if in a movie, and I had to process so much information. In the distance I could hear Mom bitterly complaining that I was very cold but all of the nurses, with donned masks over their faces, ignored her flatly and just shook their heads. It was very confusing to me.

Before long a doctor marched in and, while pulling me up to inspect the extent of the burns, barked decisive orders to the masked-faced nurses. As the nurses scrambled away, their black polished shoes were making nasty, clattering and squeaking noises down the hallway.

The doctor was alone with me, sat down next to me on the bed, bowed his head as if in prayer, touching his forehead with his left hand and shook his head from side to side, all the time avoiding eye contact with me. I was suddenly painfully aware of strong emotions all around me and got very scared when he muttered in a coarse voice: "My son now you are in the hands of Jesus".

I had learned about Jesus in Sunday school and knew exactly what the doctor meant because they taught us that if you die and you weren't naughty you would go to Jesus in heaven, otherwise you go straight to the devil to burn in hell.

I was speechless and, no matter how hard I tried, I couldn't get a word out. With tears rolling down my cheeks, fearful and trembling, I bravely looked straight into the doctor's soulful brown eyes and nodded my understanding.

In that strange environment, I felt forsaken and continuously scanned the environment for my mom, yearning to see her gentle smile, to feel her loving touch, to hear her forgiving me and I hysterically cried out: "Mommy, Mommy, Mommy…"

I wanted to ask my mom to pray that Jesus should forgive me because I had already burnt, it was pure hell and didn't want to burn again, but the nurses refused to call her. I couldn't understand their reasoning. Instead they said that, due to the seriousness of my condition, any strain would further worsen it.

When the nurses eventually put a bow-like device over the trolley and covered it with a soft blanket, I actually felt a bit more comfortable but also completely abandoned and that worsened my mood. When they wheeled me into an elevator, as it was going up, the doctor's forewarning was still ringing in my ears and, closing my eyes, I silently prayed to Jesus for forgiveness and to spare me so that I wouldn't have to face another burning.

They put me into an isolation cubicle, nobody was allowed except doctors and nurses with masked faces, which utterly freaked me out. It felt like hours that I dozed on and off.

I must have passed out, I wasn't sure whether I was dead or alive but waking up, I saw my dad standing in the corridor with tears in his eyes, staring at me through the glass window, which separated us, and that gave me a sense that I was still on earth.

Perhaps I was dreaming but it felt as if my dad continuously reached out to me with brainpower and willing me on to fight. I was so tired with such a lot of guilt feelings that it was difficult for me to look back at him and I felt so ashamed but also desperately longed to be held in my parents' caring arms.

Mom, also with tears streaming down her face, and Auntie Gwen waved goodbye and headed home to tend to my three younger brothers and sleepover friends. Later I learned that the boys, in total shock and fear of what had happened in front of their eyes, were hiding in the bushes around the house. Although Mom and Auntie Gwen were equally traumatised, they eventually managed to calm the boys down and took them back to their respective parents' homes. Afterwards I heard that the father of one of the boys was so angry at his son that he beat the living daylights out of him and scarred him for life.

The burning scene had agonisingly replayed itself in my mind until it engraved itself deep into my psyche. The thoughts were more tormenting than the physical pain and I prayed that they must please stop. I repeatedly asked for forgiveness and that the agony caused by what had happened would forever disappear.

But it didn't…

At the time in the hospital, I had not realised that in the future this burning thing would still cause mountains of pain and angst for our entire family. Unfortunately there was no "How to" manual for dealing with the emotions and consequences brought about by such a disaster and life changing moment.

But the hope that this sailing trip could be my final reprieve made the hell that I had gone through bearable. And the memories of that day, which had irrevocably changed my life and gave me a totally different world and a very scary new space to live in, only increased my resolve to persevere.

Recalling the memory of the burning incident left me emotionally drained and, when Dad returned with the spare cable, I decided to take a break and we headed home.

At the time I knew very well that with no sailing experience, no skippers' certificates plus being profoundly deaf, my dream to sail solo around the world could instantly turn into a horrible nightmare. And that I could possibly face death once more.

That night I tossed around, eventually fell asleep and for the first time in many years a particularly bad recurring nightmare, which I first had during my stay in the hospital, revisited me. In the hospital it had felt very real and totally edged itself into every grain of my consciousness. And yet again

the same nightmare haunted me…

During my coma I was vaguely aware that my parents, the doctors and nurses had many conversations with me, urging me on to be brave and to hold on. But in that unconscious state, I had to face the grim reaper as a giant trying to subdue me and wanting to sacrifice me to the devil:

In absolute horror I observed from behind a tiny shrub how a giant was slaughtering a kid. Whilst splitting a skull in half the giant's axe swung down making a swishing sound, the kid's eyes popped out of their sockets and blood splashed out.

Still the axe didn't stop and, like a hot knife going through butter, it sliced right through the chest, the abdomen and awkwardly exiting the crotch. As the killer giant continued his slaughter, the body was still upright. But slowly each part fell sideways. And when the last bit, the half torso, fell to the ground it made a flopping sound with the intestines slithering out like writhing snakes.

Then the giant slowly turned his head into my direction and I had to gasp for air. He looked straight at me with blood-stained, mean eyes and I whispered: "OH FUCK! It's the giant from Jack and the Beanstalk. He just killed Jack and was going to kill me in a similar manner!"

*"**Fee, fi, fo, fum**" he roared and began to stroll into my direction. I wanted to run but my legs froze and I tried to scream at the top of my voice. No sound came out. The giant towered over me where I was squatting under a tiny shrub, grabbed me behind my neck and with his left hand, slowly lifted me from the ground.*

My fear became so intense that my bladder and bowels released itself. Grimacing he held my head in front of his face, forcing me to look into his evil saucer-like black eyes and gave me a spine chilling wink. The giant's breath stank like the nauseating smell of my own burnt flesh.

While my legs dangled helplessly in mid-air the giant roaringly laughed and his green, slimy spit flew all over my face. He was still covered with the blood of Jack, his previous victim, and repeatedly licked his lips and made smacking sounds. Then he insolently lowered me onto a felled tree log, the same one that he had used as a chopping block to cut Jack apart. With his huge left hand, he held me down and with his right hand, he took a saw from behind his back, placed it over my belly and started to saw…

I woke up screaming! The possibility of dying must have triggered the nightmare. And the idea that I could die during this odyssey made me to wonder whether I would have a second run in with death and what the grim reaper would look like the next time we would meet.

That morning, when Dad and I returned to IT, I actually felt sick. During the course of the morning the Ragels did their usual rounds and Dad told them that I was not feeling well, but not to worry because he was keeping a close watch on me.

Lip reading his words, I recalled how he had spent hours next to my hospital bed

keeping a vigil…

After the first horrible recurring nightmare in the hospital, I woke up with a scream and it felt as if I had been sleeping for ages. Coming round, I noticed that my dad was sleeping in a lounge chair beside my bed.

My screams woke him up, giving me one surprised look, he jumped up, ran down the corridor and I could hear him calling out to the nurses. When they returned with him, they were surprised that I had awoken from my coma. Later I was informed the Doctors had told my parents, that with eighty percent burns, I had less than five percent chance to survive. During those recurring nightmares, I fought for survival and, against all odds, conquered the grim reaper. But at that point, I had no idea what anguish was still laying ahead.

My dad continued his day and night vigil beside my bed and never even took a bath. His beard had grown and, at the mere age of thirty-one, he looked like a haggard old man.

I was shaken out of my memories, lip-reading that my dad was inviting the Ragels to join us for breakfast at the local eatery. Strolling there, I thought about the many occasions in my life that the odds had been stacked in my favour but the question that lingered in my mind was, in attempting this journey, whether the gamble would remain friendly and whether my preparations were sufficient to load the dice positively.

When we were seated the Ragels were still concerned for me but I told them that I was

a fighter…

The doctors soon realised that I was not prepared to die. A couple of days after I had surfaced from the coma, I was again wheeled on a stretcher down the passage and then into the elevator.

Remembering the previous time how petrified I had been, thinking that I was going to have to face the devil for the terrible sin which I had committed, being wheeled into the elevator made me very claustrophobic.

They wheeled me into a room where I waited for what felt like hours and then into another very cold room where they placed me on a hard table. The table reminded me of the tree log which the giant in my nightmare used as a chopping block and panic overwhelmed me.

A masked man came over and with gloved hands placed a rubber mask firmly over my face. When I smelled the stinking gas, it somehow reminded me of the breath of the monster who had tried to kill me.

Despite my weakened state and the excruciating pain, the doctor was about to find out exactly what kind of a fighter I was. And in one strong movement, I ripped the mask off my face, which totally pissed him off. More determined he tried again but I ripped it off again. I was going ballistic and yelled at the bastard who was trying to suffocate me with his stinking gas.

The doctor gestured to the nurses, they held me down and when he resolutely repositioned the mask over my face, I kicked and it felt as if I was fighting for my life again. And then I knew nothing…

Sitting opposite my dad and I, the Ragels listened attentively and simply asked: "Then what?" And I continued to tell them about the

transplants...

Coming round after the first operation I carefully inspected my surroundings. I looked like a mummy with all the greased wads of gauze bandaged all over my charred body.

Beside my bed was an iron stand with a T-junction that held two look-alike steel coat hangers at its top from which two large plastic bags filled with clear liquid hung. A small plastic hose dangled down from them, connecting the liquid filled bags to a large needle that had been stabbed into the back of my left hand.

After two weeks the nurses took off the bandages and it was so painful that my screams of agony reverberated throughout the hospital corridors. I cried for my dad to come to my rescue but he had been barred from getting into the room. Dad couldn't take my cries any longer and, shielding his ears with both his hands trying to block it out, ran out of the hospital.

After the first transplant experience, I begged my parents not to allow any further operations but they had no choice, no-one can survive without skin.

Sharon offered some wisdom that I should prepare myself because there would be many occasions during the trip when one would have to fight for survival. Since I'd never even sailed offshore before this journey, I would need to realize that crossing oceans would be very hard work. When land would be left behind, I would have to keep the ship safe otherwise face disaster. The ocean, like the hospital, could be a harsh place and perhaps even tougher.

The Ragels excused themselves and when Dad and I strolled back to IT, Sharon's words of wisdom repeated itself in my mind.

During the course of that day, still on IT fixing this and fine tuning that, I was very quiet and a few times Dad slowly enquired in Afrikaans, careful to form his lips around the words so that I could read his question: "Wat is verkeerd?" (What is wrong?)

In opening the door to my memories, the self-feeding and incessant inner dialogue continued. I went to the toilet for a wee and looked at my penis

without a foreskin…

After the first traumatic transplant operation, coming round, I felt some pain around my private parts. I peeped under the sheets, saw a plastic tube had been inserted into my pee-hole, connected to a plastic bag, hanging beside my bed. I thought that was what was causing the pain. However, I consoled myself that they probably did it to help me, so that I could pee without having to get up.

On closer inspection, I was horrified to see that the goddamn doctors had cut off my penis. I couldn't believe that my mom allowed them to cut off my family jewels (as she called it). I was not prepared for it and had no idea why they did it. And I became extremely embarrassed.

It was only later at visiting hours, after crying my heart out, that my dad told me that they hadn't cut off my penis, I didn't lose my boyhood, only my foreskin which had been charred and that a circumcision was necessary to relief the contracture which had restricted my urinary flow.

But my mood lifted a little and I giggled because much later I found that there were some advantages packaged together with this burning thing and that "foreskin-less-ness" is nothing to be ashamed of. In fact my manhood looked better and also easier to keep clean. And still more years later I found that it gave me lots of pleasure when having sex.

Peeping back into the cabin I smiled and assured my dad that everything was fine. He looked a bit startled at the sudden change in my mood. Nevertheless, he just nodded. While Dad took a cat nap on the aft berth, I continued to sort out the cupboards, neatly arranging all the groceries and attended to my first aid kit.

When I stacked a pack of gloves away, a shiver went down my spine. I knew that to prevent rope burns it would be necessary for me to handle the sheets with gloves but, emanating from way back in the hospital, I have a huge

glove phobia…

Every morning there were fresh latex gloves and masks neatly stacked on a trolley. Each time a nurse would enter my isolation cubicle, a sterility ritual was followed of washing hands, putting on a mask and a fresh pair of gloves.

Before exiting, the same ceremony would ensue but in reverse: Taking off the gloves, throwing them into the dustbin, taking off the mask and washing hands. Eventually, I was so au fait with the drill that I could tell them when they had missed a step.

At the time, as an eight year old boy, I couldn't comprehend it and it made me feel really dirty. Later, I understood that it was part of the infection prevention routine but the cold, powdery feeling of the latex on my transplanted skin was very irritating.

By the end of the day, the dustbin under the basin would overflow with blood stained gloves and I would flinch at the sight of all the yucky stuff that had oozed from my burnt flesh.

As I packed the gloves into the compartment, I wondered how I would deal with them and, at that stage, I didn't realise how many times my glove phobia would become a nuisance.

It was time to head home and with my dad beside me, I jumped with my naked torso onto the quay. A stranger on the pier was watching me. And suddenly a funny memory flashed onto my internal monitor. And I hoped for the sake of the stranger

that Dad hadn't notice him

gawking…

Several times a stranger walked past my hospital room, tapped on the glass and gawked at me through the window. He gave me an awfully long disgusting stare and made the mistake to inquire from my dad, who was waiting in the corridor for the nurses to finish dressing my wounds, what had happened.

I recalled very clearly my dad's right arm shooting out and giving the stranger a straight Muhammad Ali punch, right on the nose. The stranger instantly hit the floor and in a whining heap the nurses picked him up, loaded him onto a hospital stretcher and quickly carried him away.

While I was in hospital no one, I promise you on my word of honour, absolutely nobody ever-ever gawked at me again or interfered with my Dad, not even the cops or the security guys. From then onwards, his reputation ran ahead of him. The head nurse and even the doctor kept a good safe distance and never questioned him.

However, it was impossible for my dad to forever protect me and handling gawking strangers became one of the things that I had to learn to cope with.

By now I have become so used to gazing eyes that I no longer even fear to take off my shirt. In fact, I have become quite blasé about it! But to be totally honest with you, it still hurts. And I remembered the shock of the first time I had to look at my own

scarred naked torso...

The doctors struggled to cover my torso with skin grafts taken from my lower legs, because there had simply not been enough healthy skin left. After each painful harvesting, the remaining skin had to first fully recover before they could repeat the process and it was only after the fifth major operation that I was fully covered with skin.

These transplants were very traumatic but I suffered it with the expectation that it would make me look better. But more painful than anything else I had to endure, was when I looked down at the final product on my torso. I felt it belonged to a stranger: A torso covered with a skin blanket, stitched together by a mean tempered and spiteful seamstress, who melted the pieces together with hot skin wax that had formed creases and crinkles. I was extremely disappointed and horrified, realising that I would have to carry this ugly torso around for the rest of my life.

Bumping my toe on the pier pulled me back to reality and with the realisation that things might not always turn out the way I expected it, I bumped back to reality.

The next day my dad offered to buy me some DVD's which I could watch on the laptop when I would get bored during the trip. Driving to the shop, an intense feeling of déjà vu enveloped me. I recalled the many times he had come up with

a few clever ideas…

After the final transplant the recovery process was painfully slow and although Dad and Mom read me stories and I listened to the radio (I could still hear), I was soon getting bored to tears but Dad came up with a few clever ideas:

He replaced the panel of the eating trolley, which rolls over the hospital bed, with a clear glass panel so that I could use my healthy hand to play dominoes and solitaire, upside down lying on my back.

Later he installed a mirror at the window and set it in such a position that I could see down into the parking lot, five stories below and when my parents left, after visiting hours, before disappearing in their car, I could see them waving at me.

Our 8 mm projector was positioned to reflect images onto my hospital room's ceiling by means of a mirror which had been strategically placed at a forty-five degree angle. In those days the only movies available for renting was 8 mm silent ones and I watched Charlie Chaplin; The Keystone cops; Laurel and Hardy; The Three Stooges; Woody Woodpecker; and so many other cartoons.

All these plans made it possible for me to overcome boredom for parts of the day and, once out of isolation, I was soon joined by some of the other sick kids who wanted part of the action in the makeshift movie house. My hospital room became quite popular.

My life in the hospital became tolerable and those gadgets and silent movies also helped me to laugh and stop the ceaseless rehashing of the burning accident. And eased the pain of my own guilt and my sorrow and my regret.

Since then I am a movie addict. My dad's idea with the well-stocked library of DVD's to counter boredom was a good one but, as I would later learn, DVD's loaded on a laptop on a constantly moving ocean surface would not always be compatible. What really countered my boredom would be the many books in my well-stocked library. It also helped me to catch up on reading, something which I had regrettably neglected during the preceding years.

I went back to IT and left Dad at home to watch some of the movies on the DVD's that we had bought. I was actually relieved to be alone, withdrawing into my own world on IT because having him around all the time was getting a bit much for me.

It brought back too many painful memories and sitting inside IT, I recalled how he had great difficulty in accepting my

hearing loss…

After my recuperation I had to make peace with a distorted self-image and the fact that the cute kisses and stares from little girls, admiring a charming boy were left behind in the ashes of that fire. And then, a second loss found its way into my life.

Two weeks before my discharge from hospital, Dad bought a school book of poems, translated into Afrikaans, so that I could practice my reading and not fall too far behind my peers. He read the translated poem, by Andrew Blakemore, out loud to me "When swallows grace the morning sky".

When swallows grace the morning sky

Of summer's deepest blue,

As through the air they deftly fly

I'll always think of you.

After each line he requested me to repeat the words. But when I couldn't pronounce the "es" in the word "swallow", he got seriously worried.

He made an appointment with the audiologist who confirmed that I had some hearing loss but in spite of this the audiologist assured us, that it was nothing serious and only a partial loss of hearing.

On the day of my discharge my senses were heightened and after so many months in the hospital, emerging in a wheelchair, the sun dazzled my eyes. I continuously blinked and shielded them.

One week after my discharge, I really struggled to hear and got progressively nervous because I had tremendous difficulty in following conversations which made me feel really stupid. At first I got paranoid and thought that my family was playing a prank on me by whispering all the time. Then it happened almost overnight and a great cloud of silence enveloped me.

As the days progressed, it was confirmed that I had become profoundly deaf. During the months of hospitalisation massive infections had to be countered by the strongest anti-biotic available. The nurses had emptied numerous tubes onto my burnt flesh but, unbeknown to us, it came packaged with a dreadful side-effect. It destroyed the fine hairs or cilia which picked up sound in both the cochleae of my inner ears.

I totally withdrew into my own world, became depressed and refused to join the family in the living room.

I could sense that my parents were blaming each other and the tension in the house had become unbearable. The shock of my burning accident had been one thing but then, discovering that I was deaf too was very traumatic for us. We were ill-equipped to deal with the situation but my father's reaction to my deafness was the most severe. Even though we were just boys fooling around, he blamed himself and my mother.

One afternoon, after work, my dad strolled into the lounge where he found my brothers playing records and I was silently sitting in the corner playing cards on my own. He got so furious that he ordered my brothers to turn off the music, saying that if Charl couldn't hear music, then nobody in our family would be allowed to listen to it. For more than a year, until he made peace with my disability, music was banned from our house.

I realised that he wanted a hearing world so badly for me that he was prepared to take it away from his own family. It was a nerve wrecking time and I felt so guilty for causing such distress in my family.

In my heart, I knew that he meant well but in truth it had hurt my brothers and mother and caused loads of guilt for me.

But there was no cut out and keep guidebook that could be plucked from a Reader's Digest on how to "digest" this kind of crisis.

So the struggle to reclaim my life had begun, to know what is and isn't mine. And it was my earnest desire that this crusade, this journey of discovery, would lift the curse from our family and be the end of that battle.

But when a number of my yachting friends from the Serendipity Marina came to fetch me for a bon voyage party which they were hosting in my honour at the yacht club, my guilt trip got diverted.

They were all seasoned sailors and entertained me with all kinds of myths such as cooking up a storm at sea and being extra careful on the date of the 13th. Apparently another taboo was sailing in or out of a harbour on a Friday and they gave me an extensive account of their experiences and why one shouldn't anger the sea gods.

Later, when Beverly and my dad joined us at the yacht club, the music was already vibrating on my skin. Fortunately, under those noisy conditions, I had the edge, can lip-read and they could scarcely hear each other.

The time for my departure was closing in on me, so early the next morning I was back on IT and attended to the business of making sure that everything was in order. I made a few double checks: Check sails, hull, radar, wind pilot, food, spares, water, computers and every other bloody thing. The whole lot was in order and I relaxed slightly.

The local newspaper had started to run stories which were written by Sharon, who was also a freelance journalist and she brought over "Tell-tales", a yachting magazine, which carried the story of my imminent trip. After she left, while sitting in the cabin in a habit of stroking my bare scarred chest with my right hand in anti-clockwise circling movements, I read the article.

Fingering the front page I thought back to the first time that I had made headlines…

About a month after my discharge a journalist from the daily newspaper "Die Burger" came to our house to do a story about my miraculous survival, the subsequent rehabilitation, the physiotherapy and the whole painful process of relearning to walk.

My mother did the talking and I was very self-conscious. The next day Mom proudly brought the paper to me and encouraged me to read it. I was shocked to see my picture on the front page because I looked like a badly burned skeleton with skin patched onto it.

Regardless of the shock effect of the picture, the article did carry a positive message, a lesson to parents and their children about the dangers of fire.

And the Burger article had actually planted the first seeds for me to try harder and to turn the tragedy into a meaningful experience, from which others could learn. Since that day, I had made a point of reading the newspaper and later developed a passion for newspaper delivery.

The Tell-Tale's article, similar to the article in "Die Burger" years previously, had the same effect on me and I knew then that I have a huge responsibility in fulfilling my goal, not only for myself but also for all those people who had offered their support.

The news about my planned journey had spread like a veldt fire in the local community, visitors started to flock to IT and wanted to know more about the voyage.

When yet another visitor unexpectedly showed up at IT, wanting to know more about me rather than the upcoming voyage, the elderly lady kept avoiding eye contact with me. It pained me and I remembered how Mom and Dad had helped our visitors, family and friends, not to avoid looking at me but to rather face

the sight of my badly burned body…

Slowly I relearnt to walk and rebuilt my muscle strength. My parents kept a close guard and to protect the delicate transplanted skin, any attempt from my side to play-wrestle with my brothers, like I had done before the accident, was immediately nipped in the bud.

But my energy levels started to soar and I was getting really depressed being deaf, not yet able to lip-read, feeling self-conscious about my scarred body and the worst was not being allowed to play with my brothers.

Nonetheless, as time went by, my parents realised that they couldn't keep me wrapped in cotton wool forever and, by trial and error, they slowly learned how to deal with what I could and couldn't handle. And one of the things that I couldn't stomach was visitors averting their eyes, whenever I returned their sneaking glances.

My parents used shock therapy. After the normal platitudes they would call me to greet the visitors and requested that I pull up my shirt to show my badly scarred torso.

Once the visitors had it in their face and saw that I was able to cope with them looking at me, their avoiding tactics dissipated. They treated me as "normal" and at the same time it also toughened me for the ensuing years of inevitable gawking.

Over the years, the pain of being stared at faded away in the shadows of all the other issues that I had to face but decades later on IT, watching the visitor walk away, I gazed out over Matagorda Bay and my old scars started to itch.

But I was grateful for reaching a point in my life where I had time to reflect on my convoluted life. The cards that life had dealt me dictated that I should take the road less travelled and that road took many turns before bringing me back to my sailing mission.

I hurried back home because that evening I had to go to church. Our Pastor had arranged a special service to beseech God's blessing on my endeavours and to pray for my safe return.

I knew the congregation meant well but during the service, with everybody laying their hands on my shoulders, touching me while they sang hymns and prayed, a terrible flashback entered my mind of

prayers not being answered…

After the article in "Die Burger" well-meaning friends and relatives came to our house to offer all kinds of advice for getting my hearing restored.

A distant family member had convinced Mom that, if only I have enough faith and believed strongly, there was a pastor who could bring back my hearing through prayer. I remember Dad and Mom had a huge fight over this but my mom pleaded with him not to stand in my way, to give me the chance and in the end he reluctantly agreed.

I, nine years old, enthusiastically accompanied the relative and his wife to a huge packed hall where disabled and sick people were standing in a queue, waiting to be led to the stage where a man with a long beard, dressed in a black robe, waved his arms in the air.

It was very confusing to me! I had not as yet acquired lip-reading ability and I desperately tried to understand what he was saying. Nevertheless, while he thumped the Bible, I gathered that he was doing some serious praying.

I had such high hopes and when it was my turn, I self-consciously got ready and, having just relearned to walk, painfully stumbled up the stairs towards the stage.

While his deacons put their hands on my shoulders, the Pastor laid his cold and healing hands on my head. Afterwards, my relatives wrote me a note saying that the congregation joined in singing hymns and praised the Lord for the miraculous healings that had taken place.

I had such an urgent need to be forgiven by Jesus and silently made a deal with Him that I didn't mind the scarred body but please, if He gave me back my hearing, I would never be naughty again.

After the service I was elated and upon my return home assured my parents that I was indeed about to be healed.

But, as the days progressed, reality dawned upon me: My hearing wasn't going to return. I felt even guiltier than before because perhaps I hadn't believed strongly enough. I drifted into a black depression and it took me months to again adjust to the fact that I was permanently, profoundly deaf and to get on with my life.

I didn't know whether this time round Jesus would heed to our Pastor's call for my safety and had also prayed that He would. What I did know was that it was going to take a lot of hard work from my side and I felt fully prepared to shoulder the challenge.

We all went to bed early because I had to take my dad to Houston, to take a flight back to South Africa. He couldn't stay for my departure. At the airport we hugged, saying our goodbyes and were both tearful.

Before he walked off to the departure hall, my last request to him was in the event that something would happen to me, he should take care of my wife and the kids.

WATER, WATER EVERYWHERE

FACE THE STORM AND DEFY IT

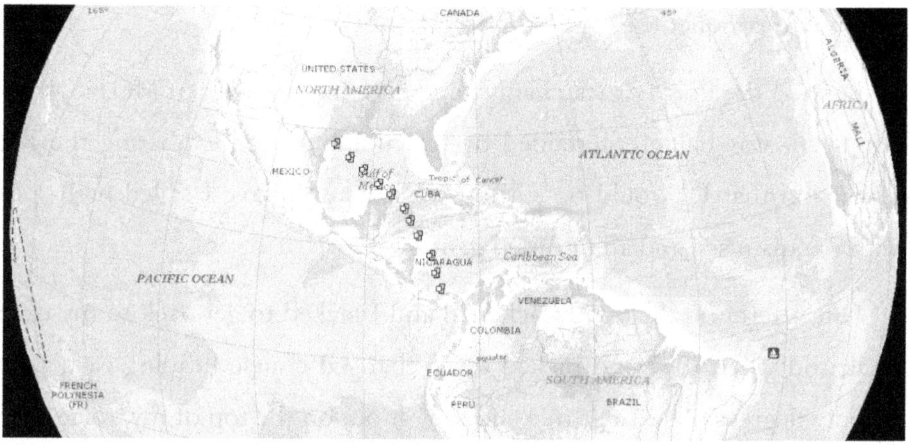

It is only in sorrow that bad weather masters us; in joy we face the storm and defy it.

Amelia Barr

When swallows grace the morning sky

On the 6th of March 2004, at seven in the morning with virtually no open sea experience, I left the safety of the familiar Serendipity Marina in Palacios, Texas to tackle the unknown. It was both exciting and unbelievably terrifying.

Waving to the small crowd of well-wishers on the pier, I set sail in memory of my beloved late mother and brother and dedicated the journey to my family and all the deaf people around the world to prove that, regardless of our silent world, we can make a loud difference.

I undertook to cast all my demons into the sea and, more than anything else, to find solace for my lacerated soul.

I sailed straight for Bird Island where Randy and his son Cory, both taught by me how to sail, eagerly awaited on their yacht "Clueless Waters" to wish me "Bon Voyage". I was so proud of my sea cadets who had since become hardened and seasoned sailors. Under their escort I motored for nine miles and, when the wind picked up, I sailed at six knots, waved ahoy and was on my own to conquer the mysterious world of the sea.

Leaving the Port Lavaca channel and entering the Gulf of Mexico, the first good sign was being entertained by two dolphins. Remembering the Ragels prediction that IT would be surfing with the dolphins, I sailed high-spirited with the main sail and an unfurled genoa.

Late afternoon the wind slackened and I tacked to get back to my original track and when the wind picked up, I changed course heading east, bearing seventy degrees. And I felt free shouting it out on the top of my voice.

A greyish bird with its white beak and prying eyes landed on IT and balanced itself on the lifelines around the cockpit. The bird made me feel in a real sailor's mood and reminded me of Gavin Sutherland's song which I had memorised as if it was a poem: "I am sailing".

Being deaf I don't know the melody but I was sailing, sailing like in the lyrics:

"home again 'cross the sea.
I am sailing stormy waters
to be near you to be **free**.
I am flying
I am flying like a **bird** 'cross the sky
I am flying passing high clouds to be with you to be free.
Can you hear me
can you hear me thro' the dark night far away.
I am dying forever trying to be with you who can say.
Oh Lord to be near you to be free"

Due to the excitement I couldn't sleep and sat the whole night watching the bird. While I was telling this experienced flyer about my hopes and fears, it listened intently. I shared the anticipation which I had felt in the built up towards my departure and the many nights I had spent worrying about the fury that the sea could unleash upon those who didn't respect it.

The bird's presence throughout my first dark night alone at sea was a blessing but perhaps I scared it off with all my stories because the next morning it suddenly took flight across the sea. I waved until I could no longer see it and prayed, flying away to be **free** and passing high clouds, it would carry the message of my journey on its wings far across the stormy waters.

Snapping out from under the spell of the bird, I got busy studying my self-steering equipment or autopilots. My three units would enable me to rest or work without me actively steering.

There were two electronic steering devices that would cause the main rudder to move according to a pre-set course: A twelve-volt wheel autopilot for fairly calm weather, which I named Andy, after my Aunt. And a twelve-volt tiller autopilot for use in light winds, or under power, which I called Tilly.

However, the third one, which I baptised Willy, was the real kingpin, designed for use in heavy weather: A mechanical wind-steering device with no electrical power, only the wind, and a real advantage for long passages. With its wind-vane and substantial rudder system bolted to the stern, it could be set at a constant angle to the wind. However, on the down side, with the wind-steering method, if the wind would shift, IT could go off course because Willy would follow the wind, whatever the direction.

From the on-set these three developed their own unique personalities and became like shipmates to me and IT. It turned out that, similar to other shipmate stories, Andy, Tilly and Willy weren't as trustworthy as I had hoped them to be. On March the 7th the first reality check knocked on my door.

Andy, the lightweight, was in charge but without continually correcting it manually, it didn't maintain our chosen course. To give me the opportunity to check Andy's problem, I locked the main rudder into position and aligned the sails, so that IT could steer herself for a time.

I opened Andy, found the autopilot belt was broken, and presto, it took me exactly nine minutes to stitch up the damaged belt. But soon the belt broke again, and hugely disappointed, I flung the bloody thing aside to deal with it later. This was only my second day out and it was already broken!

When the seas became rougher, I double-reefed the mainsail, put up the staysail and let Willy take charge of the steering work and our direction. Because the wind was up, it steered like an experienced helmsman, so I relaxed behind the laptop. Old Willy bravely slaved away to keep us on a constant angle to the wind, behaving just like a puppet. And, each time the wind shifted, Willy, willy-nilly, strung us along into the new direction.

Instead of relaxing I became exhausted from frequently having to correct Willy's settings. Nevertheless, on the tune of the rough seas, IT was performing like a real rock and roll dancer.

Things slightly relaxed and staring over the vast ocean, I was embraced by a lyrical mood, recalling the 1798 poem by Samuel Taylor Coleridge "The Ancient Mariner". I mumbled under my breath: "Water, water, everywhere, Nor any drop to drink!" But then shouted: "That prophecy is not going to work on me" and I immediately poured a glass of water down my throat.

In the certain knowledge that I had more than enough drinking water, I forced myself to refocus on the task at hand but the more I tried the less I succeeded. And I remained with a nagging feeling and hoped that, having remembered the line in "The Ancient Mariner", it wouldn't come back to haunt me.

If only I knew then that the water issue would become a curse and the words prophetic. With the wisdom of hindsight I wished that, at the time as far as drinking water was concerned, I had been better prepared for what was to follow.

Throughout the day the sea myths, which my yachting friends had told me about, haunted me. The wind had diminished, and with not enough wind to do proper sailing, the story about cooking at sea to stir up the wind particularly intrigued me. I decided to test the myth by cooking up a meal on the alcohol stove. And voila! I had my first cooked meal – rice, covered with delicious brown onion gravy, plus canned bacon.

But, when the wind died down completely, I was still three hundred nautical miles from the Northern Shelves in the Gulf of Mexico, my first waypoint, and I was not overly surprised that the storm cooking didn't work. In fact it confirmed that all those myths were absolute nonsense. So, I took a rest in the cockpit, folded my arms and pensively watched the flapping and flopping of the sails.

After endlessly staring at the open sea, being miles from everything, my mind started to drift and drove me crazy. Excuse my French but I was cursing the damn wind for staying down, using a number of elaborate swearwords and profanities.

As my irritation started to boil over, I actually felt a burning sensation in the pit of my stomach and tried to calm myself down by contemplating whether my impatience had anything to do with

my French origins…

Whenever we visited my grandmother, Ouma Agnes at her house in Komgha, I would admire her neatly embroidered de Villiers family crest where it hung on the wall in the lounge. She would proudly take it upon herself to lecture me about my French connection and that the de Villiers clan was bound by a strong sense of pride in their "aristocratic" heritage.

Pointing at the crest, she would explain the symbolism. The shield features the pastoral lamb bearing the Crusaders' symbol, a pennant with a red cross on a white background. At the helm a plumed knight's helmet and a raised armoured arm bears the sword of right-eousness to proclaim his knighthood.

To her mind the crest had confirmed our earlier membership of the Order of the Knights Templar and the Crusades on which our ancestors had embarked upon a thousand years earlier, thus setting our family on a religious path.

However, she could never give me a straight answer whether the Crusades had been suc-cessful or not but repeatedly assured me that from around that time the de Villiers clan had become successful landlords and over the centuries expert wine makers.

She told me that the Templars had questioned the Roman Catholic's interpretation of the Bible, later they were harshly persecuted, and many ended up on the guillotine paying the prize with their lives. The surviving Templars continued their underground rebellion against the Roman religion and still later, as protesting Protestants, had joined the Huguenots.

Apparently in 1686 four de Villiers brothers had relinquished their wine estates in the Bourgogne and Champagne regions of France, which had been in our family for centuries, to flee before the King's troops. They managed to side-step the guillotine, abandoned their homes and their country but had managed to retain their Protestant faith. The youngest, longing overmuch for his parents and his home, turned back and grandma said that we had lost him from our family register.

The remaining three, urged on by their passionate faith, persevered and proceeded with "joie de vivre". And emboldened by their lust for life, they opted for the Cape of Good Hope where they had successfully re-established their faith and their vineyards on three allotted farms: La Brie, Bourgogne and Champagne. She assured me that over time our family through intermarriage had lost their French language but not their impatience.

And at that point I had no doubt that I was a bloody fool attempting an impossible mission. It just goes to show that blood is thicker than water and I conveniently put the blame squarely onto the shoulders of my father's French side of the family, being renowned for their restless nature.

Anyway, there I was swearing at the elements to change their attitude and impatiently complaining about a perfectly windless day alone in a boat on the vast blue ocean. As another day passed with the wind remaining apathetic, I was between a rock and a hard place. My lifelong duel with the French impatience gene intensified and continued to plague me.

While I scooped up some salt water to wash my sneakers and to scrub the cockpit in dead calm wind, I sarcastically pondered that at that rate I would become the first deaf person, not to sail, but to drift around the world.

Waking up on the fourth day out at sea, I immediately sensed that something was seriously wrong. Staring at the GPS I screamed: "Holy-moly"! During the night, as the wind turned, Willy had just followed it and we were sailing straight back to Texas.

Suddenly force six winds hit me like a sledge hammer. I rapidly furled up the genoa, sprinted to the mast to double-reef the main and in my haste broke four mainsail tracks. I tried to console myself that they had been old and cursed for not having replaced them before leaving Texas.

I was glad that I had, before the start of the journey, devoured Chichester's books and came to appreciate the value of his information because in my first storm at sea it had become my most important tool to survive.

I tied up the reef cringles to the boom and re-hoisted the reefed main to fly in twenty-two miles per hour wind, very close-hauled and going zigzag. Poor old Willy was struggling, he constantly battled to keep on course, at times taking a strange turn.

When the storm had passed I sat back thinking about

struggling to stay on course…

When I became profoundly deaf, I already had a good vocabulary and speaking ability. Contrary to all other advice my ear, nose and throat specialist recommended that the smattering of residual hearing should be preserved. And that I should rather attend a school for partial hearing and not for profoundly deaf people.

It was quite a struggle to convince the authorities but eventually my parents succeeded to get me enrolled at The Mary Kihn School, for the Hard of Hearing in Observatory Cape Town, where my quest to reclaim my life and to master lip-reading commenced.

Walking into Mary Kihn, I felt very lonely. The whole school had less than fifty pupils, ranging from six to twelve years of age. There were only ten pupils in my class, a combination of first grades through to third grades, all bundled together into a single classroom.

Compared to what I had been used to, coming from a school with over six hundred pupils and having lots of playmates, Mary Kihn came as a big shock and I really struggled to keep on course.

Ms Groenewald, my teacher, took me under her wing and tried her utmost to smooth the transition from a big to a small school but that was not the main issue that bothered me. I had already passed grade two and what I found particularly annoying was that the plaque outside my classroom door read "Kindergarten".

During the months that I had been bedridden both my armpits and my chin grew onto my body and the contractures restricted my movement. Shortly after I joined Mary Kihn, I had to go back to the hospital three more times for further surgery to sever the contractures. As a result of my intermittent returning to hospital, I struggled with the school work and the next year repeated grade three. Fortunately, I took extra classes and managed to skip grade four and went straight onto grade five.

What kept me on course all the time was having my mother by my side, helping to steer me in the right direction. She actively got involved with Mary Kihn through the Parent's

Teacher's Association, baked cakes and held sales to augment the school's funds. And later they even managed to buy a sixteen seat bus to take us on outings to Parliament, Table Mountain and many other places.

Mom's endeavours made things slightly easier but Mary Kihn remained a struggle for me.

To help Willy with his struggle, I turned the main rudder a little to the starboard side, locked it to give him breathing space and it resulted in the sails being set much straighter.

My hands had rope burns from continuously handling the sheets and started to bleed. Even though I have a glove phobia, I resolved to at least in stormy weather handle things with gloves. So to prevent blood from smearing all over the place, I reluctantly put latex gloves on my bloody hands and, shivering from feeling the powder on them, I examined Tiggers' old charts of the Gulf of Mexico which the Ragels had lent me.

I plotted every six hours and observed that twice I had crossed Tiggers' path of December 1993, eleven years earlier. And I wondered whether Dave and Sharon would have noticed it on my Web-site.

I passed over the Northern Shelves at a depth of eighty feet and spotted a small fishing boat at anchor. I passed it within a quarter of a mile. Apart from minor hiccups, I was chuffed for safely reaching my first waypoint and my confidence was soaring.

I was closing in on the Yucatán Channel which connects the Gulf of Mexico and the Caribbean Sea between Mexico and Cuba. Close to the coast I became nervous and, due to the leeward sailing, I plotted every hour. Annoyingly the wind just didn't stop changing, so I kept sailing tight and close-hauled.

In the wee hours I spotted something on the radar and, under the cover of darkness with no deck lights to avoid detection, they slowly sneaked up on IT. I flashed my bright spotlight on them and they abruptly turned away.

Who they were, I will never know. Perhaps they were pirates of the Caribbean because the way they behaved left no doubt that they had no friendly "drop in and have a cup of tea" intentions. It placed me on high alert that modern day ship piracy is alive and well and, especially in the Caribbean, it is one of the dangers to guard against.

Finally, I couldn't take it anymore! The hard bumping, wild rocking and unforced tacks were taking their toll and, to quiet things down, I did the tried and tested old sailor's thing of a "hove-to", being equal to leaving a parked vehicle to idle on the verge of a road.

As IT's forward progress slowed down, I fixed the helm and sail positions so that there would be no need for me to actively steer. And, being dog tired, I hit the sack.

When I woke-up the wind had died down completely, the sea became as flat as a pond and looked like a huge organic mirror. I could see my own image reflected back at me and theatrically said: "Mirror, mirror on the wall, who is the greatest of them all?" It felt good to be on the biggest mirror in the world. However, there had been a time when I

hated a mirror with a passion…

At Mary Kihn, Alma Snijder, very strict but very competent, taught me to lip-read.

Standing for hours in front of the mirror, Alma formed her lips around the letters of the alphabet a, b, c, etcetera, ad infinitum. Later it was words that she formed until I could grasp and pronounce it correctly. The most difficult words were those starting with a "p" or an "m" because words like "mom or pops" begin with the lips being pressed down.

It was tough and I frequently got wrapped over the knuckles. Making the sounds was not the difficult part but having to look at my badly scarred body reflected back at me in the mirror was pure torture.

The mirror made me realise why the children kept staring at me and why, when I returned their gazes, they looked away. Every day having to face the reality of what I looked like to other people made the recovery of my self-image very painful. It took a harrowing long time before I was even vaguely socialised back into the hearing and unscarred world.

Even today I still find it hard to look into a mirror and to lip-read words starting with a “p” and a “m”. And I had already lost too much time in my life looking at a mirror, so I started the motor and put Tilly back in charge of Willy.

The calm waters gave me an opportunity to fix the mainsail slugs which I had earlier broken in my haste during the force six winds. I searched for spare mainsail slugs and found some heavy duty ones. In order not to damage the webbing, I carefully cut out the threads of the broken ones and, one by one, meticulously stitched the new slugs back onto the mainsail. It took a couple of hours but I felt pleased, getting the main back into ship-shape condition.

I went around IT to check everything, taped-up some turnbuckles, poured ten gallons of diesel into the main tank, scooped up five gallons of sea water and since departure I took my first bath. The cool water felt terrific on my sticky body and I too felt in ship-shape condition.

From nowhere a swallow appeared and landed on my bare shoulder. I yelped in surprise and it took to the sky again. As I got dressed the swallow returned and sat on my shoulder, probably reasoning by some swallow logic that I was actually harmless. Then it took off in a flash.

I spotted a Cuban ship doing a sort of survey and, after my scary visitation, I decided to rather err on the safe side by passing them at a distance of a hundred yards. However, when I waved, they politely reciprocated and waved back with their Cuban hats.

I am not superstitious but Saturday the 13th of March, bordering on a Friday, reminded me of my yachting friends at Serendipity Marina who all suffer from triskaidekaphobia. I then realised that the number thirteen is not only a baker's dozen but needed to be considered in a serious light.

Firstly, I discovered that the anemometer's reading of the wind direction was off with about thirty degrees. I dreadfully realised that, most of the time that I had confidently been sailing close-hauled in the Gulf with the wind from an easterly direction, we were actually sailing south-west.

It was a serious blunder and believing that I was on the correct course but actually not, could cause calculation mistakes and that would be hell. To avoid further blunders I undertook to always verify the wind direction with the bearing compass.

Secondly, I did not need to spot them on the radar, it was not necessary and fortunately, I was on deck with a full view of what looked like two cities afloat, coming straight at me. I had to make a difficult choice because clearly these two bastards didn't know anything about the extremis navigation rule, the point under International Navigation Rules at which the privileged vessel (floating city under power) on a collision course with a burdened vessel (IT under sail) must manoeuvre to avoid a collision.

These guys were probably from the old school because prior to extremis, the privileged vessel had to maintain course and speed and the burdened vessel had to manoeuvre to avoid collision.

I took a fat chance to sail between the two Caribbean cruising ships and, I almost broached in their wake and shuddered to think what could have happened if I hadn't spotted them on time. Although I was very rattled, I somehow still had the cool to wheel out a sarcastic grin and waved a finger to the luxury ocean liners.

The odds were once again stacked in my favour but I was a nervous wreck and after that experience, I vowed to take the advice of my yachting friends seriously and be suspicious of the number thirteen.

During the night I sailed well, and when the wind increased in the morning, I took a double reef in the main and furled the genoa up half-way. But it was not long before I faced an angry sea with twelve foot waves and lots of blowing spume, the worst I had encountered so far.

I concentrated very hard on working the sails and was twice soaked by huge waves. At about twenty-five knots the wind wasn't excessive but the sea was really wicked. The mechanical knot meter was reading five knots while the GPS speed-over-ground reading was two-and-a-half knots, indicating a strong opposing current. Eventually, we were out of the current, the wind slackened to eighteen knots and I took the staysail down.

When a surprise monster wave hit us, I resolved not to attempt anymore cooking, not that I feared that I would be feeding a storm, but because a whole pot of stew flew off the back of the stove.

Then the third horizontal seam in the genoa started to unravel. IT was keeping me busy and I wondered what the hell was going on. This was IT's and my first sea-trial and what a trial it was. I regretted that I had not made the time to do a proper ocean trial. And to take my mind off about what could go wrong next, I pondered the first time that I had learned that

time is important…

Either my mom or dad used to drop me off at Bellville station to take the train twenty-seven kilometres to Observatory. The trains were always on time, so I had learned time-

keeping was important and to respect time otherwise I would miss my train to or from school.

The train journey gave me enough time to read "Die Burger" from front to the back with the result that I became very knowledgeable about the Apartheid politics of that time in South Africa.

Once I got to Observatory station, I disembarked and walked another mile, carrying my heavy school bag to Mary Kihn. And I arrived on time before the school started.

Unfortunately, I had missed the boat where a sea trial was concerned, time and money had not permitted me that luxury.

Noticing dark specks on the radar, I thought that it was also conking in, so I took the spotlight, peered up the mast and then double-checked the radar but nothing was wrong. Then I felt on my skin how the wind ominously died down.

Rain at last! All along the dark specks on the radar were actually clouds, it rained cats and dogs. Since our departure, IT got her first free bath. There was absolutely no wind and the anemometer reading of zero confirmed the state of affairs.

As the rain slowly passed, the wind simultaneously picked up and it was not long before it was blowing at twenty-six and gusting at thirty-three miles per hour. The seas became a frightening sight to look at and on numerous occasions IT buried her bow into oncoming monsters. It resulted in water pouring under the dodger and finding its way into the companionway. In the midst of the crashing waves and strong winds there were moments that I had thought IT was going to broach.

While I was reefing the mainsail, the genoa unfurled all the way and all hell broke loose. Somehow the roller furling drum-sheet had come loose. I freaked out just from the booming vibration of the whip-cracking sail. Anyone who had ever experienced a hundred-and-fifty percent genoa loose in thirty-three mile per hour wind will know what I am talking about.

I was still in shock but the shaking and booming vibration continued its onslaught. I tried using muscle power to roll up the genoa but couldn't succeed and quickly got back into the cockpit to use the big port-side's three speed winch to roll it up. The process took a lot of teeth clenching effort and the force of the wind worn me out.

It was a terribly scary experience and I was totally exhausted. I am an adventure seeker but that was an experience for which I had been totally unprepared.

Later the seas became calmer which gave me a bit of a breather to check on things outside. I noticed that in total the main had lost nine more slugs, so I hauled the old main sail out of its bag and as before, while extracting the slugs from the old one, stitching them back onto the new main, I pondered the

shaking and booming vibration…

One day I had decided to take the Express train from Bellville to school, thinking that it would stop at Salt River Station where I could connect to Observatory Station. However, to my surprise, the Express raced past one station after another and as the landscape sped by, the shaking and booming vibration inside the train freaked me out. I helplessly watched the scenery speeding by and the next moment the train slowed down and halted at Cape Town Station.

Only eleven years old, my heart pounded in my chest and getting off at Cape Town Station I had no idea what to do. I had no money and my season ticket didn't cover the Cape Town leg. I looked at the display boards and saw that the next train back to Observatory Station was about to leave, so I quickly jumped onto it.

When the conductor approached I shivered like a leaf trying to make myself invisible but probably looked so guilty that he came straight at me. I took a fat chance and with an unsteady right hand handed him my season ticket.

However, he was a seasoned old chap and immediately saw that it was an invalid ticket. I started to cry and didn't say anything but I think that he had recognized my school uniform, identifying me as a pupil of Mary Kihn or perhaps there was another reason. I will never know.

Fortunately, he was a man of compassion and consoled me by stroking my head. And he kindly assured me, carefully forming his mouth around the Afrikaans words: "Seun moenie bang wees nie! Ek verstaan." ("Not to worry Son! I understand"). To me this experience was a very hard lesson, being on my own for the first time, facing the challenges of the scary world out there.

I verified the charts and decided to change my next waypoint. Initially I had planned to sail east of the Misteriosa Bank, a submerged atoll in the Caribbean Sea but, with the wind not cooperating, I was not going to make it. The new waypoint was set west past the Misteriosa Bank and in between the Rosario Reefs. Prudently plotting every thirty minutes, I neatly sailed through the Rosario Reefs and once through I set course for just east of the Gorda Banks.

I started the engine to charge the batteries but the alternator was not charging and it scared me. Without battery power I would have no communication with the outside world and the mere thought left me trembling, remembering a previous feeling I had of

disempowerment…

Mary Kihn was unable to compete with mainstream schools. The result was that the children competed only amongst themselves. My dad tried his best to fix some of the old gym equipment and even built parallel bars. Perhaps I had been spoiled but it really was not my style and I felt totally cut off from the world that I had known before I became deaf.

The isolation from being removed from boys of my own age at Mary Kihn made me feel disempowered and I pleaded with my parent for an opportunity to socialise.

Rugby, as contact sport, was the last thing my parents thought would be compatible with my injuries but if you are a South African male it seems to be in your blood.

In grade five I again begged my parents to request one of the local primary schools to allow me to practice rugby with their team. Eventually, Welgemoed a nearby Primary School (which my cousins Toni and Deon attended), agreed. Every Wednesday and Friday I went along to play rugby with "normal" kids. I was so proud of my rugby shorts that I even wore them to bed.

Playing rugby for Welgemoed launched me onto the trajectory of social recovery and was such an empowering experience.

Since that time I associate rugby with feelings of empowerment and being part of a team. But I was alone on IT, so I grabbed the gas generator out of the locker, connected its wires to three batteries, started it up and let it run.

I checked the faulty alternator, found that the belt was loose and retightened it with a crowbar. Within minutes the alternator was generating current again and my connection with the outside world was reinstated. However, it was a serious wake-up call and being cut off from the outside world was one of the many things that I had dreaded on this trip.

But more drama lurked around the corner and, going to the cockpit, I noticed that the radar reflector had lost a rope, madly oscillating backwards and forwards. To my absolute horror I watched the spreader arm also swinging like a drunkard, which posed a huge risk to the integrity of the mast.

I hoved-to, got my climbing gear out, took a bungee cord along and used the main halyard to lock it onto my climbing gear. The climb-up the mast to the spreaders was painfully slow and I kept one arm around the mast and with the other hand, one at a time, moved the climbing locks.

About two thirds up the mast, I finally reached the spreader. The view with the eighteen mile an hour winds in six feet swells was both scary and stunning. I secured the radar reflector with the bungee cord, extended the flag halyard with a light rope, so that I could later tie it to the railing at the stern.

The spreader arm had one bolt that needed to be tightened but, not having the right tools close by, I decided to rather climb down again. Getting down the mast was worse than going up.

Once down, I tied the rope to the railing and collected the necessary tools for fixing the spreader-arm and packed them into a shoulder bag. I put my skydiving leather helmet on and used duck-tape to secure the camcorder to the side of my head. To check that the recording light was on, I took a quick look in the mirror and, in the midst of all that drama, I couldn't help but smile at my image: I looked like Laurel and Hardy racing in their topless model-T cars in all those silent movies I had watched during my stay in the hospital.

Still hoving-to, with the same effort, I again climbed up the mast, tightened the bolt and from above captured the view on video. Having accomplished my first mast climb on this trip was a major achievement for me and while I took a well-deserved break, safely back in the cockpit, I reminisced

why sailing thrilled me so much…

She was known to all of us as the "Auntie of the Burger", the mother of Johan Goosen, one of my Dad's quantity surveying understudies. She employed newspaper delivery boys and when Uncle Johan told his mother about Gerrie's and my keenness to earn extra pocket money she warned him off, saying that we were too young.

After some arm twisting, I am still not sure whether it was from Uncle Johan's side or from my dad's, Auntie Goosen agreed and gave us the job on certain conditions. To get round the age concern she cleverly employed my dad, and in turn Dad loyally outsourced the newspaper delivery to us. So, two years after my accident, Gerrie and I started to deliver newspapers for pocket money.

Gerrie and I were doing very well with the newspaper delivery but instead of saving the money, we squandered it on hamburgers, fish and chips and sweets. In the meantime my dad's brother, Uncle Anton, cousin Toni's dad, had built himself a twelve foot sailing dingy and we occasionally spent a day sailing with them at Zeekoevlei. It was there that I first felt the thrill of the power of wind in the sails and begged my dad that we should also get our own sailboat. So, Dad suggested that we should rather save our pocket money from the newspaper delivery to buy a yacht trainer and we were sold on the idea, hook, line and sinker.

Motivated by our eagerness Dad offered to give us one Rand for every Rand that we saved and intentionally or unintentionally unleashed a serious competition between his two rivalling sons.

Gerrie and I wasted no time and with great "joie de vivre" encouraged each other to levels of near perfection. Two hours before dawn, except for Sundays, we exuberantly jumped on our respective bicycles and raced in two different directions to hastily deliver the daily newspapers.

Unbeknown to our parents we had a bet! The two of us, in mutual agreement, concurred that the last one back home with all the deliveries completed would hand over his profit for the day to the other one. However, we agreed that since we only got paid at the end of the week, we would only do a weekly reconciliation. But it was never necessary because the both of us arrived back home simultaneously. Every time!

As could be expected from high-octane sibling rivalry, to get the edge on one another, cheating surfaced. One morning I was caught by surprise. Entering the house, Gerrie sat lazily at the kitchen table, gave a big yawn of boredom and folded up the newspaper to indicate that he had already finished reading it.

I knew he had cheated but I not only had to deliver my pack of newspapers but also had to catch him out. I was absolutely determined to find out how he did it and after the third week that I had unceremoniously been dispossessed of my profit, a grand scheme had already taken shape in my head.

One morning I left together with him so that he wouldn't suspect anything and as soon as he disappeared behind the corner, I raced back, jumped into my bed faking a headache and, taking advantage of my mother's overprotection, begged her to take care of my delivery.

Peeping around the gate, I saw her car disappear, jumped back onto the bicycle and raced, following Gerrie's delivery route. He had an ingenious scheme, double outsourced, and when he had passed his stack of newspapers to his buddy, I was right at his side, caught him red-handed. He paid the buddy half of the earnings that he took from me.

In the spirit of a good loser, Gerrie paid back every cent that he took from me, which was a double blow to him because he had already parted with half of it. But we never split on each other and kept our little secret to ourselves.

There were no hard feelings but also no more fooling around with clever entrepreneurial ideas, so things worked out for us in the end. Proud was the day when we counted our money and reached our target. We quickly ran to Dad to remind him to fulfil his side of the bargain.

Finally, we had enough money and every day we searched the newspaper's smalls but couldn't find anything at the price we could afford. Then the gods smiled upon us. There was a clapped-out dabchick and trailer parked in the yard of one of the houses where I had delivered newspapers. My dad went to see the owner, bartered for a good price and we bought both the dabchick and trailer for R200.

We helped my dad to fix the dabchick and baptized it "Char-Ger", a combination of the first syllable of each of our names: Char for Charl and Ger for Gerrie. And we trans-

formed the ugly duckling into a swan and when she was ready we spent every spare moment to learn how to sail on the Sonstraal dam, just down the road from our house.

I still cherish the memory of us as two young, proud brothers buying our own little boat and learning to sail. I've read that most of the feelings we have towards "things" are caused by early association and, ever since that day, I associate sailing with a feeling of accomplishment, the same thrill I had experienced when I scaled the mast.

Seeing that it was time to tack, bumped me back to reality. However, when I tacked, IT's no-go zone (the range of directions that a sailboat cannot sail towards) was one-hundred-and-fifty degrees instead of only sixty degrees. I attempted to steer through the wind so that it could fill the sails from the opposite side but lost steerage. Locked in irons, we began to slowly drift backwards. And that situation definitely called for closer investigation. There was big trouble. It felt like something was wrong with the centreboard.

I hooked up the swim-ladder to the starboard side. With my diving goggles and a rope tied around my waist, I climbed into the water. Holding onto the ladder with my right hand, taking a deep breath, I bent over and peeked into the crystal clear water. I noticed the centreboard, the "phoenix" that had arisen out of the mud, was canted forward at a thirty degree angle instead of hanging five degrees rearward.

I got back on deck, sat down with my head in my hands and pondered my dilemma. Similar to an airplane's tail, the angle of attack and centre of thrust on a yacht's keel or centreboard is very important. No wonder we had continuously drifted sideways and had not been able to sail to windward!

I was determined to find out what the problem was. I donned my diving gear, plunged into the water and swam towards the centreboard. Once I got hold of it, I tried to swing it back into position, but it was somehow jammed and immovable.

I came back up, found some dock line and tied one end of the lines to the stern. I dove down again, all the time checking for sharks and knotted the other end of the line around the bottom of the centreboard.

Back on top, I heaved on the dock line so that it could pull the centreboard to its correct angle but the line came loose. I dove under again, this time taking a quarter inch bolt along. I fitted the bolt through a hole in the front bottom part of the centreboard and knotted the line in such a way that it wouldn't slip off again.

I got back topsides and tried to pull the centreboard back in place but it would not budge. Hard breathing and teeth clenching and wishing made no difference. It made me feel the same way as that day when

my efforts had yielded no results…

After Kobus, one of the boys who commuted on the train with me, showed up late for school I was summoned to the headmistress, Ms Schemper's, office. She asked me the reason why Kobus was late and I told her what had happened:

"The two of us played with a rubber ball on the platform of Salt river Station, bouncing it up and down. It rolled down the platform's stairs and Kobus ran downstairs, following the ball. When he returned upstairs the train doors closed right in front of him and he couldn't get in which meant that he had to wait to catch the next train, making him late for school."

I had been elected prefect in grade seven and was very proud of this achievement. Ms Schemper said that, as a prefect, I should have been more responsible and that my behaviour was unbecoming. She slowly walked up to me and with one strong movement ripped my prefect badge off my blazer. When she tore that badge off, it felt as if she pulled my heart out of my chest.

At the time, I didn't think that the justice she had meted out was justified and I started to protest vehemently, arguing that it wasn't my fault. However, she was uncompromising and regardless of how much I pleaded with her, breathed and sighed, she couldn't be swayed an inch.

She stubbornly maintained that I should have thought about the repercussions before I had engaged in such a reckless deed. She commanded me to go back to my classroom and spent more time improving my poor marks than bouncing balls on a platform.

Minus my prefect badge and my honour, I dragged myself back to the classroom, all the way sighing and breathing hard. I wanted to cry but didn't and emasculated, I sat behind my desk, totally humiliated.

I didn't know how to deal with the disgrace and from that day onwards my life at Mary Kihn became pure hell…

With those feelings springing to mind, I thought to hell with the sharks. I was not going to be stripped off my ambition by a hardnosed and unswivelling centreboard. This baby needed to be fixed, so I sprang back into the water, grabbed the centreboard, flipped my body upside down, pushed my feet hard against the hull, jerked and grunted.

Small tropical fish came to investigate the madman. I probably looked like some bare-foot, upside-down Fred Flintstone character, snorting and heaving. After a few more attempts of tugging, pulling and wrestling, I managed to force the centreboard to swing back to its correct angle.

Before going topsides, I patted the centreboard to remind her about the rescue from the mud. Back on board, I tied the line to the port side (away from the prop) to keep the board from swinging forward again.

In a final attempt to get the centreboard pendant liberated, I jumped back into the water and pulled and plucked. The damn thing remained stuck between the side of the centreboard and its housing. I checked to make sure my line would not interfere with the prop and decided to leave it until we docked in Panama.

When I sat down, I was curious to see whether my plan worked. So I set sail and within minutes we were bearing one-hundred-and-twenty-five degrees, a twenty-five degree improvement on the previous one-hundred-and-fifty degrees. So, my effort wasn't entirely successful but at least it revealed the problem and boy, oh boy, was I relieved that we were moving again.

I went into the cabin to plot my position at the navigation table and opening the lid, I saw my well-read book

"The Dove"…

After acquiring the Dabchick, the movie "The Dove" was released and both Gerrie and I became fascinated with it, watched it over and over again, probably nine times perhaps even more.

The Dove is a true story about Robin Lee Graham, a sixteen year-old boy, who set out aboard a twenty-four foot sloop determined to be the youngest person to solo circumnavigate. As he travels around the globe he experienced many adventures at sea and grew from a teenager to young adult.

Gerrie and I slept, ate, read and drank sailing! At night in bed, with the light still switched on to enable me to lip-read, our conversations invariably centred around one thing only and that was how each one of us, respectively, similar to our hero Robin Lee Graham, would sail solo around the world.

Our enthusiasm was so ignited that on our weekly library days the only books that we were interested in were sailing books and we devoured each one of them. The library soon ran out of reading material and we used our newspaper pocket money to replenish our sailing literature.

And that night I again reread "The Dove" for the umpteenth time and my thoughts were constantly with Gerrie.

When I sailed past the Gorda Banks, near the eastern tip of Honduras, we suddenly slowed down and our speed dropped from six knots to less than one knot. I walked the deck to see what was wrong. I couldn't find anything until I checked the stern. There were three white floats just under the surface and, on closer inspection, I saw that the rudder had snagged a fisherman's crab line. I took out the boat hook and tried to hook the line out of the water but it was too tight.

With the mainsail fully hoisted, I was stuck because the wind blew from behind and there was no way I could turn into the wind to lower the sail or to power around in the waves that were hitting us on the stern. So I tied a rope around my middle and mustered up enough courage to lower myself into the pitch-black water. I couldn't see anything and with the knife in my left hand, like a blind man, I felt around with my right hand for the line.

The possibility of ocean predators lurking below the dark surface scared the shit out of me and in my aggravated mood I was prepared to beat the hell out of any shark. Finally, I managed to cut away at the crab line until it parted and then IT jerked loose, sailing without me on-board.

I was holding onto the rope around my waist for dear life and was hopelessly dragged around at sea. It was a terrifying experience, I had no control over the situation and clawing, clawing, clawing, distressingly slowly, I made it back to the stern ladder. And when I eventually hauled myself aboard, I collapsed on the deck and crawling on all fours towards the cockpit, everything around me just went

pitch black…

One evening after my dad had arrived back home from work, I sensed a lot of tension. Apparently, Ms Schemper had phoned Mom earlier that day to complain about how I was doing the unforgivable "Mary Kihn School's sin" of looking away when being reprimanded. For the deaf that is tantamount to a hearing person blocking his ears and giving the speaker the finger.

The next day my dad took me to school, getting out of the car he told me to follow him to the headmistress's office and I became very scared. There Ms Schemper summoned Ms Bryant, the teacher who had complained about me and, while I waited outside, they were discussing things in the office. Of course, I couldn't hear their conversation and after some time my dad called me into the office where he instructed me to bend over.

My father took off his belt and in front of my teachers, Ms Schemper and Ms Bryant, gave me a thrashing. I accusingly looked Ms Schemper straight in the eye and then everything went pitch black.

The next moment I saw Ms Schemper yelling at him to stop. The beating wasn't that bad but nothing compared to the humiliation and for the rest of that day I sat crying in the library. I was desperate and wanted to run away but didn't know how to do it.

Years later my dad and I discussed the incident and he apologised, trying to explain that the teachers had threatened to throw me out of the school because they were of the opinion that they were doing us a special favour by allowing a profoundly deaf pupil in a school for partial hearing and that I had become unmanageable. He had also intended to get a strong message to the teachers to do their own disciplining and not to fob it off on the parents.

Whatever possessed him that day it was not the hiding but the humiliation, especially later in life…

After I came to, it was already light, I found myself lying in the cockpit and my whole body was shaking. At that point with that dark memory, I hated my father with a passion and wanted to jump over-board, abandoning my whole dream.

I crawled to the railing determined to jump. From nowhere a stealthy swallow flashed through the blue sky and perched on the three speed winch. I was sure it was the same swallow that had previously peeped in on me and probably by some swallow logic reasoned that it needed to give me some counselling.

When I offered my hand, it cautiously clambered on, gripped my index finger and while the swallow was balancing on my finger, I wondered what it sounded like. Over the years this is something that frustrated me because I can't beak-read bird sounds and it made me immensely sad. My whole life I've seen people around me being moved by the sounds of nature but I could only see the movement of the swallow's beak and had not the faintest clue what it sounded like.

Afterwards it made itself at home under the spray dodger where I put out some water and crackers for it to feed on. Watching the swallow pecking on my offerings, I couldn't help but wonder where it came from and why it came at the precise moment that I had so desperately needed it. It saved my life!

It stayed with me for a number of hours before it took off with a flash and as it flew away, I thanked the swallow for its unexpected company. While throwing it a farewell kiss, I recited the first verse of "When swallows grace the morning sky".

When swallows grace the morning sky
Of summer's deepest blue,
As through the air they deftly fly
I'll always think of you.

Later that morning, when the temperature reached an unbelievable eighty-five degrees Fahrenheit, I was forced to shower. Ever since the burning thing I can't stand heat, not just due to my fear of fire, but because my skin lost eighty present of its pores. It limits my perspiration ability and consequently my cooling down mechanism.

And in that unbearable, humid heat the prophetic words "Water, water, everywhere, Nor any drop to drink" became fulfilled.

The water in the tanks was awfully dirty and I tried to boil it but it still had a foul taste. The drinks were warm and yucky. I also ran out of bottled water and, similar to the day of my burning, my thirst became unbearable.

I packed all the food in the refrigerator, switched it on, put all the drinks and canned fruit inside and started it up. Within two hours I had a cold drink and as I poured a cold, orange flavoured river of salvation down my throat it tasted absolutely divine.

But little did I know then, that somewhere in the near future, I would still be haunted by the lack of water.

Rehydrated, I pushed IT hard to reach our first big Milestone. The next forty-eight hours we devoured one-hundred-and-forty miles of ocean to hit our last waypoint for the first leg of my journey. And there she was in all her majestic glory: "Look Pa, look Ma there is Pa-na-Ma!"

On the 20th of March, two weeks after my departure from Palacios, in a magnificent sunset, I sailed into Cristóbal's harbour on the Atlantic side of the Panama Canal.

And I could confidently assert that the past two weeks had taught me much about myself and moulded me sufficiently to begin the transformation from novice to experienced sailor.

Blood Suckers

I cautiously approached the Yacht Club, searching for a vacant slip. Not finding one, I was at a loss. However, it was not long before an elderly man in his dinghy rowed past me and, after I explained to him that I was deaf, he conveyed the obvious fact that the marina was chock-a-block full and advised that I should rather go and wait at the anchorage area.

Dropping anchor in the bay, I morosely waited at the navigation table with my head on my arms and reflected on the adrenalin pumping events of the past fifteen days, the things I had gone through and all the difficult decisions that had to be made.

But, it wasn't long before Jerry Logan, a yachtsman from Georgia, came over in his dinghy and kindly offered me a ride to the club. I locked up and went with him, explaining that I was looking for an agent going by the name of "Peter". Before taking leave, Jerry invited me to join the party that he would be hosting later that evening. I didn't wait long for agent Peter to show up. He handed me a package from home, containing charts and a book on the Samoan Islands.

Later that evening I went over to where Jerry's yacht was moored. He was on a three year circumnavigation with three friends and, before the other visitors would arrive, he gave me a guided tour of his luxury fifty-five foot ketch, fitted out with the latest navigation equipment. When people from all over the world started to arrive for the party, he introduced me to them.

There were many Frenchmen. I gathered that they didn't like the English very much because they were reluctant to speak their language. However, when I explained to them that I am an Afrikaner of French origin, they accepted my bona fides. It was only then that they made the effort to speak English to me. I told them that they should speak slowly and carefully form their words. At times it was difficult to understand their lip-curve French accent and they often had to spell out the words, writing it on my palms with their fingers, but in the end it all worked out well.

During the course of that evening I enquired from the French why they hated the English so much but I think they had forgotten because they couldn't really give me a satisfactory answer. It is so silly! But to avoid confrontation I **didn't** tell them that I had very good memories of an English country village.

Together with all my newly acquired friends, we celebrated the successful completion of my passage from Texas to Panama. I had no problem fitting in and at that moment I was immensely grateful for the opportunities I had to

re-socialise back into the hearing world…

At the time Mary Kihn School only taught up to grade seven and when the time had come for me to go to High School, my parents faced a huge dilemma because there was not much of a choice as far as schools were concerned.

Except for Worcester, a school for profoundly deaf-born pupils, the mainstream schools in our vicinity were big and, although my parents by that time had enough confidence in my lip-reading ability, they also realised that it would be hard for me to compete in such an environment.

Ouma Agnes de Villiers was also a retired teacher and my parents had decided to rather send me to her in Komgha, more than a thousand kilometres away from our home in Cape Town. They reasoned that since the two of us had a special bond, she could assist me with upping my marks. I lodged with Ouma in her house, "Saamstaan" (standing together), and attended the Komgha Secondary School, being a much smaller ordinary school for mainstream education.

The Eastern Cape border town of Komgha, established during the time of the frontier wars between European settlers and the Xhosas, in many respects mimic an English coun-

try village. The town is surrounded by a commonage where the villagers' sheep and lowing herds wound slowly o'er the lea.

After coming from a "deaf" school and, even though it was difficult to cope with being away from my parents, it was a time I recall with fond memories. In this town I had been re-launched into the world of the hearing and I will always cherish the place where my late grandfather had been mayor for twenty years, followed by my grandmother for another two years.

Mary Kihn had taught me how to lip-read but it was at Komgha that I honed my people skills. Initially, socialising amongst hearing people was very limited but gradually, as I got to know more people in Komgha, it became easier which had resulted in a lot of interaction with hearing people. Something that I had greatly missed at Mary Kihn.

Anyway back to the party. It was great, clean fun and afterwards Jerry arranged for me to be taken back to IT where I slept non-stop for a straight, magnificent eight wholly hours.

Before first light many yachts were leaving to go to the first set of locks of the Canal. After coffee, I felt refreshed and waited for the authorities to clear customs. Agent Peter had arranged a vacant berth for me and Americo, one of my new friends, docked right opposite me. Americo and I immediately jelled and when I had difficulty understanding people, it was his easy-going manner which helped me a lot.

The tall masts of the large sailboats surrounding IT at the marina caused reception problems for the Iridium Sat phone. So, with my laptop under my arm, I jumped onto the quay and went to an open grassy knoll behind the club, but still there was just no reception. Eventually, I managed to send messages from Americo's boat's portside where there were no obstructions.

I took the badly damaged genoa down from the mast and hailed a taxi so that I could take it to the repair shop for the necessary mending. A taxi driver by the name of Dracula came by and seeing him gave me goose bumps because he looked very close to the real thing.

Anyway, as it turned out he was not a blood sucker and was indeed very helpful. During my stopover in Panama, Dracula became one of my closest buddies and I still remember him with fondness.

After dropping off the genoa, I went to the supermarket for the necessary supplies. Dracula questioned me about the copious amounts of bottled water that I had purchased and in turn I shared with him the very hard lesson I had learned when the water in the tanks got spoiled. But when I told him about my fear of thirst and how it came about, a sympathetic gaze lit up his eyes, actually making his Dracula-like face look quite handsome.

Resourceful old Dracula also bought me a cheap-cheap carton of Marlboros at $1.00 per pack on the black market and he charged me only three bucks for the taxi ride. Nevertheless, I tipped him another two for his excellent services.

Back at the marina, at the fuel depot, I poured ten gallons of diesel into the main tank, filled up the four empty five gallon jerry cans for $37 and strapped the full ones where they belonged.

Carlos, the ad-measurer, arrived and took extensive measurements of IT, asked numerous questions, checked the navigation equipment on board and wrote down detailed notes about everything. In the sweltering Panamanian heat he was dripping with sweat and I soon over-heated. We decided to take refuge in the cool air-conditioned bar where we continued our discussions.

He took great trouble to advise me about the rules and procedures during the transit. I would need extra fenders and line which I could rent from the yacht club. Just to complete the necessary paperwork took more than an hour: Sign here, sign there, ad infinitum. My impatience resurfaced and I guess it was because I had been hanging out with too many Frenchmen at Jerry's party which in turn ignited my own intolerant French blood.

While filling out all the forms, I recited the words in my head:

Patience is a virtue…

When I lodged with Ouma in Komgha and things didn't go according to my wishes, she used to say: "Patience is a virtue, virtue is a grace and Grace is a little girl who didn't wash her face". And that drove me crazier than any sailor would ever imagine to be.

Every time I think of how I got back at Ouma Agnes, I chuckled. While a lot of people have the choice of selective hearing, I have the choice of selective lip-reading, being able to choose not to see what people are saying.

At Mary Kihn it was a sin to do so and I knew it was spiteful to turn my head away, refusing to look at Ouma so that I couldn't read her lips. But I couldn't help myself and in turn that drove her up the wall.

Despite my visible irritation and exasperated sighs, Carlos was not intimidated and politely continued with the task at hand. I genuinely felt envious of Carlos, every day tolerantly dealing with hundreds of people and keeping his cool. Heaven only knows where he got his coolheaded manner from, interacting with so many stubborn, bad-tempered and downright rude people. Everything took time and I swore to acquire the flair for patience. And I fancied myself emerging from this journey as an easy-going and lackadaisical old chap.

He enquired whether I wanted a speed transit but with my sail in the shop, I told him that once everything would be ready, I would rather contact him.

After Carlos had left, three Englishmen and I, the lonely Texan Afrikaner Boer, sat at the bar and argued animatedly about our common history of more than a hundred years ago. I patriotically played along pretending to be angry with the devious way the sly English had snatched our country from right under our noses and in turn they vehemently argued about the brutal way the English soldiers had been treated by the Boers. Nevertheless, we ended up as pals, forgiving our respective ancestors and enjoyed each other's company.

That evening, back at IT, I had time to reflect on my afternoon's conversation with the Englishmen. Unbelievably after so many years subsequent to the Anglo Boer War, many Afrikaners still have not forgiven the English. It is so silly, but there you have it!

During the Anglo Boer War our great-grandfathers had either killed each other or locked each other up as Prisoners of War in various camps around the world. One such camp where the Boers had been imprisoned was at St Helena, where my van der Merwe great-grandfather had been kept behind barbed wires. I had informed my English friends that I would visit there during my last leg on my way home.

What I didn't tell them was that I didn't hate the English at all, in truth, my own grandmother was English and I remembered the many stories she had told me about the English/Afrikaner conflict during and in the aftermath of

the Anglo-Boer War…

In the evenings after supper Ouma Agnes poured herself a nightcap and, with the two of us sitting at the dining room table, she would tell me many family stories. One of her stories, in particular, fascinated me.

Ouma's mother, a Miss La Grange (also of Huguenot extraction and with the same French rebelling streak), was brought up in a conservative Afrikaner home. When her mother married an Englishman, and that during the Anglo-Boer War, it was deemed to be treason by her family. My great-grandma had been severely punished, disinherited, disowned and renounced for unwittingly allowing her French rebelling genes to take control of her.

Each of the La Grange daughters inherited a farm but my poor great- grandma had been showed the road with a measly roll of linen.

Although my de Villiers grandparents were married a full thirty years after the Boer War, there was still a lot of doubt, on my Afrikaans grandfather's side of the family, as to whether he wasn't perhaps courting trouble. But in Ouma's lifetime, for fear of my grand-dad exercising his vast vocabulary, none of his family had ever dared to say a slanted word about my half-bred grandmother.

Ouma had been requested to play the organ during the sermon on Dingaan's Day (then viewed by the Afrikaners as a Sabbath, in thankful remembrance of their victory over the Zulus). She had soon sensed that big trouble was looming, especially when the visiting preacher beseeched the Lord to bless Nazi-Germany and to save the Afrikaner Nation from the Jews and the English by chasing them into the sea.

With each "into-the-sea-chasing" request Ouma said she got more and more upset. After the third request she slammed the organ shut, got up and furiously marched out of the open-sided festival hall.

Due to work commitments my granddad couldn't attend the function but three of his sisters had showed intrepid courage by demonstrating their kinship solidarity and without hesitation had followed their sister-in-law out of the hall.

The annoyed Preacher had discordantly tried to lead his distracted congregation in singing a psalm without the aid of the pedal organ. My gran's sisters-in-law, in whispering voices, had berated the tactless man and wiped the tears from Ouma's cheeks.

Only when it became known years later that two of those sisters-in-laws had husbands who were members of the "Ossewa Brandwag", a militant fascist and fanatic anti-British organisation, did Ouma Agnes came to appreciate the extent of their courage, in protecting the family unity.

At the time, staying with her, I had made friends with many bilingual English families and at Komgha the English spoke better Xhosa than Afrikaans and the Afrikaners spoke better Xhosa than English. But it was at Komgha that I had really started to learn English and I fell asleep pondering this story.

I was painfully aware that my transmitted logs were falling behind but leaping three feet from the bow to the dockside with the laptop and satellite phone tucked under my arm, had become very risky. And then time and again to try unsuccessfully to acquire a signal, became a huge schlep.

So, I reverted to using the office computer at the yacht club to check my website and to send emails. However, after only three attempts my dilemma worsened when I was unceremoniously kicked out by the boss, an elderly lady with a very nasty temper, bitterly complaining that I had over-utilised their office computer.

But I was no stranger to

old ladies with flaring tempers…

The year before my burning accident Dad had invited my English cousins, Alan sixteen and Chris fourteen years old, to join us for the June holidays visiting my Afrikaner mother's van der Merwe family on their farms.

One evening, my dad had psyched the two cousins up to both wrestle with him and pin him down on a bed in my grandmother's house. One cousin on the left and the other on the right arm tried their utmost to keep him down. Time and again, with deep animated lion-like roars, he shook them both off.

My brothers and I were the inciting bystanders and had a lot of fun watching Dad fling them aside like wet rags. We had belly-aching laughs and cheered him on to do it all over again and to add renewed vigour to the wrestling. After an hour or so, the well-used antique bed-base snapped in half with a loud crack.

Ouma Das van der Merwe burst into the room in a bedevilled rage. The three of them were on the floor, hugged by the broken bed, struggling to get up. We scampered out of the room, laughing our hearts out because Dad received such a heated scolding from his mother-in-law for behaving like a child.

Having been on the receiving end of Dad's vast and furious vocabulary we never thought that the day would come that he, a grown man of stature, be belittled by an old lady.

I loved my grandma Das very much but there I was as a forty-three year old man, treated as if I was a little boy that couldn't keep my hands out of the cookie jar and getting medicine from an old lady too.

Dracula took me to the sail repairer and I was confident enough with the progress to send a message to Carlos that he could proceed with the arrangements for my transit.

The following day Dracula took me to an internet café and finally, I succeeded to send my logs. I was on-line long enough to attentively read all the encouragement posted on my website, loved the Guest Book and responded to each of the messages. As I was going through all the well-wishing emails from family and friends, out of sheer gratitude for their support, I silently wept.

I received word that the transit would take place on Wednesday, March 31st, and according to Carlos's detailed instructions, seriously started to prepare IT.

Dracula took me to town for the last time where I bought the necessary food and drinks for the transit pilot. The four line-handlers, charging $60 each, would be responsible for their own food and I didn't cater for them.

We went via the sail repair shop only to find that my sail was not yet ready. Can you imagine how my impatience played havoc with me? But the owner promised to personally deliver the repaired genoa to me during the course of that afternoon.

Back at the marina, Americo, Kevin, Becky and Russ, sporting their new Panama hats, came round to IT to say their goodbyes. By then we had become very close friends and my bond with them made me feel as if I was part of a gang again. Still waiting for the sail to be delivered and to get rid of my frustration, I showed them how to rip a fresh bread apart and eat it like

an African hyena…

During my first year at Komgha I made lots of friends and we had innocent, naughty and fun-filled days. One of my friends Wayne Chemmaly, or Scoopy (his nick name), and I used to slip out at night and organise a gang of other boys to raid the fruit orchards of the locals.

During the night the local bakery also baked bread for the next day. We used to go round to the bakery and coaxed the baker into giving us one of his freshly baked loaves. We took the warm bread, made a tunnel with our bare hands, filled it with butter and syrup, ripped it apart and ate it like real African Hyenas.

And I was about to give up that my sail would ever arrive but then, unexpectantly, Dracula showed up. Lo and behold, he was proudly carrying my genoa on his shoulders. I was actually tearful saying goodbye to Dracula and told him how much I appreciated his assistance. He is such an amazing fellow and after my encounter with this incredible guy I no longer fear vampires.

My newly formed gang and I said our "au revoirs" and "bon voyages" and clicking our fists together like real gangsters do.

In preparing for the transit we were instructed to lie at anchor, so I vacated my slip, motored all the way to the bay and dropped anchor. I went to bed early, ready to move on and after the eleven day stopover at the marina in Cristóbal, I excitedly looked forward to the transit experience.

Des popped in at four o' clock in the morning of transit day to alert me that the line-handlers had called him over his radio because they couldn't get hold of me over mine. Des was requested to give me a message that they were waiting for me at the yacht club.

There had been a serious communication breakdown because I thought that the line-handlers would come together with the pilot but apparently the two groups moved in separate classes. So I motored to the yacht club to collect them and reversed back to the flats with all my navigation lights on.

I on IT, Des and Alison on Alii Nui, Ron and Suzanne on Tapasya were in position when the crew boat took turns to stop beside each of us for the pilots allocated to our respective yachts to get on-board.

My pilot asked for my horn and took over the command of IT. Although I was thoroughly briefed by agent Peter on the procedures during the transit, I had no idea how over-protective and possessive I had become of IT. It was only with sheer teeth grinding that I stayed behind the wheel to steer while the new captain barked the orders.

Following the lit markers we soon approached the first set of brightly lit locks at Gatun and the pilot commanded me to slow down. "Tapasya" also slowed down and I came onto her portside with the eight experienced line-handlers on our respective yachts, operating like a team, to secure the yachts onto each other.

When the boats moved too much, either to port or starboard, my pilot shouted commands for Des to reverse and Ron to run full speed ahead, keeping us in a straight line. Although it was early morning, I was already overheating from the exhaustion.

The Gatun locks slowly closed and we were lifted for thirty feet. Once through we proceeded to the next gate and in a similar manner repeated the same process. We eventually ended up in Gatun Lake, a freshwater lake, where we were separated.

After all the intense steering and concentrating, I relaxed for the first time. The line handlers were just hanging around, making small talk and telling jokes. Thinking about the absurdity of calling a deaf person over the radio, I asked them: "What kind of a joke did you try to make to call a deaf person over a radio?" And they laughed their hearts out and thought it was extremely funny when I asked them:

"How stupid could you be?"

After one year at Komgha I completed grade eight with flying colours. However, my Ouma Agnes, already in her late sixties, had become a bit frail and moved to Oudtshoorn where my aunt Andy (after whom I named Andy, the autopilot) could take care of her. That left my parents very little option but to put me in the hostel at Worcester, a school for profoundly deaf-born pupils.

After the very first day at Worcester, I realised that it was going to be very hard for me to adjust. The maths that they taught was on a very low level and I got bored, arrogantly thinking that these pupils were not only deaf but also stupid.

Worcester could teach me nothing new. Every standard could only be completed in two years and all the matrics were already adults. I calculated that I would be twenty-three years old before I would leave school and it was a very scary thought.

Furthermore, the Komgha experience had spoilt me and although I can use sign language, I prefer to lip-read. So communication was very difficult at Worcester because the pupils and teachers could not lip-read and only used sign language. The school's focus was on practical work with very little academic grounding. They spent only two hours in the morning in class and the rest of the day in the workshop. It was a good thing for those pupils because they would leave school as skilled artisans.

After one week at Worcester my dad attended a function at the school and could clearly see that I was extremely unhappy. The next morning he came to fetch me, donated my brand new uniform to the school and said that they must give it to someone who really needed it.

But I was the stupid one and, only after I had gone to America did I acquire a certificate as a coded welder. If I had obtained one earlier, my adjustment to America would have been far easier and perhaps I would have been a happier guy.

While shaking my head, I accepted that Carlos must have forgotten to mention this bit of important detail to them or, alternatively, he didn't believe that I was really deaf.

I dropped the joke when tankers, freighters and a Caribbean cruise ship passed, getting closer to Pacific locks. Following the pilots' instructions to the T we docked behind a big freighter from Singapore which left very little manoeuvring space. We waited for it to go ahead of us and as a precaution a tugboat came between us and the freighter.

We entered the Pedro Miguel lock on the Pacific side and went through the same process but this time in the opposite direction going down through sets of locks located on the smaller Miraflores Lake. Safely through all the locks we separated and headed out into the Pacific.

Late on the 31st of March I motored into Balboa's marina on the Pacific side of the Panama Canal.

Arriving at Balboa's yacht club I offloaded the line-handlers who were supposed to have brought their own food but the joke was on me, they had eaten mine. I greeted the pilot and admitted that it would have been difficult, if not impossible, to have transited without him.

The next morning after a cold shower at the yacht club, I waited for agent Peter to settle the final account for the transit. Seeing the bill, I almost had a heart attack: A grand total of $2,650. It was only then that I came to appreciate that Dracula had actually protected me against the expensive Panamanian blood suckers.

The shock of the expenses was gnawing at me, so I walked over to IT thinking about all the cost that must still be incurred and as a worried man I eventually crashed.

When dawn broke on the 4th of April, I did a few last minute checks on IT, waved farewell to bloodsucking country and set sail to attempt my second leg.

ADJUSTING MY SAILS

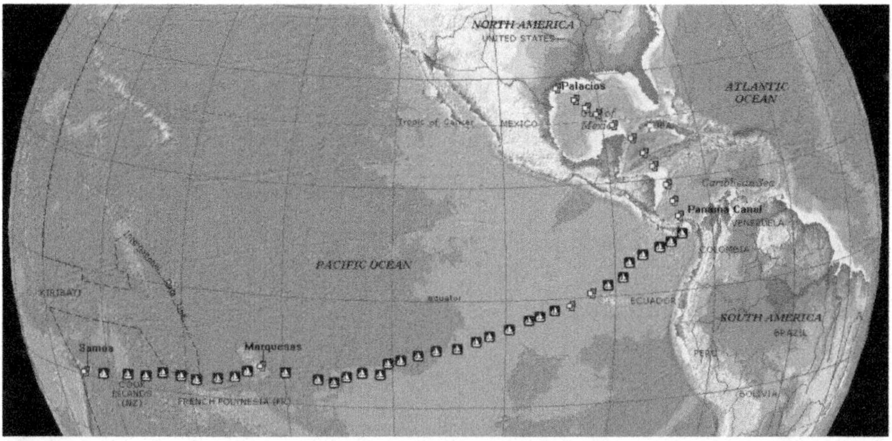

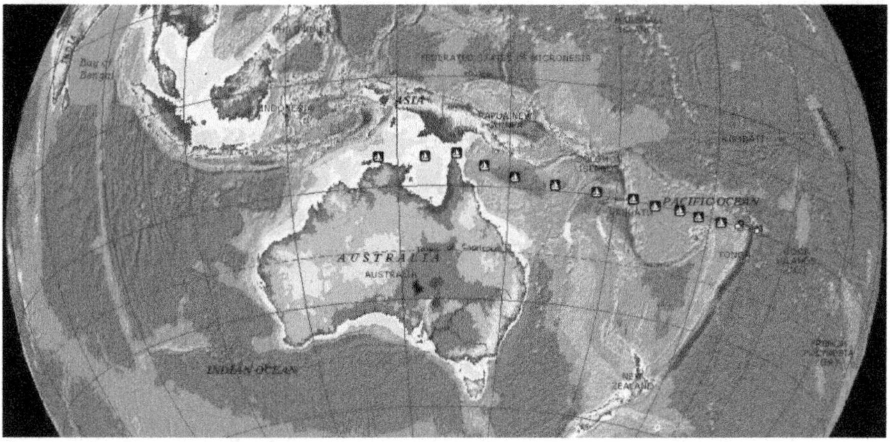

I can't change the direction of the wind, but I can adjust my sails to always reach my destination.

***Jimmy Dean** (August 10, 1928 – June 13, 2010, American country music singer, television host, actor and businessman)*

Not a drop to drink

Heading for Samoa the heavy burden of the expensive transit started to dwindle when I looked back at the beach and saw spray being spectacularly swept along in the breeze, just above the top of the breakers.

With their white plumes dissolving in the air, I wished that the expenses of the transit could also melt away, just like that. As the plumes waved farewell kisses at me, I returned them dramatically, kissing my finger tips and blew three sweeping smooches back at them.

It had been Paulie back at the club in Cristóbal, a real Don Juan, who had showed me how to throw those melodramatic kisses at the passing girls. Once they were out of sight Paulie had

elbowed me for information…

After the Worcester fiasco my dad had organised with the school principal, Mr Algie, that I go back to Komgha. My mother was protesting and didn't want me to go so far away again, but she had also realised that my mind was made up.

I was elated when Mr Algie said that he was very happy to have me because the school needed me for their rugby team. And everyone at school wholeheartedly welcomed me back. I stayed at the hostel which was a great experience and only a five minute walk to school.

My buddies soon realised that they could use my lip-reading ability to their dating advantage. When a group of girls across the room flirtatiously stared at us, my buddies elbowed the fourteen year old me for inside information.

Putting my lip-reading ability into operation, I could quickly determine the content of the girls' conversation. I could instantly tell who's hot for whom and whose time would be better spent dancing the evening away with somebody else. For instance: "The blond says Morné is cute, the short brunette says Alan Coetzer has a nice ass but his nose is a bit too long."

I only gave the information but the buddies still had to do the hard work and under those circumstances there were no guarantees. For example, Alan Coetzer still had to make a judgement call on whether his supposedly nice ass outweighs his long nose and could land him a good old fashioned snog.

Needless to say, I did play a few pranks. Sometimes a girl would say she thought one of my buddies was gorgeous but, contrary to her opinion, I would tell him that she said he was stupid.

When it came to my own tactical advantage where the girls were concerned, I could snog one with my eyes closed and wouldn't know whether she was saying "yes" or "no". It was only if she pushed or pulled that I got the message but sometimes I got it wrong and later defended my misinterpretation of the rapid movements as spasms of passion.

"Hey, give me a break, I am deaf not impotent!"

But I got jerked out of my amorous memory and wishful thinking about disappearing expenses when two ships came straight at me. One approached from the front and one from the rear. Remembering the incident on the 13th of March, when I had nearly been run over by two luxury liners, I nervously kept a close guard and was ready to give way.

I watched them cautiously but, a quarter of a mile away, they changed direction to avoid me. At least, they knew the correct version of the seafarer's "Rules of the Road". I became increasingly anxious with all that ocean traffic, recalling it was one of the main reasons why I had not wanted to take the northerly route but that was water under the bridge.

That evening the colour of the water became much darker, the shape and attitude of the ocean strongly reminded me of Matagorda Bay in Texas where one often finds that there is a smooth transition between no swells and long smooth ones.

And then the full moon revealed her face in all her glory, illuminating the water so that her white and yellow lunar path was reflected in a hazy mirror image on the ocean's smooth surface. Staring at the undertows and riptides rushing by, a type of mystery was reflected back at me and I marvelled at the scenic beauty.

The stunning vista switched the poet on in me and I composed a poem for myself:

Cautiously in a quiet moonlit night, I was sailing along
bright stars sparkling
At the helm all night, singing a silent full moon song
with lips quivering
Adjusting my sailing
and willing myself to be strong
whilst my eyelids started flickering
I moved on dingily-dong
thinking about my last experiences, shuddering
hoping that my solo silent mission won't go wrong

Having composed the poem in that glorious full moon setting, my memory was jogged about a time when I was so love-stricken that I had written a secret weekly poem and when

a whole village had raised a boy…

Being without any family, the whole Komgha village had taken me under its wing, ensuring that I would not feel lonely. They opened not only their homes but also their hearts to me and every weekend I was invited to somebody's home.

One such family was Willem and Dottie Fourie. They had a farm near Komgha and another one, not far from Morgan Bay at Double Mouth. The Fourie's daughter, Thea, and I were in the same class. Alas, we were merely good friends

She taught me how to ride a horse but unbeknown to her, I secretly had a crush on her. Every week during that short period, before she got a new boyfriend, I had composed a poem dedicated to her but regrettably, I never had the guts to give it to her.

I fell asleep trying to remember some of the poems that I had written to Thea, so many years ago, but couldn't. And thought that perhaps I got moonstroke.

Ever since my departure, I had only been able to read wind-speed in miles per hour, not knots, resulting in me manually calculating the conversions which gave me headaches. There had been a lot of enquiries on my website and I decided to make sure that I hadn't suffered any moon stroke from the previous evening's full moon. So, I seriously focused my mind on the operation of the weather station. And at last I figured out how to read, not only knots but also kilometres per hour. It just goes to show what can be done if one applies your mind. No moon stroke here!

While in the cockpit the wind kept me cool but entering the cabin, shielded from the wind, the heat became unbearable. To cool down in the cabin, I opened the hatch but the waves leaked into the cabin and forced me to keep it closed.

The falling barometer meant that I would soon be facing a storm. The smooth Pacific swells of earlier were replaced by waves of almost ten feet high and I sailed close-hauled trying to stay on course but it was almost impossible.

Then, three days after leaving Balboa, I went through the worst storm since leaving Texas. I managed to get the genoa furled up on time but, with winds up to thirty-three knots and waves constantly hitting IT from every side, it became impossible to get the main sail down.

The night was pitch black and the skies were ablaze with lightning. I locked myself up in the cabin where the up and down punishment flung me out of the bunk. So, I threw a mattress on the sole, checked the radar and went to lie down trying to sleep out the storm.

When IT splashed down, I was intensely aware of the continuous see-sawing and crashing of her bow, hitting wave after wave. I got tremendously worried whether she would be strong enough to withstand the torture.

When the wind dwindled at daybreak I inspected the damage. In the storm pots, pans, canned food, charts and almost everything, that had previously been secured into their places, came loose and were scattered all over the cabin. I also discovered that during the storm I had lost fifteen feet of Danworth anchor and chain. Fortunately, there was a spare anchor with twenty feet of chain.

For about fifteen minutes two brownish seabirds circled around and I wished that Morné, my school pal from Komgha, was with me to help identify the birds. And I made a promise that next time I wouldn't think of his profession as stupid

bird watching…

The head boy of Komgha School, Morné Du Plessis, and I had become best friends. Since a young age Morné was a keen birder. At that stage, I guess even today, it had been quite a weird thing for a teenager to be more interested in bird watching than doing other teenage stuff. I had been very keen to find out what about it intrigued him so much, so I followed him around on his birding expeditions. While he was following and watching birds, he used to put his finger to his mouth, indicating that I should shut up. At the time having to shut up for hours while he stalked the birds, wasn't really fun for me.

Afterwards, questioning him about the birding, he shared his dream with me to become a professional bird watcher and in turn, I shared with him my desire to become the first deaf person to solo circumnavigate.

Long before I had even attempted mine, he already had realised his dream and, at the youthful age of twenty-seven, became Professor of Ornithology at Cape Town University (currently the Chief Executive of the World Wildlife Fund).

Being a healthy teenager, I was more interested in other kinds of birds and it was only much later in life that I did some serious bird watching. Fortunately, Morné and I had kept contact and I hoped that I would be able to see him during my stopover at Cape Town.

When the birds flew away, similar to the other birds that had visited me, I wondered what news these two unidentified seabirds brought. But if only I knew then what I was about to discover, I would have seen them as an omen, giving me a warning.

As I was cleaning up, I checked the bilge and found more water than should have been there, even accounting for the storm. That was not a good sign. I turned on the bilge pump and then proceeded to find the source. I inspected the stuffing box on the propeller shaft and the centreboard's pennant tube. Everything looked good.

Opening the water tanks, I was flabbergasted! Almost all of my ninety gallons of water was gone. I had fixed the water tanks during my preparation, before I left Texas. I couldn't understand what had gone wrong. And why the hell the water prophecy kept haunting me?

My predicament was so huge that there was no time to feel sorry for myself. I altered the sun cover to make it droop in the middle, so that it could act as a rain catcher. There were already two small holes that had been caused by chafing, so I used those holes to insert two plastic thru-hull fittings.

I attached a hose to each fitting and sailed straight for a dark cloud on the horizon. When rain poured down, the water got pooled in the sun-cover and flowed through the hoses, straight into my empty containers. I managed to yield seven gallons of pure, clean water and it tasted like honey.

Using one gallon of rainwater I washed my hair and the rest of my body. Stark naked, cleaned and refreshed, the relief for harvesting the fresh water lifted my spirit and like in my youth

I danced…

We had many school dances at Komgha and by standing barefoot on the wooden floor, I could feel the vibrations of the music and mimicked the moves of the couples, dancing away. I felt the rhythm and swayed in unison with the music.

It was in that English country village that they had allowed me to be part of their parties, where I pranced, hipped, skipped and jumped like a real expert dancer.

But I was flipped back into reality when the flapping and flopping of the genoa started to decrease. Since leaving Balboa it was my first cloudless day.

I could kill for a cold soda and turned on the refrigerator, popped in some and waited until they were cold enough to drink. The cold drink came at a heavy price because the batteries got depleted and, even though I tried for three hours, their power couldn't be restored.

In the end I strongly suspected a wiring problem because all the instruments were dead and the tachometer also conked in. Having no power to switch on the instruments and lights, I stayed up all night lying on my back in the cockpit, identifying the stars and the constellations.

Being in the dark, I went on survival overdrive and did what the olden day's sailors used to do. I used a plumb bob, a kind of weight with a pointed tip suspended on the bottom, hanging from a string as a vertical reference point and tried to get a fix to navigate in that way. Awesome!

Came day break I tackled the alternator problem and installed the spare alternator but it had an altogether different wiring system to the old one. If all else fails, read the manual! Trying to figure out how exactly an alternator works, I read and reread the chapter on alternators in the Boat Owner's Mechanical and Electrical Manual until I could finally grasp it.

I made some wire connectors and extended the engine's wiring. While the engine was running, I got behind the alternator for the umpteenth time, leopard crawling under the galley sink through the small, twelve by eighteen inch cabinet door. It was very hot under the galley sink but I was determined to fix it. Using my tiny tester, I cautiously held each connector in front of me, carefully tested them for voltage and reconnected the life wires.

Peeking from under the galley sink, watching the voltmeter on the navigation table I attached the last wire to its terminal. And whoosh, up shot the voltmeter dial to a whopping fourteen volts, I screamed: "Hello Houston, we have a lift-off!" However, I couldn't run the motor for long because the diesel levels were worryingly low.

Satisfied with my work, I sat in the companionway eating my first food in twelve hours; two pieces of biltong (jerky), a few olives and pickled onions.

I tackled the mess putting everything back, cleaning up the oil smears and gave the cockpit a complete scrub with saltwater and soap. After an entire day of repairing and cleaning, I was exhausted and when my head hit the pillow I was instantly snoozing.

During the night I became acutely aware of a bad vibration originating from the engine and in the morning I switched it off, hoved-to, took a dive into the Pacific and checked whether the trouble could have been caused by the prop.

The water was even clearer than those of the Caribbean and I couldn't find anything wrong. But when I checked the engine's mounting bolt nuts, I found that two were a little loose, tightened it and gone was the vibration. Afterwards, I sat back in the cockpit, contemplating the issue of

Sunday sins…

Morné and I did a lot swimming and fishing in the sea at the nearby seaside resort of Morgan Bay. However, Morné had not been allowed to swim or fish on Sundays because his father was a God fearing Christian and believed it was a sin.

Having been raised in a family where doing fun things on Sundays didn't constitute a sin, it was something I had found difficult to comprehend.

According to our family anecdotes, it was my grandfather Tony de Villiers who had liberated us from Sunday sins. He had been the mayor of Komgha for twenty years and to this day, his legacy still lives on in the Komgha community. Thanks to Oupa Tony, my father had been raised with interdenominational exposure and in our house Dad had continued this tradition of being liberated from Sunday sins.

The story goes that while Oupa Tony had been mayor he had a squabble with a "holier-than-thou" bucolic NG Church Dominee and in rebelling against the insulting way that the Padre had addressed him, he declared a number of activities on a Sunday to no longer constitute a sin. After that incident Dad, his brother and sister could enjoy fun things which hadn't been within the realm of their other more conservative Afrikaner cousins.

And we had been allowed to swim, fish, play golf and snooker on Sundays.

And I wondered what Morné's dad would have said and whether he would forgive me for taking a dip in the Pacific on a Sunday.

Then I saw something strange on the horizon, got out the binoculars, had a good look and unexpectedly, spotted land. Worrying that I might be on a wrong course, I checked the coordinates on the GPS, plotted my position and double-checked it on the charts.

The land mass appeared to be twenty nautical miles away and I guessed that it might be Isla Culpepper but was unsure. The radar gave an exact distance and bearing but what confused me was that the charts and the radar readings were not the same as the GPS.

"Culpepper" appeared to be fifty instead of twenty nautical miles away. It baffled me and for the next three hours, I felt disorientated and confused. Being lost at sea was one of the things I dreaded and my pulse started to race, feeling the terror of being lost.

Eventually at noon I figured out that it was actually not "Culpepper" but a smaller island, "Isla Wenman", which I couldn't previously pinpoint. Both islands are just north-west of the Galapagos of which they are a part. Plotting again I was relieved to see that I was indeed on the correct track.

I was grateful for the charts which were a great help especially when I started to doubt my gadgets. When the Ragels had lent them to me, I had no idea how often that would happen and usually at the most critical times.

For two reasons the 12th of April was a special day for me.

Firstly, I crossed the equator. It was very quiet with almost no wind, sailing at an average speed of three-and-a-half knots, passing over the equator at 10:15. I took footage of the GPS going through 0.00.000, 94:53:7:45 degrees west. As had been agreed with Sharon and Dave, it would only be at the equator that I would be allowed to open their surprise box. The box contained sailing magazines, nuts, dried cherries, sweets, a jester's hat and a toilet scrubber. And a small bottle of rum for Neptune!

They had wisely coached me how to perform "The Crossing of the Line Ceremony", an initiation rite that commemorates a sailor's first crossing of the Equator to ensure that Neptune, who rules the southern seas, would not be affronted. Sailors who have already crossed the Equator are nicknamed Trusty Shellbacks or Sons of Neptune and those who haven't are nicknamed Slimy Pollywogs.

I felt a bit silly, but as per the instructions, it was a serious rite and because I respected their guidance, I didn't want to confront Neptune's fury by entering without his permission. So, I went a little crazy and as a Slimy Pollywog with the jester's hat on my head and the toilet scrubber as sceptre, I went on deck and dramatically poured the rum for Neptune into the sea. While I earnestly requested his blessing to enter the southern hemisphere, I swallowed the last few drops.

Secondly, the 12th of April was also my late mother's birthday and as night fell, looking at the skies, I saw her smiling face amongst the stars and my thoughts were with her all the time. I remembered how she had agonised, how she had always been there for me and on each holiday returning from Komgha, how she had welcomed me back with

yellow ribbons…

As an unaccompanied minor I used to fly back home from the nearest airport to Komgha, East London to Cape Town for school holidays. Returning home for the first holiday, Mom had tied yellow ribbons around the pine trees standing in the circular drive-way in front of our Durbanville house.

At first, not knowing the lyrics of the song "Tie a yellow ribbon round the old oak tree", I didn't get it. But after some explaining that the hit song was about a released prisoner who had been welcomed home by his beloved with yellow ribbons around a tree, I grasped the meaning.

Subsequently, each time I returned home after the school's quarter, I looked forward to the yellow ribbons. And I too felt welcomed and ready to reclaim my life.

That evening I was sad and over the years my longing for Mom never dissipated, in fact, I miss her even more than ever before.

"Water, water everywhere, Nor any drop to drink", those prophetic words haunted me yet again but at the time, I kept the truth to myself, fearing that I would scare the folks back home. On the 13th of April my biggest terror materialised: The little I had left in my tanks and the harvested rainwater, finally ran out!!!

I felt at my wits end and desperately looked around for ideas on how to handle the matter at hand. I searched in my small library and found Wilbur Smith's "Blue Horizon", turning the book over, the fact that it dealt with an epic journey on the high seas to the Cape of Good Hope, grabbed me.

I spent the rest of the day at the navigation table with the radar on standby and pushed my nose into the book.

For three days without water, I made little progress, a frustrating three hundred nautical miles. The wind was down and it felt almost like we were in the Doldrums. I calculated that at that pace it was going to take forty days and forty nights to reach Samoa.

Realising that with a depleted water supply and dwindling diesel levels, I would be unable to safely reach Samoa, I changed course and entered new waypoints on my GPS to rather opt for a stopover at the Marquesas. Once I made that decision the turmoil in my heart started to disperse and my despondency got diluted.

The next morning I saw real, famous Pacific swells: Looking up in the trough it looked like distant hills and when on top, looking down a beautiful valley appeared below. Every swell gave a different picture, awesome but also very scary. I switched on the masthead tri-colour light so that we would be visible in the deep swells. I was in a quandary, still had a very long way to go and didn't want to unnecessarily burn up valuable diesel to charge the batteries. But in the end logic prevailed and I started the engine to keep the tri-colour switched on.

I managed to keep IT steady in the swells but suddenly she came to an abrupt standstill and the wind shifted so fast that it locked us in irons. The whole genoa got stuck against the starboard rigging! We were on a port tack and no matter how hard I tried to roll up the genoa in the pouring rain with twenty four knot winds, I didn't succeed. To get the genoa off the rigging, I started the engine, ran IT upwind and back to the original port tack.

Once the genoa was sorted out, I gave my full attention to gather as much water as possible and managed to get a sufficient supply to hopefully last me to Marquesas.

In the evening skimming through the deep water on a beam-reach, I watched intently as millions of shining plankton particles followed in IT's wake, generating incredible luminescence. The current in the surrounding water propelled them, dispersing the organisms throughout the water. The stars were amazingly bright and sparkled in unison with the plankton.

I had once before in my life witnessed

shining plankton

Just before we were to complete our schooling at Komgha, Morné and I had decided to hike the "Strandloper (Beachcomber) Trail" which stretches for eighty kilometres between Kei Mouth and East London.

Geared with back-packs, sleeping bags, enough food and ample water the two of us had been dropped off at Keimouth from where we started our hike.

Those days Morné and I had been super-fit (and super-young) and on our first evening we had easily reached the halfway mark between Morgan Bay and East London. We slept on the sand of a lonely beach, made a fire and the stars were amazingly bright.

At midnight Morné woke me up and pointed towards the glittering plankton in the breakers. When I left Komgha that "glittering plankton hike" from Morgan Bay to East London became a special highlight for me and an experience that I will never forget.

The next couple of days I spent time fixing things, putting all the tools back into their boxes and generally just got some of the nitti-gritty stuff done which I had earlier postponed.

The seas were as they should be: "Hills and Valleys!" In strong wind IT performed very well, the swells lifted her from behind and we surfed at speeds of up to eight knots.

I desperately wanted IT to make haste for the Marquesas, so I took the spinnaker out and it was time to learn, because in my entire life I had never used that kind of sail. Despite a lot of tangling, I managed to hoist it up and when the spinnaker finally flew, I stood back and was delighted in conquering it.

However, the uneven wind caused the spinnaker to tangle up around the roller furling and it took me a whole hour to get the mess straightened out before it flew again. But just as I hurried back to the cockpit to adjust a sheet, it got entangled again. I aborted the flying attempt, had enough of the stupid spinnaker and as I got it off it fell into the sea. At that stage, I didn't know that this kind of weird spinnaker behaviour would become a huge irritation along the way, but I managed to fish it out and dumped it hastily into the fore hatchway.

I unfurled the genoa and set a westerly course bearing two-hundred-and-fifty degrees, making a run for the Marquesas.

When a pod of dolphins, similar to my departure from Palacios, came to encourage me, it was probably the happiest day since I had left Balboa and I once more recalled the Ragels' forecast that IT would surf along with dolphins.

It was beautiful to see nine of them swimming shoulder to shoulder in front of IT, riding the bow wave and at times leaping into the air, diving back into the water, all the time playfully interacting with each other.

The dolphins brought good luck and late afternoon the wind picked up, occasionally shifting throughout the night accompanied by heavy squalls which was a relief, giving me the opportunity to catch fifteen more gallons of rainwater. In the distance I could see a funnel cloud and watched it closely but it didn't threaten us.

But still we were not covering enough sea miles to my taste and I urgently wanted IT to fly again. So, I rolled up the genoa and got the bloody spinnaker out of the hatchway. It was still wet and tangled up from the previous time I had to fish it out of the ocean. I dragged it up to the bow, sorted it out and hauled it up. And I was delighted that IT was flying again and sailed on a run for the Marquesas.

I relied heavily on my daily weather fax and when I couldn't obtain one, I was very concerned. My closest station was Honolulu, Hawaii but the blinking light on the fax machine indicated that the signal was too weak. So, I just kept it on automatic and while I cooked some rice and brown gravy, I waited.

When the weather fax finally came through it predicted strong winds and heavy weather. To prepare, I hastily hauled down the spinnaker and I again forgot to put on gloves. Due to the friction of the quick release of the rope, I burnt all my fingers. Looking intently at the blisters I swore at myself: "Damn it, when are you ever going to learn to handle things with gloves?"

The 3rd of May will go down in my memory as "The day of the Squalls" but little did I know then that there would be yet more squall days, actually beating this one.

Each time a squall hit us the wind was up to thirty knots and we roared sideways down big waves at a speed of up to nine knots. On numerous occasions, IT came close to broaching but quickly corrected herself. I closed-up the cabin to block out the falling rain from dripping onto the bunk where I was reading under a flashlight and sporadically checked the radar for passing ships.

Then the bloody Randy Andy, stupid auto helm (my apologies Aunt Andy) stripped her gears again and I was fed-up with her. I took her down and bandaged her, using anything I could lay my hands on, even duck-tape. So we sailed with Andy in bandages doing the steering but during the next squall Andy exploded, popped open and the belt simply fell off like a snake's skin.

Although I felt annoyed, I realised that she had probably not been designed for this kind of weather. Seemingly the poor old shipmate of mine was too much of a softy for this sailing job and I tossed her aside. Locking the wheel, I put Willy to work and he was doing a sterling job and only on a few occasions did I need to correct him.

Over twenty-four hours, I had counted fourteen squalls with the longest one lasting two hours. At night the squalls took their toll and I called it quits. So I hoved-to with only the mainsail up, fell onto the bunk and, before my head hit the pillow, I was fast asleep.

Waking up at dawn the weather was calm and a lone swallow flew low over IT. I threw a kiss at it with an invite to stay for breakfast. I didn't see it as a bad sign when it hurriedly flew away because from my previous experience with a swallow I knew that it was a lifesaver. In fact my mood lifted and despite the water and diesel dilemma I had a good feeling about it and I trusted my

sixth sense

Komgha's School only went as far as grade nine and at the time my father had sold his Quantity Surveying practice in Cape Town to go farming in the Bushveld, close to my mother's parents.

In the late seventies and eighties the government had given subsidised loans to encourage farmers into permanent residence as a strategy to form a bulwark against the returning A.N.C's freedom fighters who were crossing the border from Zimbabwe to South Africa. There on the border, my dad had bought a farm on the banks of the Limpopo River and named it Ravyn.

That gave me the opportunity to go to school with Gerrie in a medium sized, mainstream High School at the nearby town of Mussina where Christa, my mother's sister, also schooled and could keep an eye on us.

At the same time my two younger brothers, Francois and Christo, attended the adjacent primary school. Distant cousins of my mother were also teachers at Eric Louw and gave my parents the assurance that they would look out for us. My brothers and I stayed in the hostel during the week and went to the farm over weekends.

It was a new experience for my brothers to have me around all the time, not only during school holidays. After Komgha, arriving at Eric Louw, my lip-reading ability had already been so well established that the children at school often teased me that I was faking deafness.

My brothers used to play along and during school breaks frequently tried to demonstrate to the other children that I was not deaf. They followed me around on the playground, talking and gesturing behind my back where I couldn't see them, thereby disabling my lip-reading ability.

However, what confused them was that I had developed a kind of sixth sense, peripheral vision and an accurate perception of depth, enabling me to notice the slightest movement, reading any situation and detecting any change in the atmosphere.

I would immediately notice them sneaking up behind me and following me but I played along and gave them the chance to make their silly movements behind my back. But when I had enough, I would swing around and that, apparently, demonstrated to the other children that I could indeed hear.

At that moment I missed my brothers and looked forward to meeting them when I would get to South Africa.

I caught sight of the four islands which make up the Marquesas. Although I had beforehand carefully studied the entry instructions, it was still very tricky. With the wind down and another twenty five nautical miles to go, I manoeuvred to side-step all the tiny islands, which are scattered alongside the main island.

Finally, I saw the pilot light against the cliff and the flickering lights of the small town beckoned me. Then with a huge sigh of relief, the green light of the small harbour entrance appeared.

After thirty-one days at sea, battling with the batteries, not having enough solar power, wasting valuable diesel and yet again, struggling to survive on the bare minimum of water, I was about to find out how wrong my sixth sense could be…

Smuggling Merchandise

On the 5th of May at two o' clock in the morning, I steered with the port's navigation lights and my radar into Atuona's little harbour, situated on the south side of Hiva Oa Island. The waxing moon was hiding behind roaming clouds and threw ghostly images of the steep cliffs onto the quiet surface of the water.

I motored around for about twenty minutes with my spotlight, feverishly searching for a place to anchor. I couldn't find any but saw a small buoy, hooked IT up to its chain and, after that harrowing passage from Balboa, I immediately fell asleep.

I was anxious to find the cause for the water leak and the next morning, on closer inspection, I found that the tanks' caps had cracked and when toppling over in rough seas the water from the one side had syphoned from starboard side to port side and vice versa. After I sealed both of the valves I turned my eyes heavenwards and prayed for this water nightmare to take flight.

I hauled out my inflatable dingy, installed the floorboards and foot-pumped it up. I emptied the remaining four, five gallon water containers into the tank and rowed the two-hundred yards to the quay with the empty containers. I filled them up at a tap, rowed back to IT, emptied them, rowed back to the quay again, filled them up and frantically repeated the process until the tanks were full.

I walked with passport in hand for about two miles to town. Without any hiccups I got my passport stamped at the Gendarmes' office. Strolling back to the harbour the sweet aroma exuded by the indigenous palms enveloped me and I was fascinated by the adjacent thick green forest. After my water ordeal during the last leg, the walking actually helped me to get rid of the cob webs and I was just admiring the beauty of the Island.

When I got back to IT, I was sufficiently de-stressed to haul out the gear and climbed to the top of the mast. Although, the swells gave me a hard time, I managed to put the two lost spinnaker halyards back through their blocks. After being sea-bound for so long, scaling the mast and being high up in the sky was pretty fun.

Afterwards I took the empty jerry cans to the fuel depot but the lady in charge refused to sell me any diesel or gas. I couldn't understand it and tried every trick in the book, from being nice to nasty, to convince her of my predicament. But she pigheadedly bitched that she was out of stock and indifferently told me in broken English that I should come back the next week.

My soaring mood of earlier swung from being light hearted to steaming anger. I was totally dumbstruck watching from the side-line how she openly sold to others, filling up their cars and trucks but flatly ignored me.

Disgusted I went into town and walked around like a beggar pleading for diesel or gas but absolutely nobody was prepared to sell any to me. I am used to discrimination but that was the ultimate power insult.

In a very dark mood, I hitched a ride back to the harbour and when I got there found that IT had drifted away a hundred meters. I rowed out like a maniac, motored her back to the original spot and dropped anchor again. Disheartened I went back to town, hitching a ride and did some more begging.

Upon my return IT did it again! Having lost my big Danworth anchor during the last leg, obviously the spare anchor was too small to keep her from running away in the current and the wind. And in a mutinous mood she AWOL-LED and after some serious pillow-talk, I understood that it was her way of telling me that she didn't feel welcome in the Marquesas and therefore voted for a departure. I got her close to the horseshoe-shaped breakwater and dropped anchor again.

Further on in the journey she would time and again sensitively read my mood and before I could depart she would let me know it was time to go by going a-drift.

Doggone tired I fell asleep in the cockpit, occasionally waking up to check that IT wasn't running off but with me on board my old seahorse decided to stay put. When I eventually woke up at four o' clock in the morning I felt refreshed enough to write my logs.

With renewed vigour I hastily got dressed and was determined to find a solution for the diesel shortage and hitched a ride back to town. By then I knew that no amount of begging was going to yield any results and that I had to change my tactics.

At a small eatery I ordered an ice cold beer, the owner spoke perfect English and marketed the Island as the famous final resting place of the French Painter Paul Gauguin (1848 - 1903) and Belgium singer Jacques Brel (1929 - 1978). They were buried amongst the flowers, trees and ferns in Calvary Cemetery, overlooking Atuona. Having read-up beforehand about the Marquesas, I knew all of this but still I pretended that I knew nothing about all the interesting things and that it was news to me.

I am a great fan of both Gauguin and Brel and had vowed that I would visit the cemetery while in the Marquesas. There had been a book of Gauguin's paintings in our house and, although I couldn't hear the music, I remembered the many records of Jacques Brel too. So, a visit to the cemetery was a must for me.

The owner of the eatery was in a conversational mood and took a keen interest in my silent voyage but I had another burning issue on my mind before I could go sightseeing. I took him into my confidence telling him about my diesel obtaining predicament. I offered to pay him $60 (6,000 francs), if he would assist me. He became very quiet, looked sympathetically at me and said he could get into serious trouble if he helped me but, in any case, that he would.

However, he warned me that after he helped me, I wouldn't be able to stay and would have to run away otherwise he and I would be running the risk of being caught out by the diesel mafia. Apparently the diesel mafia was a group of government officials who controlled the limited diesel supply on the Island and only sell to locals.

I weighed up my options and although, I was disappointed for going to miss the opportunity to visit the cemetery, I opted to rather go with his suggestion. He took me back to the harbour where I hastily rowed to IT and collected the empty jerry cans.

As a stowaway hiding under the canvass on the back of his pick-up, he went to the same fuel depot where the lady previously had refused to sell diesel to me. Peeping from under the canvass I could see the eatery owner pumping ten gallons of diesel without any resistance from the bitching lady.

Back at his eatery he requested his friend to go and fetch me five more gallons. When his friend returned with the smuggled merchandise the eatery owner made haste to the bank where I withdrew the cash to pay him.

I could see that the eatery owner had become very nervous, he asked me to hurry-up and I quickly dashed into a store for some last minute items. Since my bribed guardian angel could get into serious trouble with the fuel mafia, he also requested me that he should remain anonymous.

Back at the harbour we gave each other bear hugs, I thanked him for helping me out and putting his safety on the line, smuggling the fuel for me.

Having barely recovered from the arduous previous passage, I scurried back to IT thinking about the missed opportunity to visit the Cemetery where a great painter and a singer were buried.

On the 6th of May, after two weird days in the Marquesas, feeling a bit like a pirate with the smuggled merchandise and really distrusting my sixth sense, I hauled up anchor and slipped away.

"So that's the Pacific Captain Cook, Piece of Cake!"

When I anxiously hauled-up my sails to run off, a catamaran and two sloops simultaneously and suspiciously also hoisted their sails. Not trusting my sixth sense any longer, I got very worried that it could be the diesel mafia that had found out about the smuggling and decided to follow IT into the coastal waters where they would confiscate her and put me behind bars. I contemplated how I would deal with being jailed in the Marquesas, thought that scared the shit out of me.

The catamaran didn't make much progress and I thought I gave it the slip but as we rounded the head of the island, going on a beam-reach, the cat got the upper hand, closing in on me. After what my eatery friend told me about the diesel mafia I nearly fainted and, as I helplessly watched it closing in on me, I really panicked. Then suddenly the cat passed, its passengers waved at me and it was soon just a speck on the horizon.

Peeping backwards, I saw the two sloops had turned towards a small bay with white sandy beaches and then they dropped anchor. Phew!!! Wiping my brow I collapsed in the cockpit. I had not been followed, it was only

my guilty conscience…

As a teenager I was very active in sport and developed a huge appetite. The food was nice at the hostel in Mussina but never enough and I also got bored with the predictable menu.

Mom used to pack a Tupperware container full of food for each of my brothers and me to snack on and if one of my parents would come to town during the week they usually topped-up our supplies.

One particular week the tin of sweetened condensed milk was finished on the first day, the last of the cookies and biltong (jerky) ran out by the Wednesday. There was still plenty of coffee and milk but no sugar.

My parents didn't come by with the usual top-up and I had squandered my pocket money on cigarettes. I begged my brothers and Christa for snacks but they were very tight fisted. By Thursday evening after study, the hunger pains were seriously gnawing. All that my junior, nicknamed "Jakkals" and I could talk about was food.

Our yearning for something sweet had infiltrated our conversation to the extent that it became pure torture. Subjects like a thick slice of home-baked bread with lots of butter and fig jam, peanut butter or honey took centre stage. In fact it made us so mad with hunger that we slipped out of our hostel in desperate search for food.

The Primary School's hostel was situated next to the High School's Hostel and we spotted that its kitchen window was open. As Jakkals stood on my shoulders he peeped through the open window, noticed a big tin of syrup and a glass bottle with peanut butter, left behind on the sink. And that set our minds on fire, aggravating our hunger pains and like alcoholics the temptation was just too much, we couldn't help ourselves.

With Jakkals still standing on my shoulders, he climbed head first through the open window and grabbed the two containers. After passing them to me, he reversed out and back onto my shoulders.

That night we feasted on peanut butter and syrup until sweet behind our ears. However the containers were so large that we couldn't finish it off, so I invited Jakkals to spend the weekend on the farm with us. When my mother came on the Friday afternoon from the farm to collect us from school, we had already stashed the stolen merchandise in our suitcases to take along. During that weekend, when nobody was looking, the two of us eventually managed to clean out the stolen containers and threw the evidence away.

Came Monday morning, as we arrived back at school, there was pandemonium. A police pickup was parked in front of the hostel and having a guilty conscience, we started to panic. During school opening, the hostel master announced that there had been a break-in at the Primary school's hostel kitchen and that all the boys must line up for an identification parade. Apparently they had finger-prints and one by one the boys were asked to show their hands. When they came to the two of us we panicked like hell but when they passed us, we relaxed slightly and gave each other knowing looks.

Nevertheless, when they completed the line-up, the police pointed at the two of us and while all the other boys were sent back to their respective classrooms, Jakkals and I were requested to stay behind. How they identified us I still don't know. We probably looked so guilty that it was easy to spot us. They took us to the police station for interrogation but we immediately spilled the beans and they called our parents.

Jakkals' mother, Auntie Anna Smith, arrived before mine and cried her heart out, all the time asking: "Charl how could you?" But when my mother arrived, after I told her what had happened, she bent over and started to cry, not from sorrow but laughter. She patted the hysterical Auntie Anna on the back and consolingly said: "Don't worry, it's no big deal, only teenage mischief, when I was young I did it lots of times!" And then Auntie Anna started to laugh too.

On our behalf the two mothers positively proceeded to engage the police and like true legal experts they argued that the window was open, therefore it couldn't constitute a break-in. Consequently the Police dropped the case but insisted to escort us back to school.

Although, we were greatly relieved, the real humiliation was being dropped off by the police in full view of all the children and teachers hanging out of the classroom windows.

And I could just imagine the pandemonium it would cause if I would have been caught out.

But then it was suddenly just me on the big blue again!

The next day I needed to gather my thoughts and concentrate because we were close to the atolls requiring careful sailing. I plotted more frequently and was already miserably tired when the Pacific exchanged her pacifying mood for one with bitching strong winds accompanied by an antagonistic sea.

Then a second "Day of the Squalls" hit me, making the first one of the 3rd of May to look like a purring kitten. During twenty-four hours I went through a total of twenty squalls and each time a squall hit us the wind went up to thirty knots with IT roaring sideways down big waves, coming close to broaching. But by that time I had more confidence in IT's ability to correct herself.

I quickly got into the cockpit to furl the genoa but was too late. The wind punched me in the face with a whopping thirty-five knots and as I got the sheet into the three speed winch slowly furling it the starboard sheet got entangled. The remaining genoa madly flapped around the roller furling and violently shook the rigging.

And before my eyes, the whole genoa forcefully burst apart, ripping from the top halfway down, slowly tearing, more and more. And to rub salt into my wounds, nature further raised the stakes and lightning started to strike all around IT, blinding me. When the rain poured down in buckets, I had no choice and, badly in need of a rest, I closed-up the cabin but it was too moist and impossible to sleep the storm out.

With both hands clamped to my face I was dumbstruck, repeatedly shook my head and sighed, all I could do was to wait for calmer conditions.

Peering towards the east through the hatch I saw yet another black cloud approaching us from behind. I threw a finger at the black cloud, dared it to raise the stakes and to hit me before it would burst, stupidly arguing that at least I would have a better chance if the storm and I could

play blackjack…

While schooling at Mussina I started experimenting with Blackjack. After a hard week at school returning home to our farm we usually sat outside at sunset so that the breeze could cool us down and every night we barbequed.

After careful preparation everybody sat down to a fantastic family feast and there was always too much food. If a guest was not able to dish up seconds or thirds it was deemed an enormous slap in the face of the host and, especially in our Afrikaans culture, it was an unlikely occurrence. A true feeling of belonging would engulf me when so many of the people I love had a blast in the African bushveld.

When darkness broke, the table cleared, all the adults and children took a seat around the leadwood fire. We chatted away, sometimes about menial issues, other times laughing about family stories and taking shots at forecasting our and our countries future.

But when the strongest flames of the fire died down, it became impossible for me to lip-read the conversation. So, I used to slip into my father's study, switched on his old floppy-driven computer and played blackjack.

I played for hours on end, stretching my legs only at short intervals to check on everybody at the fire-side and to pour myself a cold drink. I soon understood the game pretty well and won a lot of electronic fake dollars.

I over-played my hand and felt totally distressed. I should not have gambled with nature because this was no "push" where the player and dealer got the same point total. Nature is clearly an advantaged card counter, who could track the profile of the cards that had already been dealt and it cunningly adapted its playing strategies.

Flabbergasted, I kept a luff in the main and studied the torturing weather. Even the rain moved horizontally! It definitely wasn't what I thought it should be and dashing back into the cabin, I remained perplexed with many questions circling around my head. Could the blackjack game have angered nature so much or was the bullying weather just as spiteful as the teacher

who had unleashed his fury upon us?

During our physical training period we were doing fitness exercises on the rugby field but the temperature outside reached an unbelievable, torturing 45 degrees Celsius. It became dangerously hot to practice outside. So, to keep us occupied, our teacher sent us to the gym to do some donkey work, cleaning up the storage area.

The teacher, with his cigarette in his mouth, was ordering us around. We lethargically rearranged all the equipment and reluctantly re-packed the storeroom. When he turned his back on us, I bounced one of the gym sling balls up and down and pretended to aim it at him.

Zake Pretorius, the head boy, dared me to hurl the ball at the teacher. Zake's mother was our English teacher and I was always in trouble with her for reading Wilbur Smith rather than trying to follow her lesson. I admired Zake, always trying to impress him, but also didn't want to get into any more trouble. So I told him: "No-way".

But when the other boys joined in and started to heckle me, mouthing that I didn't have the guts and was a sissy, that day took a turn for the worse. Being called a sissy, for us as youngsters, was deemed to be the worst possible insult. Without thinking twice, I hurled the ball, aiming for the teacher's head. As the ball connected with its target, he nearly swallowed his cigarette, furiously spun around and demanded to know who did it.

I looked around, saw that everybody kept their lips tight and so, I did the same. The fuming teacher exploded and unleashed his fury upon us, chasing us out of the gym and into the boiling African heat. He ordered us to leopard crawl about half a kilometre to the Baobab tree and to run back, adamant that his torture would not stop until somebody would come forward to face the music.

After the umpteenth time of crawling and running, the boys especially the fat ones, started to complain bitterly but the teacher, bending the tips of his cane backward and forwards with both his hands still visibly shaking, continued the punishment.

Seeing that the teacher was unrelenting in exercising his fury, the boys started to plea with me to confess. In the end their whining and piteous gestures got to me. I strolled up to the teacher and told him that it was I who did it. Very upset he commanded me to go to his classroom and wait for him.

Arriving at his classroom the teacher slammed the door shut. He turned to me and bristling with self-importance, he confronted me: "Hoekom het jy dit gedoen?" (Why did you do it?). Although I didn't feel it, I answered with confidence: "I was dared to throw the ball at you and they called me a sissy and nobody calls me that". He asked me who dared me and I told him everybody did.

Still steaming with anger he looked me straight in the eyes and used one hand to hold onto my dishevelled collar and with the other hand rhythmically ticked the rod on his desk. During that high voltage situation I kept my cool. After a few seconds, feeling more like an hour, he threw his rod down, opened the classroom door and harshly pushed me out.

That incident did not only teach me how to stare somebody down but also how to test another person's willpower. But I still had to face the consequences of the terrible weather.

As the waves increased in size they occasionally hit us square on the portside, releasing an avalanche of water all over the deck. The water eerily splattered onto my legs, inside the companionway, where I was typing on the laptop. And I was still left with more questions than the answers.

When the wind shifted coming from the south, blowing at thirty knots and gusting to thirty-five knots, it was time for me to face more music. And with a sinking feeling I watched the sinking barometer and the increasing wind. When nature raised the stakes once more with not only incomprehensible bad weather but a furious full force roaring gale, my first one on the journey, I had very little willpower left.

Whatever I tried to think of to cheer me up tended to make things worse. And I seriously thought about

throwing in the towel…

Christa, my mother's sister, being only eighteen months my senior, was in the girls' hostel. My mom got special permission from the headmaster that I could visit her during the afternoons, so that she could help me with history and maths.

Initially Christa showed some patience with my dreamy attention span and the difficulty I had in matching her lips with the written mathematical equations. But it soon turned into frustration and finally into pencil-chucking exasperation.

But she was on a mission and forced me, repeatedly saying: "Only a sissy throws in the towel and Charl, failing is not an option!" And she persevered with her tuition.

And I hate to be called a sissy and failing not being an option I scraped through.

And looking at the date, yet again the 13th of May, a Thursday bordering on a Friday and similar to the 13th of March when I narrowly escaped the ocean liner, also the 13th of April when I ran out of water, it definitely confirmed to me that the Pacific is a bitch and that my sailing friends back at the

Serendipity yacht club were right: There is something wicked about the number thirteen! And sailing is not for sissys!

At a loss for answers, I went back inside the cabin to wait for a weather fax, so that I could, at least, get some indication of what the hell was going on and why I could not

read the signs of nature…

My parents were confident enough in my hunting ability to allow me to go on my own into the bush, usually on either my grandfather's or father's farm near Mussina.

On one particular cloudy day I misjudged the bush, endlessly milled around in circles and by noon I was totally disorientated. Fortunately for me Dawid Sokker, one of my dad's farm workers, was also hunting with his pack of mongrel dogs for wild boar that had caused havoc to our sweetcorn the previous night.

Dawid was an expert tracker! It was child's play for him to isolate and pinpoint a specific spoor amongst dozens of others. He could not only accurately tell what animal it was but also its sex and size. Within minutes he could tell how old a fresh spoor was, how fast the animal was running, whether it was getting tired and in which direction it was heading. And he had quickly deciphered my spoor, detected that I was lost and came to my rescue.

For the rest of that day Dawid taught me how to read the signs of nature. At a fast pace, eyes on the ground, he effortlessly trotted along the kudu spoor and skilfully sidestepped the Mopani trees. Riffle on the shoulder, I followed him and although I was superfit, I struggled to keep up with his pace.

Then up shot his hand, indicating that I should halt and with his left palm he patted trice towards the ground, signalling that I should sit down. While I squatted down beside him, he put his right index finger to his lips, gesturing that I should be silent. With the same finger he tapped on his ear and then into the direction he wanted me to take note. He crooked his left index finger downwards and then jabbed it sideways pointing towards a thicket where the kudus were hiding.

Dawid bowed forward, pointing at one specific set of tracks on the ground and standing up straight again, he used both index fingers to make a spiralling movement above his head, mimicking the two-and-a-half turns of the horns of the kudu bull.

I wanted to get up from my squatting position but he put his right index finger to his lips again and with his left hand slapped three times hard towards the ground. I obeyed his orders, stayed down and kept my mouth shut.

Throughout the whole episode I carefully watched his lips but Dawid did not move them a single time. Yet, I clearly got the picture. It is amazing that Dawid couldn't read any written word, yet the veldt was an open book to him.

That afternoon Dawid and I went back to the farm to collect my father's old Landrover, loaded the dead kudus where we had left them lying in the veldt and returned as heroes with two trophy sized kudu bulls.

When at last a blurry weather fax arrived from New Zealand the penny dropped, I got the answer that had kept on avoiding me and then I realised that there is a big difference between the signs of the veldt and the sea. Without comprehending it, it was I who took a silly gamble. I actually sailed slam-bam right into the middle of a low pressure system without being able to decipher the signs of nature.

The next day, late in the afternoon, when the weather became somewhat better I tackled the mess on the roller furling system. I tied a knife with duck-tape to the end of the boat-hook, reached twelve feet up to the torn genoa and started to cut away at the ripped canvas.

After two frustrating hours, as the sun was setting, I finally managed to salvage some canvass and sheets from the furling system. It baffled me how a sail could get so knotted and messed-up!

Everything was scattered all over the floor and the cabin was a complete mess. Nevertheless, I continued to sail on a run with the headsail goose-winged to the portside and the mainsail to starboard, going at seven knots. Despite the bullying weather I calculated that since leaving the Marquesas I had sailed 1,059 nautical miles in seven days, definitely a personal best for me.

As soon as the sun, for the first time in how many days, showed his pretty face I immediately packed out all the damp mattresses, towels, linen and pillows to dry out on the deck. IT looked like a Gypsy caravan! I filled up the generator and started it to charge the batteries so that I could later switch on the laptop.

Suddenly something in the water caught my attention, so I held onto the stanchions bowing over the railings and watched in amazement as flying squid started to jet-propel themselves out of the current by expanding and contracting their mantle cloaks. They were soon joined by flying fish and in their getaway effort, chased by predators, the flying squid and fish behaved like kamikazes. They jumped onto IT and left a slimy battlefield on the deck.

I started to clean up the mess, slipped on the slime, fell backwards and was lights out for a few seconds. When I came round, stumbling disorientated towards the cockpit, sitting down for a moment, I thought back to how those two seemingly unconnected phenomena had previously weirdly combined in my life,

slipping and being lights out…

In matric I had been elected hostel prefect. It was a serious responsibility and doubts had been raised by some of my teachers whether, as a deaf person, I would really be up to the task. But eventually I earned the confidence of my hostel father and mathematics teacher, Frans Venter. He and his wife, Saartjie, stayed in the apartment right underneath my room.

Every Wednesday evening they went to the open air movie theatre in town and he left the duty of supervising the students in my "capable hands". However, being a movie addict myself, I showed a keen interest in their pastime and used to quiz him about what movies were showing and who starred in them. On one particular night, the temptation became too big, an international movie "The Wild Geese", which had been filmed near Mussina, was going to be the main feature. Knowing, thus far, during Frans' absence nothing really bad had happened and that the students were generally well behaved, I slipped out and trotted the three kilometres to reach the theatre.

Being interval there was nobody to check the tickets and I sat at the back where I made myself invisible and watched the main movie, lip-reading all the way through. As the message: "The end" got displayed, I sprinted back to the hostel and was thrilled with my first successful free theatre movie.

But, as it goes with any addiction, it became a bad habit and I couldn't wait for Wednesday evenings.

Frans and Saartjie used to take seats right in the middle of the amphitheatre. They usually stayed longer, probably visiting with their friends. But I would rush back and after climbing the flight of stairs, three steps at a time, I crawled into my bed. Upon their return, mostly an hour or so later, Frans would open the door, pop in and enquire whether everything was in order. Of course, while remaining in bed, sheets tucked under my chin, I would respectfully confirm that everything was honky-dory.

But one evening my mischievous slipping in and out of the hostel backfired! They must have decided not to visit with their friends and I miscalculated my timing. As he opened the door to my room, I dived backwards onto my bed but misjudged the distance to it, fell flat on my back onto the floor and was lights out.

When I came round, kneeling over me, Frans's face was right in front of mine and he asked: "And now?" I wasn't compos mentos enough to conjure up a lie, so I told him that I had slipped which of course was the truth but when he raised his eyebrows into a frown on his forehead I quickly added: "On something slimy on the floor". I knew that he suspected something fishy. And after that incident, in fear that he would really catch me out, sadly my free-bee movie days were over.

While I continued the clean-up operation, this time more cautious not to slip on the slimy mess, three brownish seabirds showed a keen interest and for about twenty minutes helped themselves to the offerings of the free-bee kamikaze squid and fish.

The smooth sailing that followed all night long gave me a chance to have a good sleep. The next day I finished Alan Villiers' masterpiece "Captain James Cook" and all the Captain's escapades inspired me. He was a man who had no fear to tackle the high seas and I drew courage from The Captain's brave example. I found it fascinating that the Captain had to douse his pipe because the locals on the Islands that he visited thought it was devilish and threatened to make trouble for him. The story jogged my memory of my own

smoking trouble…

Sometime after I had commenced my schooling in Mussina, similar to most of the hostel boys, I started to smoke in secret. We knew that if we would get caught, we would be in serious trouble, so we smoked outside behind the toilet block in a secluded spot.

Later as a hostel prefect, for the upcoming final exams, I was allowed to study late with only my desk lamp on. One evening after general lights out, knowing that everybody was asleep, I lit a cigarette and was happily puffing away when suddenly Frans Venter opened the door.

When he walked up to my desk, I knew that he must have smelled the smoke. I quickly spit the cigarette into my palm and formed a fist around it. He cornered me with the half smothered cigarette burning my right palm, like hell. But he said nothing about the smell and rather enquired about what I was busy studying. And he encouraged me to try harder. When he left I was as scared as a rabbit corned in his hole but as the days went by, it turned out that he was not going to make any smoking trouble for me.

I suspected that Frans liked me and opted not to take the matter any further.

And to this day I am still grateful to Frans for protecting me against more trouble at school.

I lit my pipe but after the third pull, yet again, the barometer started to fall and regardless of the Captain's sterling example and against all my resolutions, I became as scared as a rabbit cornered in his hole.

The trauma of that unexpected gale hadn't worn off as yet and I was still hung-over from it. I slapped myself in the face for undertaking this voyage and I could kick myself that I had even imagined that it was actually my burning desire to do a solo circumnavigation: "How bloody stupid could I be? ^&@!!!"

So I went outside and this time round while watching the dark stormy clouds behind me, I shouted repeatedly with raised arms: "You have trapped me Jezebel!" Sickeningly, a realisation entered my mind that I had been enticed into unsuspected degradation and annihilation.

And in that irrational state of mind I decided to try and twist the stormy weather's arm to my advantage because I seriously feared for my own sanity. I knew very well that to put the spinnaker up in such stormy weather would be total madness and would be against all sailing rules but I wanted to make haste for Samoa. And in an effort to get a one knot increase in speed I hauled out the spinnaker.

In a mad frenzy I lifted the pole, snapped it to the pad eye on the mast and hauled up the spinnaker. I ran the sheets from the cockpit, snapped the knot, tack and clew onto the lazy sheet and hooked up the main halyard.

I sank down in the cockpit to admire my work, poured a gallon of water over my head and wished for a beer. That wish was not fulfilled but low and behold my effort actually yielded a one knot increase. Wow! And a smattering of hope resurfaced that the tide would someday turn for me.

But my glee and gloating didn't last very long. And I was not at the helm when the spinnaker beast decided to wrap itself around the shrouds, the mid-stay and the roller furling.

Seeing what had happened I cursed, let go of the main halyard and untangled the mess. I ran back to the cockpit, adjusted the course, ran up front, hauled up the spinnaker, cleated the main halyard, ran back to the cockpit and adjusted the sheets so that I could set course with Willy.

I sailed all day long with the spinnaker, hand-steered most of the time and when the sun went down I got the spinnaker down too. But I couldn't believe it when again it slipped into the water and after a lot of grunting, I fished it out again. I went to the cockpit, unfurled the little genoa and set sail on a broad-reach with a port tack.

Approaching Suwarrow a low coral atoll, part of the Southern Cook Islands, a line of squalls constantly hit us from behind and in that kind of weather my radar was useless. I navigated with my GPS constantly plotting our position on the paper chart and decided to run south.

To add insult to injury a heavy thunderstorm with lightning and heavy downpours followed the squalls. Being very close to the atoll it was stressful and my nerves were in total shatters.

To accommodate the thirty knot wind I furled up the headsail and staysail and double-reefed the main. IT was screaming along at seven knots. When the barometer started to drop again I was at the end of my tether, going crazy and knew that if I didn't want to go totally berserk I had to get on land. Fast! I cursed and yelled on top of my voice: "So, that's the Pacific, hey Captain Cook? Nice man, piece of cake!!!"

Having been forced to flee the Marquesas and after fourteen harrowing days in angry squalls and a monster gale, making me doubt the rationality of my mission and thinking about the advice of all those doomsday prophets who had forewarned me against undertaking this hedonistic trip, the cold black ink of depression coursed through my veins.

Once again failing not being an option but still fearing my own demise, I spotted "Tutuila" Island containing Pago Pago's main harbour which was still twenty-five nautical miles in the distance.

A Bird Whispered in my Ear

On the 21st of May at nine 'o clock at night, after a dreadful time at sea, I motored into Pago Pago harbour where a Friday evening party was in full swing with lots of people in attendance.

I explained to a bunch of happy guys who were loitering around, smoking under the lamplight, that I was deaf and enquired whether it was safe to dock there for the night. I didn't even think twice about their eager response in broken English: "No problema! No problema! No problema!"

I was seriously fatigued, locked the washboards from the outside, got inside IT through the front hatch and locked it. I immediately fell into a deep comatose sleep but I was constantly plagued by a horrible nightmare:

"The same greyish white bird which had joined me on my first night out at sea after my departure from Palacios was inside the cabin with me. It balanced itself on top of the navigation table scanning its surroundings with its prying eyes. Its beak was moving all the time as if it was trying to tell me something. It frustrated me because I couldn't read its beak sounds and when it suddenly took flight out of the open cabin towards the lamplight on the dock, I ran after it shouting for it to come back!"

I screamed myself awake and sitting up straight I noticed that the light from the lamp on the dock was streaming through the open cabin into IT. For a moment I was totally baffled, I was sure that I had locked the wash-boards but then it clicked: The washboards had been removed from the out-side to force an entry into IT.

I gave one startled yelp and hastily jumped off my bunk. I immediately re-alised that the "No problema!" of the previous night was a "Big problema"! During my night-time slumber an ethically challenged somebody or some-bodies, who had the privileged information that I was deaf and wouldn't be able to hear them, entered IT without permission.

When I saw the mess around me a feeling of doom gripped me in the pit of my stomach because I knew that I was in big trouble. After fleeing Mar-quesas and the taxing fourteen days at sea I thought nothing, absolutely "no-thing", could rattle me anymore but, oh man, I was wrong! I feverishly checked for my wallet and found it under my pillow. I went to the navigation station, looking for my passport but it was missing.

I did a quick reconnaissance and found that all the charts, the radar, the GPS, the weather fax and my satellite phone were intact. However the thieves had helped themselves to some canned food, the DVD player and even my shoes. All my distress flares and flare guns had also been taken! But I went totally off my rocker discovering that my laptops together with the data kit and camcorder had been stolen. And I nearly cried discovering that my only record of all my trials and tribulations, the eleven disposable cameras with their films full of my memories, had been taken.

Looking outside I saw the life raft had been ripped out of its holding bolts but was too heavy for the thieves to carry and appeared to be in good order. After the step-on-board ladder had been used to smash open the washboards, which were nowhere in sight, it was discarded and the ditch-bag's contents were strewn all over the place!

I was in two minds what to do, whether to call for help or stay put, fearing that the thieves could return and help themselves to the rest of the goodies. On the verge of hysteria I scanned my environment, saw a small shop, ran over, asked them to call the police and, fortunately at that very moment, a police officer stepped into the shop to buy coffee.

I explained to the officer what had happened and he requested me to slow down because he couldn't understand a word that I had said, apparently I was babbling too fast. He gave me a ride to the police station where another officer took over and after I had filled out a formal complaint they escorted me back to IT. While I miserably hung around, the police thoroughly inspected the ins and outs of IT and wrote a lengthy report.

When the police left I cleaned up inside IT and low and behold at the bottom of all the mess, right inside the navigation table, I found my discarded passport. It gave me hope that the thieves might also have dumped the other stuff and I started to anxiously search around in the vicinity. However all that I could find was the two badly damaged washboards and the empty emergency flare containers, forlornly floating on the west side of the harbour.

During the hunt around the harbour for my lost cargo I befriended a number of yachties including Eric and Ann Nesbitt from Michigan on-board Temerarius.

Later that day Eric helped me to get IT to safety and with everyone's assistance we tied her up in front of their yacht. Their neighbourly support meant a lot to me and made the blow of the break-in more bearable.

But I needed to refocus so I filled the water tanks, cleaned the slime out of the bilges, took the sails down and generally inspected IT for damages. I fixed the washboards, fitted them with new locks and generally beefed-up the security on IT.

That night, while Eric kept a watch on our yachts, I dined out with Josh, Suzy, Hank and Nicole. I was craving fresh parboiled vegetables and it was my first real food since I had left Balboa. During supper I was very tense and everybody tried their utmost to get me to relax.

Afterwards we joined Ann, Karyn and Cliff on board Temerarius and after Eric gave me a shot of Tequila, which quickly took effect, I strolled back to IT where I rolled around for hours. What my newly acquired friends didn't realise was with that burglary I had reached the end of the road.

Contemplating my dilemma I decided to forget about failing not being an option and that only sissys throw in the towel. I honestly wasn't sure whether it was worth continuing and whether I was really up to it:

The first stretch from Texas to Panama wasn't that bad but the expenses with the transit had far exceeded my budget. On my journey from Panama to Samoa, the stormiest stretch thus far, had made me to constantly slave to keep IT safe. And my initial optimism that the Pacific would be peaceful and the trades steady had been replaced by the reality of the incessant rolling caused by bad weather and in turn that had driven me crazy.

The thing that I had dreaded most was heat and thirst and it had materialized when I ran out of water forcing me to stopover at Marquesas where I had to smuggle diesel to run away like a thief.

I had worried about pirates on the high seas but the real villains had been on land in Marquesas and right here in Pago Pago. The pain in the arse squalls, the gale and the spinnaker weirdness taught me a hard lesson. And with my genoa in tatters I was also falling apart because I had no clue how I was going to fix it.

I had learned that I could dry my computer in the engine compartment to keep myself connected to the information and communication highway but the theft of the valuable equipment, my critical link with the outside world, was a crippling blow. In order for me to realise my dream the computers and flares needed to be found or replaced and I had no hope that they would be recovered. And there was no space in my budget to do so.

I had intended to stop-over at Pago Pago for only three days but was stranded and as a worried man I eventually dozed off, dreaming that the same greyish white bird had returned but this time round I was able to read her beak. She no longer had black eyes but my mother's stunning blue eyes and even spoke in her kind voice, saying that I should hush, all the time assuring me that everything would be alright.

Waking up the next morning, despite my desperate situation, I actually felt calm and chit-chatted with all my yachting neighbours. Suzy dared me to shave off all my hair, Mohawk style, and offered to do it for me. I protested like hell but before they departed on Suela she got at me and turned me into a rebelling sailor.

As the day progressed the cloud of doom and gloom hanging over me dissipated, especially after the support everyone gave me. I felt very grateful, reciprocated and invited them all to a late afternoon barbeque, the South African way, right there on the wharf. Everybody brought a side dish and the yachties loved the lamb chops.

The next morning the tide started to turn and from that point onwards things changed dramatically in my favour. I received a message from Monica Miller, the news Director of 93 KHJ Radio in American Samoa, who had heard about the break-in from the police and requested an interview. During the interview I shared my story with her and that due to the theft, the torn genoa and my tight budget I would unfortunately have to abort my solo mission.

I was told that she had broadcasted my story and made a plea that my stolen equipment should be returned. Ana, a Samoan woman, who had heard the broadcast decided to pay me a surprise visit. She kindly offered to repair my torn genoa and as she eagerly set up her sewing machine on the dock, right next to IT, a smattering of hope flared up that I might still be able to continue the trip.

I was totally stunned watching Ana working non-stop, diligently, painstakingly and patiently, hours on end, mending the sail. The picture of her, serenely turning the wheel of her old manual sewing machine burned itself into my memory. I didn't have words to thank this kind woman, just stood around admiring her genius, at a certain point something snapped inside and into my head popped the image of my mom behind her

sewing machine...

After I had passed matric my mother decided that it was time to make me a set of brand new curtains for my room at the University.

Mom sat for hours behind her sewing machine, saying she wanted me to feel that it was a new beginning with new curtains to kiss my innocent school days goodbye.

She knew very well how thrilled I had been for passing matric first class with university exemption at the usual age of eighteen and in that way she celebrated with me in achieving my first big milestone in life.

And Ana's sewing did introduce a new beginning for me because the next morning I received yet another message from Monica with the news that my camcorder and laptops had been found. When the police returned them I reclaimed my stolen goodies, jumped up and down with joy, tested them and was elated to be back on line.

In the afternoon I got another message that the Samoan newspaper had requested me to come to their offices and when I arrived they took pictures of me and handed me a cheque of $500, a donation made by Mrs Wanda Alofa and her daughter Aitulagi of Malaeimi. They had written a letter to the newspaper that they wanted to help me to complete my journey and to demonstrate to the world that Samoans are kind. And what happened to me was the work of a few bad apples. The donors also expressed their hope that others in the community would come to my aid and that the police would find the culprits and prosecute them.

The next morning when I picked up the newspaper from the office my story was on the front page and I knew then that it was all worth it. Similar to being on the front page after my discharge from the hospital and more recently in Palacios, the flame to complete the journey had been rekindled. With renewed vigour I spent the rest of the day re-organizing IT to get her in shipshape condition so that I could press forward in attempting my solo, silent sailing.

During the course of that afternoon a forty-two year old Marine patrol officer by the name of Michael Nix came over to show me some more items that he had recovered and I identified them as mine. There were flares, some of the ditch bag's contents and one crashed camera with the film ripped out.

Michael Nix and I became close friends. He spoke English very well and I could easily read his lips. His six feet muscular physique stood testimony to his rugby heydays when he had played as a superb flanker.

I received an invitation to dinner from the First Lady and the Chief of Police. That evening a banquet was hosted in my honour by the First Lady and Governor of Pago Pago. They went out of their way to show me a different side of the Samoan people. And during the function Michael Nix acted as my interpreter.

The morning after Ana, my sail mending goddess, gave me a ride to a wholesale food store near the airport where I bought the necessary supplies for the ensuing leg of my journey. Upon our return I fitted the repaired genoa onto IT's roller furling system and, as her handy work was hoisted, Ana proudly watched from the wharf. A group of yachties gathered around and applauded her.

I celebrated the mended sail with Ana, her husband Richard and their teenage daughters Lisa and Diane. While they sang cheerful island songs, which I couldn't hear, I rejoiced by taking pictures and serving snacks.

During the celebrations I enquired from Ana why she had taken all the trouble mending my sails without any remuneration. She mouthed something about a little bird that had whispered in her ear and I left it at that. I will never forget Ana selflessly repairing my genoa, not charging me a dime and her kindness will remain in my memory banks forever.

Duncan from Florida on a two year job contract in Pago Pago and his girlfriend Anita, a local, had heard about my plight on the radio and came over in their jeep to present me with a "lava-lava", a traditional sarong worn by the Samoan people.

With the lava-lava around my waist they took me for a ride around the island. We stopped at the world famous Tisa's Barefoot Bar where I met the owners, Tiss and Candyman, who had also heard about me. They presented me with a nice T-shirt, card and a donation. Thereafter Duncan and Anita took me up the mountain where I could see the ocean on both sides and it was truly a breathtakingly, beautiful scene.

And the following morning when Duncan, Anita and their friend Michael came to pick me up, we drove to the other side of the island. On our way Anita bought a bunch of island flowers to put on her mother's grave. Seeing the thoughtful gesture reminded me to put flowers on my mother's grave the next time that I would visit Mussina.

Anita's cousin, called Bird, joined us and armed with surfboards and body-boards we went to their favourite surfing spot. We swam and paddled with a long loop to get behind the reef and waited for the waves. The surfing distance was short and breaking away, the reef came up very fast. When the tide came in, in lovely warm and crystal clear water, it was show-time! We caught the powerful waves and several times I was washed out, right to the shore.

Our energies were sapped and as I wrapped my "lava-lava" back on, a relaxed island time feeling washed over me. On our way back we stopped at Duncan's house where he made some Kava, a traditional drink with a bitter after taste. And I appreciated it so much that they used their valuable time to show me a different facet of the true beauty of this strange island.

Back at IT, I was still contemplating how kind Anita and Duncan were but I pondered about Bird, his nickname for having a bird-like face, who couldn't speak any English and I was quite intrigued when Anita told me that Bird could mimic all the sounds of the birds on the Island.

At the crack of dawn I went to the harbour master to settle the bill and a pleasant surprise awaited me. Chris King informed me that Terry Hunkin, the president of the local Lions Club, had already taken care of the bill. The gesture not only bowled me over but also gave me a knot in my throat: Although I did send Terry and the Lions a thank-you card, still I don't think they know how much I appreciated it and how much it was a lifesaver for me!

Upon my return there was a lot of activity around Temerarius, I went round and was shocked to hear that there was yet another break-in. While Eric and Ann had been asleep their cash was stolen, they were fed-up, got ready and in a fury departed from Pago Pago. I was still flabbergasted standing forlornly on the pier, waving them off and didn't know what to think.

Temerarius's sudden departure had not yet fully sank in when the final nail in the coffin was hammered in. While I visited Duncan for lunch the sons of bitches broke into IT again but only took a flashlight.

Temerarius's place had been taken by Wolf Muller-Fabian and Barbara Miroslaw and during that night I had a horrible nightmare. I dreamt that Bird was trying to wake me up by mimicking bird sounds but I couldn't understand him, so he started to flash a torch light into my eyes.

I woke up with a jerk from the flashing police lights that were streaming onto IT. Wolf had caught the thief red-handed. But while Wolf was busy calling the police the thief got away. Fortunately nothing valuable had been taken and I couldn't believe it when they found my discarded stolen flashlight had been used to break into Wolf and Barbara's yacht.

Poor Barbara was really freaked out and wanted to leave immediately but it being Memorial Day everything was closed and we all had to wait until the next day for immigration clearance.

That evening the contrast of this beautiful Island with its thieving people on the one hand and then again the very kind people puzzled me. After I took the necessary precautions against another break-in by locking the boat from the outside then climbing in at the front hatch to lock it from the inside, I eventually fell asleep with a feeling of disillusionment.

When Duncan, Anita and Bird came round for a farewell lunch on board IT, I requested Anita to translate to Bird my nightmare which I had told them about and that had Bird in it. After Anita translated my account from English to Samoan, he looked sympathetically at me, pulled up his shoulders and just smiled.

I carefully checked IT's dock-lines before I caught a lift with them back to town to post a package, containing videos, disposable cameras with pictures of the island and the newspaper clips.

When I got back from town I was shocked to see Karyn and Cliff fighting with IT. One of the dock-lines had chafed through and IT was swinging like a pendulum crashing back and forth into Odyssey and it was only after a huge struggle that we got IT tied up at a safe distance.

Yip!!! IT was reading my mood again and similar to Marquesas she rebelled. I surveyed the damage and was devastated to see that during the pendulum swinging, Willy had been pretty badly busted up.

The last thing I had to do before I could depart was to get some spare fuel. Then more shit! Due to the time lost in fighting with Island Time I was not on time and the fuel station was closed. It was a terrible disappointment and I had no choice but to wait until the next morning.

Early bird catches the worm! But so fucking what? In a very foul mood and last minute makeshift repairs, I got Willy sort of wired together. Pumping ninety gallons of fuel at one gallon a minute took a frustrating ninety minutes because the bloody nozzle was too big for the hole and kept slipping out!

And on the 2nd of June after wasting valuable time to top up my tanks and, after a twelve day stopover, I played with the words "Island" and "Time" and said out loud: "My time on my Island Time, IT for short, on this Tutuila Island, TI for short, is over".

Torture Strait

I dashed out of Pago Pago and headed straight for Thursday Island in Australia. Like a cannonball the twenty-five knot winds blasted me out of the harbour and at the exit angry squalls and moody seas emulated my gloomy state of mind.

Against all better judgement and sailing taboos I had chosen shitty weather plus a Friday to sail away. I trusted my own ability to tackle the dangerous seas more than further exposing IT's safety to petty thieves and thereby risking the shattering of my dream.

While the headsail was up in heavy seas we screamed along on a beam-reach. I got so aggravated that I started swearing at the squalls ordering them to f-off. But the words spoken by King Canute entered my mind and calmed me down:

"Well, my friends, it seems I do not have quite so much power as you would have me believe. Perhaps you have learned something today. Perhaps now you will remember there is only one King who is all-powerful, and it is he who rules the sea, and holds the ocean in the hollow of his hand. I suggest you reserve your praises for him."

I immediately stopped the swearing and I made a dramatic bow to apologise to the almighty ruler of the seas. But King Canute's words became prophetic, applying to me rather than to his friends. The bitching squalls did not accept my whimpering apology, if anything they became more outraged with one after another, endlessly harassing me.

I was grateful for all the emails but replying to them became absolutely impossible. While typing the squalls interfered with me pressing on the QWERTY keyboard and the moment that I had succeeded to finish a word, it used those same fingers to scramble the letters. The typing looked like gibberish and I abandoned the effort.

In the end the squalls' nagging presence managed to attack my computer, the dampness caused it to flicker on and off and the error messages scared the shit out of me! I could fix anything on the boat but was no tech expert and if my computer would shut down I wouldn't have a clue how to fix it. And would be incommunicado!

I was totally at the mercy of the squalls and technology. I had grown up hunting pigeons and guinea fowl with a pellet gun, building model airplanes but it had only been in later life that I played computer games and only after going to America that I had the privilege to watch television with sub-titles.

And I was unsuccessful in dodging the squalls so I went inside the cabin, closed the hatches, made myself as comfortable as I could on the sole and pleaded for a break.

Still, the squalls continued their relentless onslaught, they reminded me of

a packman game…

After I had passed matric, I decided to go to Stellenbosch University to attempt a degree in Agriculture.

Separated from the protection of my family and our helpful small and fun loving Mussina community, University came as a bit of a culture shock. I found it extremely difficult to cope with an unaccommodating University that catered exclusively for the hearing and during lectures lost critical information but still I recall it as a valuable life experience.

In the eighties, not like presently, a personal computer had been an oddity. Although my father had one on the farm I didn't have one at University but my roommate had a floppy-driven one and for hours on end, instead of studying, he played Packman.

A few times I played with him but, compared to blackjack, found it such an irritating game with the Packman having to gobble up dots and having to run away all the time, while being chased by ghosts who wanted to eat him up.

Different from blackjack, there is no skill involved. And in the end the Packman can't escape and inevitably got eaten up.

But, as I woke up in the morning, the squalls got even angrier and the wind was soaring at a vigorous thirty-eight knots. There was no time to get dressed, so I hurried stark naked to get the headsail down because I had learned my lesson that any delay to make myself presentable for the big blue lady would later cause me great anguish.

Later, when the squall battering slightly dissipated, I got the break that I had pleaded for and reflecting on my last day in Pago Pago with the pumping incident, I actually giggled because size did matter where a pump was concerned... And I was on my way to the place where people apparently talk funny and the South Africans seemingly flock to like bees around a queen.

I was in the cabin when we sailed over the International Dateline with my GPS reading 17:40 Greenwich Time and then I got a little confused and couldn't comprehend what day of the week it was. Was it Saturday or Sunday, when I had crossed it on the 4th of June? I imagined the confusion that this would cause in an ordinary suburban settlement: Saturday or Sunday. Do we party or pray?

Regardless of my disorientation I felt an enormous thrill for achieving that wonderful milestone and a pleasurable buzz droned through my nervous system, shuddering through my veins and gave me squirts of pleasure giving brain juices.

But at the heart of all hypocrisy lies the ability to justify behaviour and I so prayed for a brandy to celebrate that achievement. And I would even pray pouring it down my throat.

But the thrill and pleasurable feeling soon started to wear off and as my excitement dissipated

I no longer felt special…

I would have given up after the first semester at Varsity but what kept me going was meeting a special friend, Rozanne Botha, who did duty at the student support group.

Being very compassionate she always made a point to chat with me, encouraging me to hold on. And despite my handicap she made every effort to treat me as a deserving human being.

When I had later accidently found out that she was the daughter of the Prime Minister of South Africa, P W Botha, my respect for her only increased because she behaved as if there was nothing special about her and that she was only an ordinary girl.

And after all the crossing of the dateline wasn't that extra-ordinary and I should rather have saved my breath than wishing for a brandy but still next thing I screamed out loud: "Sun, Oh Sun, where art thou!" Everything was damp and I was willing the cosmos to canvass the sun on my behalf so that it would lend me its heat.

It worked because an hour later I went outside and noticed that the wind was starting to relax, eventually the ocean became placid and the sun shone again! Soaking up the sun's nourishing rays I ceremonially laid out my clothing and other wet stuff to dry on the deck. In a thawing mood I basked in the sun content to absorb its warming rays and rested before tackling more canvass.

I woke up to the odious fact that all night long I had been drifting around in circles and made absolutely no progress. There was barely any wind and on the second day of drifting the realization hit me that I was seriously trapped in the doldrums, noted for calm periods when the winds disappear altogether, ensnaring a sail-powered boat for periods of days or weeks on end.

And for days on end there were no swells, the colour of the sky was reflected in the water and at night time the same effect. And the absence of clouds gave me a feeling of floating in space. After milling around in the doldrums my mind started to wander and in that place where "nothing ever happens and nothing ever changes" I found it hard to concentrate on even the bare necessities.

My emotional state of mind started to seriously worry me and when my mood started to swing like a pendulum,

red lights started to flash…

Except for a few very special friends, the students at Varsity gave me a hard time for being deaf and badly burned. Their attitude towards me had further exacerbated my already skewed self-image. I even played rugby for the hostel's third team but it didn't soften their stance.

And where the girls were concerned I developed an obsession that the only reason why a girl would show interest in me would be because she felt sorry for me. And the one time that I had accompanied a girl to a varsity dance I made sure that she felt at liberty to dance with the other males and not feel compelled to attach her to me, a horribly scarred person.

But, on our way back on the bus from an Intervarsity in Pretoria where Stellenbosch University (Maties) and Pretoria University (Tukkies) had played their annual rugby match, I met a girl who took the effort to form the words with her mouth which made it easier for me to lip-read and understand her.

She really made me comfortable and I didn't feel like a freak but appreciated as a human being. I had later learned that her family own lots of land and wineries in the Worcester area, not that it made any difference to me.

Thrice a week the two of us got together for a game of squash. Super-fit, I would jog a long distance uphill to collect her at the female hostel, then downhill to the squash court where we played a heavy game of squash and then uphill again and after dropping her off at the hostel, I again jogged downhill back to my hostel.

But a badly burned and deaf first year student dating a fourth year student is courting trouble and can ignite the wrath of the seniors. I should have seen the red lights flashing, they gave me a really hard time so I decided to rather back off from our weekly get-togethers which resulted in us losing touch.

It took a number of years before I could gather enough courage to allow myself to even think about dating.

Having had this little conversation with myself slightly pacified me and the doom and gloom of my own doldrums all those years ago assisted with knocking some sense back into me.

Noticing that my batteries were low I started the engine and motored for two hours with Andy at the helm but when she started to give problems again, I stripped her and discovered that the tiny plastic gears inside the gear-box had stripped. And I eagerly tossed her aside because at that very moment the wind suddenly picked up and I sailed with Tilly connected to Willy. Halle-lujah! IT was galloping at five knots out of the doldrums. And it was so satis-fying and so very beautiful.

Although it was taxing sailing with the indecisive wind that kept changing its mood and direction, I didn't mind. At least I was out of the bloody dol-drums. I was happily sailing along in a seventeen knot when a total wind standstill caught me by surprize. The anemometer reading was zero, zilch, nothing! Then the sea started to bubble and there was no way to tell which way the waves were rolling.

I was hypnotised by the phenomenon! It looked like we were in a cauldron of boiling hot water and it bubbled so fast that IT danced around in circles. To get out of my mesmerised state I slapped myself against the head, started the motor but at that moment there was a malfunction and it was only after the third attempt that the engine started. I gave it full throttle and made a run.

Yes that boiling pot of water nearly crisped me and made the adrenaline to pump! Later I tried to figure it out! It was probably a hydrothermal vent where sea water seeped down into the cracks created by the spreading of the sea floor. As the water came into contact with the veins and channels of superheated molten magma the sea water started to boil. Whatever the explanation it had scared the shit out of me, thinking that I was going to be cooked alive! Again!

After Willy's crashing accident, when IT had wanted to run away from Pago Pago Harbour, I had tried several times to repair him but he was in a real bad shape and I continued more makeshift work on the poor thing. All the time Willy's oar was going zigzag, the old fella was a Humpty Dumpty hovering on the wall and waiting for his great fall. I tried to patch the Humpty Dumpty together again and, to stabilise it, I fixed the oar with duck-tape around the shaft.

When we sailed close-hauled past the De Horne Islands of Futuna and Alofi, I was a happy man.

And in that exuberant mood I entertained myself and played announcer:

" …standing 762 meters tall in the northern corner, weighing in at an amazing billion tons is the monstrous Futuna, flanked by the small yet very potent Alofi, weighing in at half as much and standing half as tall. Ladies and gentlemen taking on these two giants in the southern corner, all the way from Palacios Texas, is the explosively deaf maniac Charl De Villiers on the back of his sea horse, called Island Time. The two of them have a combined weight of approximately 8,000 kg. While waving his toilet scrubber cum sceptre, Charl is riding through the amazing six meters deep waters towards the battle ground. But place your bets because Charl and Island Time's ability to drift at more than an inch a year clearly gives them the advantage…"

After my colossal battle with the doldrums and the imaginary fight with the De Horne Islands, I cleaned out the hellhole with a moronic smile, managed to get the laptop dry and charged the batteries.

We had a noon to noon run of a hundred miles. Not too bad. After the doldrums sailing all day on a broad reach with the spinnaker pulling like a Budweiser Clydesdale team of horses, was great fun.

When the wind picked up I went upfront and took the spinnaker down. Initially it had been hard as hell because I didn't have a dowser sock or a scoop but, after all the previous horrendous attempts, I got the hang of it. And by then I had made peace with the fact that half of spinnaker would always fall into the water, so I took down the half wet spinnaker with the halyard and sheets still attached to it and dumped it into the hellhole.

Suddenly the northern sky turned its blue into black eyes and with my blue eyes I winked and confidently returned its dark-eyed gaze. When the rain eventually dissipated a spectacular rainbow was unveiled, spanning over the blue skies. And it carried a feeling of fortuity, the probability of a fortune at its feet mystified me.

The wind was shifting and shifting towards Santa Maria Island, part of the Vanuatu Islands. It resulted in me doing continuous tacking which also slowed us down. I pondered how we were ever going to get to the land of

OZ because at that rate I would probably only make it in time for the next year's 2005 Currie Cup rugby finals in South Africa.

When the wind eventually stopped its hysterics I took all the damp mattresses, linens and towels to dry on the deck. We were drift-sailing at two knots and it gave me the opportunity to take down the main. While replacing a lost batten I reflected on the two days of continuous tacking, going zigzag all the time. It felt like I was

chasing game…

Nico de Kock who had studied agricultural management with me became one of the few students that took me under his wing. In those days his friendship meant a lot to me and when I couldn't keep up with the lectures he lent me his notes.

During our first winter break at Varsity I invited Nico to come and hunt on our farm in the African bush where I acted as his guide.

After driving along a bush track in a Landrover, going zigzag with two trackers on the back of the vehicle checking for spoor, it was not long before they spotted fresh tracks and pointed in the direction of the unseen herd.

I spun the steering wheel and floored the accelerator and the Landrover crashed into the thick Mopani bush. Following the trackers' pointed instructions left or right the old Landover's bull-bars whipped the younger trees flat and swerving through the bush I barely missed the thicker Mopani and the occasional ant-bear hole.

The adrenaline was pumping, Nico clung on for dear life, the two trackers ducked away from the thorn branches but for the rest of the time they stood on the back of the Landrover as if on tour on a luxury bus and easily swayed their bodies in unison with the speeding and bumping Landrover, going zigzag all the time.

As soon as the herd was spotted, I slammed on the brakes, told Nico to grab his rifle and we quietly sneaked up, with the trackers fanning out behind us. We both got a clear shot and when the animals dropped, Nico was so thrilled that he jumped up and down.

After taking photos we returned triumphantly to our camp in the bush where the game was slaughtered into biltong strips, salted and hung up to dry. And that evening we celebrated his first successful hunt.

But something on the horizon disturbed my thoughts. It was a dark shadow stretching from the east all the way to the west. Rubbing my eyes over and over I could not make out what the hell it was. I flippantly thought that it was perhaps just another squall and to my own detriment I didn't pay further attention to it because I got side-tracked by an oil leak from the engine which nearly freaked me out. I quickly removed everything around the engine, sniffed out the problem and speedily fixed it.

The next moment the dark shadow was upon me and loomed almost on top of me. Then a forty knot wind hit me with a punching blow and caught me with all my sails up. IT took off as if her tail was on fire! It took a while for me to realize that it was a front heralding the south-east trade winds. With a super-human effort I managed to furl up the headsail, loosened the mainsail's sheets, set Willy up and fastened the wheel to keep IT on a beam-reach.

That whole night I shouldered rough seas and cursed for not being better prepared, especially, on a date like the 13th. Midway between the Santa Maria and Vanua Lava Islands I could clearly feel the change in climate and for the first time since I had left Panama I covered myself with a blanket.

With dawn breaking and the sun peering over the horizon I clearly saw the breath-taking Santa Maria and Vanua Lava Islands, forming part of the Banks Islands. I was relieved that the islands were visible and throughout the night I constantly plotted, double-checking to avoid a collision with all the small islands scattered around the main island.

But the wind became lethargic at four knots and unfortunately so was our speed. To get an increase in speed I hauled out the spinnaker again, clipped on the sheets and up-hauled the halyard's lazy sheet. And I just hoped that it wouldn't turn out to be

a futile exercise…

I didn't pass my first year at Varsity, not for a lack of trying but the pace in Academic Lane was just too fast for me. I couldn't keep up with lip-reading the lectures and had missed out on a lot of vital information. After failing my first year my dad encouraged me to try again but harder and to put in a lot of effort in increasing my marks.

And in the second year I put my nose to the grindstone, went for extra classes, borrowed notes, knocked on the doors of the lecturers, studied in the library so that my Packman-crazed roommate couldn't disturb me, asked for advice from the student support group and even went to church to pray for a miracle.

By the end of my second year I managed to substantially increase my marks but when the results came out I still failed. It was a futile exercise and after all that effort I missed the pass rate with just one percentage point. So, hugely disheartened, I decided to call it quits and that was the end of my pain in Varsity lane.

Occasionally a wave came on the quarter to let us roll down it, the spinnaker waltzed one step on the way down and two, three steps hitting the trough. But it was a futile exercise, in yet another wind shift the spinnaker started to do a serious waltz and wrapped itself around the furling system as if it was madly in love with it. It took me two hellish hours to untangle the two lovers. When I finally got the spinnaker down I was so fed up with its amorous behaviour that I dumped it through the front hatch.

But on father's day, Sunday the 19th of June the winds were down again and, when we were sailing at one knot, I was joined by two duck-like birds. The ducks displayed an amazing balance and while positioning themselves on the bowsprit, they slept with their heads tucked under their wings.

It was a really a pity that I didn't have a book about sea birds with me, so I just called them "Ocean ducks". Not that there is any connection between ducks and duck-tape but, for no reason at all, I felt compelled to explain to them how much I used duck-tape, my panacea for bandaging anything and everything.

I wondered whether it was father's day for ducks as well or whether they showed their fathers' gratitude throughout the year. Father's day is a lot like Sundays but for the wrong reasons. People go to church on Sundays and think they are off the hook for the rest of the week and so too children treat their dad's on father's day. And think they are off the hook for the rest of the year, I was pointing fingers right back at myself!

When I flipped over my chart, it grabbed me that I had entered the Coral Sea two days ago without even noticing it and belatedly I saluted: "Au revoir Mr Pacific and Aloha Miss Coral Sea!"

Waking up I watched a flock of birds diving down, then swooping low over the water like dive-bombers and circle-diving they went up again. I couldn't understand what they were doing but a closer look revealed that they were fishing and used their wing shadows to spook a shoal of baby flying fish. In turn used the flying fish used their wings to get airborne and were then snatched by the swooping birds. Fascinated by nature's way, I watched this feeding frenzy for quite a while.

But the goddamn wind started to behave like a bloody shape-shifter again and kept on changing and it was only with a hell of a lot of effort that I managed to keep IT on the desired course. When I woke up I was seriously pissed off! Despite all my effort we had sailed in the opposite direction than intended. Doing some heavy breathing I managed to get us back on track and we sailed hard again. The waves kept crashing over the boat forcing me to sit at the navigation station and to avoid being soaked, I closed all the hatches.

Always expect the unexpected! With land on the lee I spurred IT on hard. The Invisible Reefs were just thirty miles north of us, too close for comfort and I attempted a safer distance.

There was no sun for almost five days and I was virtually on my knees praying for it to dry up the soggy mess. I didn't think that the weather could get any worse but Murphy is a bastard. And my afternoon consisted of a score of butch squalls waiting in line behind us, each having a whack at us with their gigantic water batons.

My spirit was totally dampened by the constant rocking and rolling under the squalls that had battered us at a rate of one every half an hour. During the squall onslaught the winds reached up to thirty-six knots, lasting for half an hour at a time. Still, there was a little bit of a light at the end of the tunnel: I had a noon to noon run of one-hundred-and forty miles!

I got the fright of my life when I received a weather report that typhoon Dianmu was reaching a destructive one-hundred knots accompanied by a gale warning with clockwise winds of up to forty-five knots. The gale winds would be bearable but if I would get caught in the middle of a typhoon it would take a miracle to save IT and myself. Fortunately the typhoon and the gale were far from us and we weren't yet in harm's way.

In the meanwhile I took the new genoa out to do an investigation of it and discovered that the luff was too long. The tack of the sail was tied down at the bow and this meant that I wouldn't be able to furl it up in time when the wind would increase. But my biggest concern was that if it was all the way up and a squall would creep up on us I would be in serious trouble! However the problem had to be considered and some kind of plan devised.

I used most of the day practicing how to use the new genoa and eventually developed a feel for it. But practice makes perfect and the more you practice the luckier you get (a Gary Player saying). So I practiced repeatedly to get it furled up, rushing to the front, loosening the tack, clipping it on the furling system, rushing to the cockpit and furling it up again.

By the end of the day the repetitive furling took its toll and with all the practicing I lost a part on the furling system. Lucky for me I had the mariner's fix-it-all, old duck-tape, handy and it seemed to be fine for the time being.

But thanks to the monstrous new genoa we were at least making some headway in very light winds and the next day in smooth seas, cloudless skies, it was a beautiful day for sailing or perhaps drifting, even living or maybe dying. Depending on whichever way one looked at it.

So I wrapped the Lava-Lava, which Anita and Duncan had given to me, around my waist and it occurred to me that I was not really a novice in wear-ing

a sarong…

While I had been at Varsity, my Aunt Christa had qualified as an air hostess with the South African Airways. After I had botched my attempt and the pain in varsity lane, the two of us went hiking in the Zoutpansberg. During the hike she enquired from me what I had planned to do and, realising that I was not yet sure, she enticed me to join her on one of her flights.

Upon my return from the hiking expedition I wasn't very hopeful that it would materi-alise but resourceful Aunt Christa got a bee in her bonnet. She actually managed to con-vince my parents and bought a ticket to take the twenty year old me along with her as a guest on a flight to Mauritius. There it would change crew and I would get off before the flight would proceed to Hong Kong.

Initially, when we landed in Mauritius, I stood out like a sore finger because I was too shy to take off my shirt and rather covered my burnt body with as much clothes as possible.

Before Christa departed together with a fresh crew to Hong Kong, we had a huge fight. She was irritated with me and pointed out my folly: Ironically people were staring at me not because of my badly burnt body but for being covered up like a mullah.

As Christa boarded the shuttle to the airport and waved goodbye she pleaded with me to behave myself. Paradoxically the moment her aeroplane was airborne I managed to shed off my shyness. I only wore a speedo under a Mauritian sarong which is similar to a Lava-Lava and swam without a shirt.

Nobody was really noticing my scars except for a few children. When they stared at me I invited them to take a closer look and showed them the consequences of playing with fire. Due to the scarring, my torso looks a bit like a map of Africa and I also gave them a geography lesson, pointing to my belly button, representing Cape Town and travelling all the way up to my left shoulder where Mussina is situated.

In recalling this interlude in my life I relaxed. When the ocean wasn't trying to gulp me up and sailing was smooth, small things amused me.

In fact I was having a ball, personalising some of my sails, calling the big genoa Obelix and the small staysail Asterix after the comics that had portrayed the two as tough Gauls. A had a long conversation with both of them enquiring why they had given the Romans such a hard time. It dawned on me that if the sails were Asterix and Obelix then the wind would be Getafix, the magician with its

magic potion…

When Christa had left for Hong Kong, she was soon out of sight and out of mind. And the real fun started for me in Mauritius. It was my first time overseas and as excited as a little boy with a brand new toy, I made lots of friends. In truth I had a ball, it was my first exposure to real life gambling and alcohol served in an open pineapple, a kind of magic potion.

I met a whole bunch of crew from Air France and British Airways. The hostesses from both the crews invited me along to a remote spot on the Island where they swam topless. There I was testosterone-loaded but badly burned and deaf with a bunch of beautiful topless girls. However nothing happened between us and we just had clean fun. Really!

Afterwards I met a guy and his wife from South Africa who were accompanied by an attractive female friend. She was engaged but wanted to experiment a bit before getting married. While swimming and snorkelling I explored her breasts but that was it… Really!

I opened a tin of spaghetti and meatballs but craved for an enormous hand-eaten meal of Gaulish wild boar, baked potatoes the size of a baby's head with cream cheese, cooked pumpkin, beans and large flagons of ale and magic potion to swallow it in celebration of some kind of victory over some kind of foe. But I was about to find out that my two Gaul' sails were going to give me a hard time.

Obelix did most of the pulling but it turned out that Obelix wasn't ideal for winds of more than fifteen knots. IT started to yaw heavily but when I fixed the wheel to counteract the strong breeze, we made good on some lost miles.

However the wind became too strong and I wanted to put Asterix up but to make matters worse its halyard came off the mast. With big waves passing underneath us, there was no way I would have been able to climb up the mast and fix it.

Counting to ten or backwards didn't even calm me down so I started counting in multiples of ten and eventually relaxed. What a hellish night it was!

The next morning I hauled up Asterix and it came as no damn surprise that the clamp for the torque tube had come loose during the previous night and went for a swim. The missing part was a heavy blow and I just hoped they would have parts in OZ.

In the meantime I reverted back to the old repair king, duck-tape, but knew very well that it would only serve as an interim solution because with the strong winds and wet weather the chance of the duck-tape coming loose was highly probable.

At midnight the whole rigging started to shake as if a pit-bull was tearing away at a slipper. This was unusual and I donned my foul weather gear to go up front. Upon closer inspection I saw that Obelix had come all the way out of the roller system and that the drum sheet had snapped off. Next thing my torch blew its bulb which meant that I had to get Obelix off the roller in the pitch dark with waves crashing over me the entire time. But after a titanic struggle I managed to get the job done and dumped Obelix into the front hatch.

When it became light, I took the old genoa out, which Ana had sat for hours to alter into a storm sail. Preparing it for hoisting, my thoughts were with her all the time. Suddenly IT went sliding down a big wave. I grabbed onto the railing to avoid being launched into the ocean. Afterwards, when IT levelled out, the sail had disappeared. I searched for Ana's sail and spotted it as man-over-board. My heart ached but, I couldn't understand it, at the same time a feeling of great calmness enveloped me. All Ana's hard work had hopelessly disappeared into the water but I knew that what she represented to me would never slip my mind. Ana's light-hearted and joyful spirit somehow gave me enough courage to recite the well-known playground poem:

"Whether the weather be fine, or whether not, we'll weather the weather, whatever the weather, whether we like it or not."

But as the reality sank in, it became obvious that I would have to face a new dilemma: Obelix was basically rendered useless. There was a huge question mark how long Asterix would last. Plus the loss of Ana's genoa made me feel at a loss too. I was so damn tired and longed to be on the safety of land, my land, South Africa.

Suddenly my thoughts got interrupted by a few baby tunas happily frolicking alongside IT and a tremendous guilt overwhelmed me. While tears streamed down my cheeks I fell onto my knees asking their forgiveness for mixing their friends with mayonnaise and eating them on crackers.

At midnight I passed just north of the Portlock Reefs which are amongst the most northerly reefs of the Coral Sea and entered the channel. I didn't see any markers, which were nerve wrecking, and I became a quivering emotional wreck realising that, in that reef-infested waters, I would have to navigate blindly.

Then almost disaster! In the six feet water the centreboard hit the reef and I could easily feel the vibration of the bump shaking down my spine. Thinking about the previous time when I had ran IT aground in the shallow Matagorda Bay waters, nearly wrecking my dream by badly damaging the old centre-board, I screamed out loud: "Please God not again!"

He must have heeded to my call because as I turned the helm hard to starboard the depth slowly increased from six to twenty-five feet. Heavens it was a close call and I just hoped that I hadn't damaged the centre-board again because that would definitely be the end of my journey.

When I checked the charts I got it all figured out and resumed sailing in eighty feet of water. And I couldn't believe it, there were still no markers. I plotted every fifteen minutes and it was all blind sailing in a whole different world. But as it became dark the markers lighted up and I navigated smoothly all night through those tricky waters with reefs scattered everywhere.

Dealing with the oncoming freighters was very difficult and where the channel took a loop I decided I had enough of the traffic and took my own route through the reefs.

On the 28th of June at two o' clock in the morning, with about twenty miles to go, looking south I saw the lights of Cape York Peninsula, the administrative and commercial centre of the Torture Strait (my name for the Torres Strait).

After twenty-five days at sea, approaching the harbour, I had never before been so tense in my whole life! And I blamed my father, it was his fault! He convinced me not to take the seemingly dangerous route round Cape Horn, in fear of the monster waves. Granted, in the end it was my choice and a tough one but give me Cape Horn any day. Juxtaposed against the squalls, the doldrums, the dangers posed by the barrier reef and the ocean traffic, Cape Horn would have been child's play for me.

Dropping anchor I was tired, frustrated, stressed out and close to breaking point!

However, later when customs came on-board, I already felt slightly better but, unfortunately, they confiscated some of my foodstuff.

I was particularly anguished to part with the mayonnaise that had made many a meal on-board IT more palatable but it contained dairy products and that was forbidden. Remembering my promise to the baby tunas not to have their family with mayonnaise, I didn't argue. At least the temptation had been removed. Being dog-tired, I fully cooperated and was just grateful for small mercies. At least I wasn't harassed during the search and after all it was only mayonnaise, tempting but not dangerous.

With the paperwork completed customs gave me a ride on their zodiac to their offices and later I was dropped off at the hotel. After that hellish leg through the "Torture Strait", I was exhausted but just happy to be alive. With a bloody Mary on the hotel deck, I thought back at my ordeal and couldn't believe that I nearly wrecked IT, colliding with the reef. The alcohol started to take effect and in a more relaxed mood, I recalled a previous experience I had of

blind navigation…

After nine days Aunt Christa returned from Hong Kong, the aeroplane landed at Mauritius to refuel and I was the only passenger to board the flight.

On take-off the commanding pilot Jan Lategan, a kind of no-nonsense Afrikaner, called me to take the co-pilot's seat next to him and he winked at me and put my hands on the throttle. As I slowly opened the throttle I felt the power of the machine vibrating underneath me. It was an amazing feeling to be in control of such an aeroplane with all the passengers on-board. And it was a great thrill and a once in a lifetime experience!

After I had returned to my seat Christa came to fetch me from economy to be seated in the gold class where I was one of only two passengers being pampered and spoiled. Christa gave me a double bloody Mary and I dozed off. When we approached Johannesburg in very cloudy and rainy weather, Jan Lategan commanded me back into the cockpit to observe how he navigated blindly, assisted only by communicating with the Air Traffic Control Tower.

As he unseeingly maneuvered through the danger, putting the aeroplane into automatic landing mode, I carefully observed how the plane landed itself. When the plane eventually smoothly touched down, Captain Lategan with a grin on his face looked chuffed, especially when all the passengers clapped hands for him.

That fantastic trip gave me a glimpse into Christa's glamorous job and a taste of the life of the rich but it also taught me the value of reliable navigation equipment.

Even though I had not slept for twenty-four hours, I could still appreciate the beauty of Thursday Island and the view overlooking the bay, was absolutely stunning. The climate reminded me of Mussina in South Africa, as hot but with a much cooler breeze. The main difference being that the island is encircled by water, while Mussina is surrounded by the African bush. The mere thought of the bushveld brought on a sudden, overwhelming yearning for those dulcet years on the banks of the Limpopo.

Looking around I felt appropriately dressed in my favourite rugby shorts and sandals because everyone else wore them too. Afterwards the customs' officials took me back to IT and, I hadn't notice it before, they drove on the left-hand side of the road, just like in South Africa. And the longing to be in my country of birth only intensified.

Back in the harbour I inspected IT and found that during the many squalls and storms and the close call with the reef, she was really badly busted up. I was told to wait, until business hours on Monday morning, for customs to take care of the rest of the bureaucratic stuff, so I focussed on a series of repairs to get her back into shape, before tackling the trip to Darwin.

When customs returned on Monday morning I had sufficiently recovered from my ordeal and wasn't so rattled anymore. The custom guys, knowing how to talk rugby, made me feel at home and we exchanged views about our respective countries' favourite sport. Because they had been so helpful I went back to thank them and presented them with a signed Texas Kwagga rugby T-shirt. They reciprocated and gave me a nice cap, some souvenirs and bag of ice.

I went to the Laundromat where I met Andrea from Germany and Natalie from the UK who were on a coastal cruise around Australia with four other persons. They were very friendly. Andrea reminded me of Ana, my sail mending goddess. But they had so much dirty laundry that they occupied all the washing machines and, while we made small talk, I patiently waited in the wings for them to finish. When they departed, I tackled my washing.

While loading the front-end loader, I thought about Ana in Mauritius and my heart ached for the loss of the genoa. At that very moment I experienced a dramatic shift in my consciousness. I couldn't believe it! I didn't get impatient while I had to wait for the ladies to finish their washing. And new hope surfaced that, at the same time that I had lost Ana's genoa, that I had also lost my intolerant demon. Perhaps that was the real influence she had on me.

It was a brief two day stopover but a refreshing one and I realised that without this salvaging recuperation I wouldn't have been able to make it in one piece to Darwin.

Independence Day

Four o' clock in the morning of the 30th of June, I left the harbour of Thursday Island, on a Tuesday morning. I again played with similar words as those that I had used when I left Tutuila Island (TI) and thanked Thursday Island (TI) for giving me a good "time" on my Island Time (IT).

And sailed under a double-reefed main and staysail, happily galloping along at about seven knots, all day long in the Arafura Sea. When the wind subsided, the seas became very calm.

Closing in on Cape Wessel, the skies were clear, the wind weak and at nightfall I sailed under a full main. At daybreak I hauled up the spinnaker but the wind was insufficient for IT to be controlled by Willy and I steered manually. For the first time in ages the skies were clear and the sailing smooth, which emulated my relaxed mood.

When I had passed Cape Don, leading me into the Dundas Strait and over to the Van Diemen Gulf, I was still elated. Calm seas followed and I took a shot at fishing. I caught a wahoo and a shark but when I tried to haul them on-board, I lost both. I didn't have a gaff on board. And I didn't care because it was just great fun.

Independence is one of the most important things in the world to me, being able to fend for myself using my own skills and competencies. Initially, being deaf, made me completely reliant on the people around me who had to help me with communication, but as time went by I adapted and fought back to regain my independence. And on the 4th of July, Independence Day in America, I was completely alone on IT, taking on the world and it was the most independent I had ever felt in my entire life.

As the days flowed one into another the flat seas made it feel as if IT was gliding on air and I wasn't making enormous progress in terms of nautical miles but the new found calmness that enveloped my psyche did me a world of good.

And I couldn't believe it but I was already within sight of Darwin. I emailed customs to verify my arrival and with their help arranged for a slip at the Tipper Waters Marina. However all the yachts from overseas were still required to undergo a fourteen hour quarantine period before entering any of the marinas.

With some more e-mailing back and forth I took off for Hill Wharf, three miles down Fannie Bay where customs came alongside in their Zodiac and deployed a pilot on board to guide me through the very shallow waters towards the quarantine anchorage area situated before the harbour's entrance.

The seven day stretch on the open sea from Thursday Island to Darwin heralded a totally new beginning for me and entering the safety of the anchorage with the assistance of the pilot, I knew then that I had irrevocably changed.

Ship Shape

After I had completed the compulsory quarantine period, a marine officer came aboard and we set out for two miles through the shallow waters towards the marina. While I circled around, Hans and Soren Anderson went first through the lock and then it was my turn.

I took a shuttle to an internet café to post my logs and received a surprising message that my family was on their way to Darwin. While waiting for them, I hastily took stock of the damage on IT.

Bev, Sharleen, Gideon and Joy, my mother in law, arrived on-board a red-eye flight from Sydney. Having been away from them for four months, it was good to see them all. Gideon had grown and was almost as tall as I. Sharleen was still my princess.

We took a shuttle to the motel where they had been booked in, chatted for a while and then Beverly and I took another shuttle back to the marina to have alone time on IT.

During my stopover at Darwin the main focus was to get IT back into shipshape condition and it left very little time for anything else. However, during the family's visit, we did manage to do some sightseeing. When they departed, after six days, I felt lonely but knew that it was only a matter of time before I would be re-united with them.

The day after their departure, I could finally give my full attention to IT and I pedalled with a rented bicycle two kilometres down the road to the sail maker's shop where I gave instructions for Obelix to be modified. I spoke to the technician at a Furuno dealer who recommended that I should take out the radar monitor and the old bed-shaker so that he could modify it into a super bed-shaker. This I did and it turned out to be an impressive boat shaker but still, its real test would come on the next leg, tackling the open seas again.

I climbed the mast and while aloft, at the top, checked all the pulleys and cotter pins. I carefully took Willy's mechanical gear apart but, in the process, I accidently dropped the stainless steel rod into the water. I immediately pulled off my shirt and dove into the water to salvage the rod. Halfway down something bit my lower right calf and I sky-rocketed out of the water. Bloody Hell!!! I couldn't believe it: I had been bitten by a crocodile! Fortunately, it was still small and its teeth left only shallow penetrations. I disinfected the wounds and after a while the bleeding stopped.

Luckily Dietmar from Germany swam by with his scuba gear, doing an underwater propeller job, so I asked him to do a quick dive down to retrieve the rod for me. For some unknown reason the crocs didn't like the taste of Germans and he could roam in the waters unscathed.

Still rattled about the croc incident, I gave IT a good scrubbing and a shiver went down my spine, recalling the stupid stunt I had done on another

"crocodile Dundee" day…

Gerrie and I, along with two friends, did the craziest thing that you can ever imagine. With the crocodile invested Limpopo River in full flood, we went to the cliff at Spies' place on my dad's farm and jumped twenty meters down. While hanging onto logs, we floated for two kilometres, until we reached the banks of the river, next to the farm's pack shed.

We were idiots but apparently that day the crocs had also lost their appetite for South Africans. Just to be spiteful, I felt like having crocodile steaks, a local delicacy. Instead, I headed for the harbour, buying a kilo of medium-sized prawns and fried them in garlic butter, served on a bed of rice. And what a gorgeous meal that was. I doubted whether crocodile steaks would have tasted nearly as delicious.

I was up early, hosed down the sails to get rid of the salt and scrubbed the mould off the ice chests. One of the yachties was so kind to lend me his bike and I peddled over the hill to Fannie Bay, following the shoreline to Cullen Bay Marina, to check if my packages with the parts for Andy had arrived. On the way back, I got lost and ended up carrying the bike through a muddy swamp, all the time looking out for crocodiles. Nevertheless, the peddling was good exercise and did me wonders.

As a farewell gesture, I cooked pap, a kind of maize meal porridge, and minced meat with brown onion gravy. I took it over to the Australians to taste this traditional South African cuisine. Everybody licked off their fingers, helping themselves to seconds.

After the eighteen day stopover in Darwin, IT was properly refurbished, in ship shape condition and I felt less apprehensive to tackle the third leg of my journey.

ALL I ASK IS A TALL SHIP AND A STAR TO STEER HER

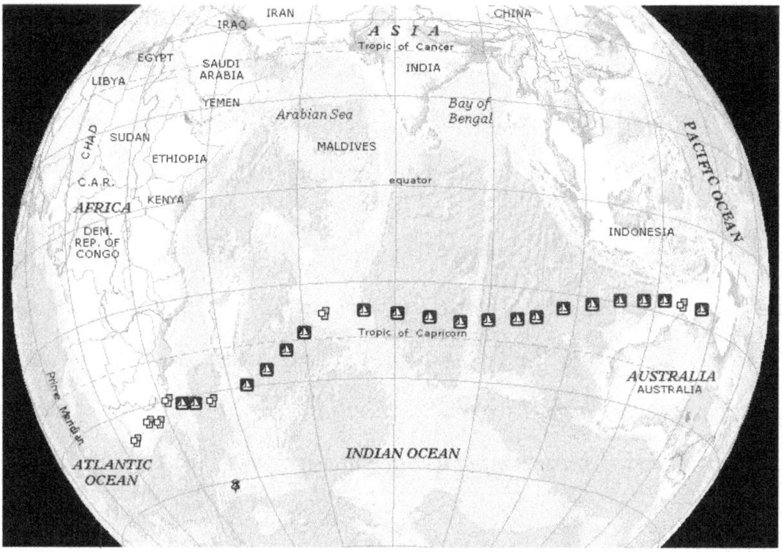

I must go down to the sea again, to the lonely sea and the sky.

And all I ask is a tall ship and a star to steer her by.

John Masefield

Jury-Rigged

On Sunday morning, the 25th of July, I left Darwin heading for South Africa. Looking back towards Fannie Bay, watching thirty-seven yachts simultaneously hoisting their sails, was an awesome sight. Until a few of the racing boats in the regatta caught up with me, I kept sailing with the spinnaker.

The sailing was smooth and I had time to reminisce about Darwin and all the people that I had met. Other than when meeting a non-sailor with whom you first have to find a common interest, sailors are bonded by their love of sailing. We immediately have a connection which makes it easy to get along and become good friends.

The next morning the wind started to relax, the ocean became placid and the sun started to rise. I sat in the cockpit, content to absorb the sun's nourishing rays which reflected silvery orange highlights on the water.

The way that the glimmering rays were dancing on the water's surface reminded me of how I had been fascinated by such radiances on a trickle stream in the dry Limpopo riverbed. So, I let my eyes roam over the water to soak in the vastness of the ocean and recalled that long, long ago, I too, had

a farm in Africa…

After my Mauritian stint it was time for me to face reality. I joined my dad, farming. After one year farming on Ravyn, we bought a farm twenty kilos further down the river. On my newly acquired farm, Overvlakte, situated below the confluence of the great Shashi and Limpopo Rivers, I started to plant cotton and irrigated it with water pumped out of the Limpopo aquifer.

The Limpopo valley lies well north of the Tropic of Capricorn and well below the surrounding countryside. Any breeze, from whatever direction, is in essence a berg wind, and if the summer turns really nasty, the valley can hit maximum daily temperatures of well over forty degrees Celsius. And with the resultant high evaporation rate, it was important to have a sufficient and constant water supply. My uncle, George van der Merwe, specially came to help me to put up an extensive irrigation system.

And in that searing heat I hoed my first crop.

Karin Blixen in "Out of Africa" said: "I had a farm in Africa…" And I thanked God and could also say: "I too have a farm in Africa and this was what I love!"

I must have dozed off because when I woke up, it was already ten o'clock in the morning. But the thoughts about my African farm lingered on. And being on my way to South Africa, having opened that memory, I knew that it was going to be one of my toughest passages, facing a whole bunch of old demons.

When it became dark, I set the radar connected to the newly modified bed-shaker, on a fifteen-mile guard zone. At midnight it alerted me that a ship had entered the guard zone. It was the first test for the bed-shaker, and it worked. I quickly went outside but it passed at a comfortable and safe distance.

After reading a number of emails that had made enquiries about my new bed-shaker, I decided it was time to reveal the big mystery and logged a quick lesson on "The super, dooper bed-shaker":

"Firstly, one sets a guard zone on the radar, anywhere between four and twenty-four miles. Secondly, since it was impossible to run the radar continuously, as it would use too much battery power, I put the radar on "watchman" mode. I would set it for twenty minutes which would put the radar on standby for twenty minutes. Then it would activate itself for one minute, to scan the environment. It would go on standby for twenty minutes again, and so on. If the radar detected anything inside the guard zone, the bed-shaker vibrated vigorously to wake me."

After the lesson, I couldn't fall asleep again. Strangely, instead of reassuring me, the watchman mode of the radar made me paranoid. After the near collisions I had on my previous legs, I felt like a soft target.

A feeling of intense isolation enveloped me. I shivered and the shadows of the clouds passing over IT, created an intense fear. It was as if there was a presence that I couldn't identify. There were no ships and no land around me. I switched on the light inside the cabin, crawled under the blanket, pulled it over me and hugged myself into a foetus position. In drifting in and out of sleep, I wished I had a gun to protect me against all these

unseen enemies…

Terrorists had sporadically crossed our farms' borders but fortunately, years later, we were corrected and informed that they were actually "liberation fighters". However, government propaganda had brainwashed our family to the extent that we decided that we weren't going to be the softest targets around, armed ourselves and kept our own watch.

The erstwhile SA Defence Force was unable to patrol the vast border and had erected an expensive, high voltage security fence. But the ultra-expensive army fence also had other unintended consequences.

Against that fence we witnessed a small herd of zebra self-destruct in their attempt to move south. And the fence couldn't endure the onslaught of a well-oiled elephant war machine. The elephants effortlessly trampled the electrified fence and then slowly marched to their target. Without trumpeting, they silently devoured three hectares of mature sweet corn and, as quietly as they had come and without even being noticed, they casually followed the dry river bed and slipped back into Botswana.

But the real terrorists were the baboons. Three troops of baboons settled in the sandstone hills around my dad's farm and deployed their spies to survey the area. Like decent, ecologically-aware, human beings we did not declare war on them and limited our counterattacks to when they would enter our lands or the garden. The baboons had no such sentiments, they exploited our weakness. Whenever anyone emerged from the house, a single high-pitched bark was all that was required to put them on high alert.

In all those years we never fired a gun shot in anger at anything but the baboons, and needlessly carried our firearms in their holsters. But, regardless of our paranoia or watchfulness, the liberation fighters still managed to plant landmines on our farms.

As the reality sank in that it was just me on the vast ocean in a pitch dark night, I decided to be more vigilant and not solely rely on the watchman. I took the flashlight and went outside again. I beamed the powerful light in a circle around IT but there were no ships or unseen enemies.

In twenty-four hours, I only managed to cover eighty-five miles. I was plodding along at three-and-a-half knots. And then it hit me. For some reason I naively thought that the doldrums were left behind in the Pacific. But boy, oh boy was I wrong. I was right back in the middle of it. At that moment the feeling of severe loneliness that I experienced was so intense that I momentarily wept.

After the stopover in Darwin, having been in social contact with my family and so many people, the disappointment of unexpectedly being marooned in the doldrums was overwhelmingly painful. The doldrums made me feel incompetent and

medically unfit…

I had been declared medically unfit to be conscripted for army duty. Consequently, I was privileged (or unprivileged) to have never done military duty except as a home guard during the period when the terrorist (or freedom fighters) were planting landmines.

But although the army had labelled me as medically incompetent, they soon discovered my hidden talents and regularly called on me to use my skills, which I had learned from Dawid Sokker the expert tracker, to identify and track the spoor of the enemy.

With that bit of trivia floating around in my mind, I felt less emotional and more competent to make proper decisions. By then, I knew that the doldrums could play havoc with my mind and that I needed to find a way to snap out of it. So, for boredom therapy, I braided my first eye splice, following the instructions in a book I had borrowed.

I plaited the ends of the rope back into the standing end to form a circle. However, I didn't exactly succeed, and after a number of blood splattering attempts, I abandoned the splicing effort. The sharp "pusher," that came with the kit, ended up in my fingers. Blood was dripping from my hands. I swore like a sailor and it messed up the whole idea of taking my mind off the doldrums.

The following days weren't much better. As the one day rolled into the next, my mood deteriorated. Milling around in circles, I thought that it would be critical for me to snap out of it. I was poking around, looking for something to do and found the head gear which I had used for

skydiving…

After moving to Overvlakte, on the remote banks of the Limpopo, I soon realised that if I wanted to lead a balanced life, I needed a hobby. One of my friends invited me to a skydiving event. Without telling my parents where I was headed, I joined him.

I was immediately attracted to the sport. However, I hadn't as yet reached the legally mature age of twenty-one and couldn't jump without my parents' consent. To say the least, they weren't impressed and no matter how hard I tried to convince them that I would be OK, they were just saying: "A BIG NO!"

So, I waited in the wings and the moment I turned twenty-one, the 5th of November 1981, I didn't need their permission anymore and, without their knowledge, went for a one day training course.

I also needed a doctor's certificate to declare that I was fit for skydiving. The first three refused, but I managed to convince the fourth doctor that my disability would not jeopardize me.

Later, when I told my parents, they were furious and said a big: "LAST TIME, NO MORE!!!" But of course their reaction, instead of stopping me, motivated me to continue.

Being deaf proved to be an advantage, because with the door removed from the aeroplane, it was surprisingly noisy and skydivers generally have difficulty hearing each other. But I could lip-read regardless of the noise.

But returning to reality, the wind was still ominously down. I received an email from Hans with the news that he was six-hundred miles North West of my location, cruising in twenty knot winds which didn't exactly cheer me up. But, made me to realise that if a storm would suddenly show its pretty face, I would be unprepared. The idea of a storm launched me into a better mood.

I enthusiastically read Coles and Bruce's heavy weather sailing tactics. And in anticipation of more wind I prepared all the sails, got everything ready for the probable storm and went inside the cabin. I waited and waited but it soon became clear that it was just wishful thinking. The wind remained lifeless, so I tried to start the engine to charge the batteries. I couldn't believe it. It wouldn't start, no matter how hard I tried. I became very scared and knew then that if something is not going to happen soon, I will mentally seriously start to

malfunction…

On my seventeenth jump, there was a malfunction on my main parachute. I took a risky decision to do a cut-away and successfully opened my back-up parachute.

It scared the shit out of me, and when I told my parents, a huge argument ensued. This time round, they begged me to quit. They said they had almost lost me in that fire and I shouldn't do it to them again. But I couldn't stop.

I continued skydiving, but in secret, so my parents didn't know what happened on my forty-second jump, when there was yet another malfunction. I did a successful cut-away and to land between power lines, I had to lift my legs to miss them.

However, one of my friends spilled the beans and my parents were outraged. Still, I couldn't stop, the adrenalin rush was not the only reason but to, at last, compete on even terms with others, was.

I again tried to start the engine, I couldn't believe it, with the first turn it purred and I couldn't find the reason why it malfunctioned in the first place.

After a week of mental malfunctioning in the doldrums, worrying about reaching the United States by my target date of December 2004, I passed the Hibernia, and then Scott Reefs. I was out of the Timor Sea and into the Indian Ocean proper.

I became very excited, adrenaline was pumping. And I couldn't fathom why I had malfunctioned in the doldrums. The wind was blowing at twenty-five knots, and I didn't mind that IT's tumultuous movements kept hurling me from side to side, making it tough to even get up from the berth. It also didn't concern me that my whole body was aching from the constant knocks against the sides. What I did care about was that the strong winds enhanced my progress.

The following morning, I could see swells in the distance, indicating that the wind would soon be coming from there. The seas were very different to those in the Pacific, and I spent much of my time in the companionway, studying the waves. The effect of the cross-swells intrigued me, and I wasn't afraid anymore. It actually excited me to find new ways to adapt my sailing methods to a new

rhythm…

Our Pietersburg skydiving team was called Team Rhythm. We did show jumps at numerous agricultural shows, rugby finals and even night jumps, wearing day-glow jumpsuits. I loved my black and pink day-glows, with flares attached to my feet or smoke bombs on day jumps, mostly orange.

Those days we were very popular and the spectators loved our team! Three of us sometimes performed a three-way compressed stack, which basically looked like one skydiver was sitting on the chute of the one below him, and that diver was sitting on the chute of the one below him. When we landed in front of the crowds, they cheered and cheered.

Team Rhythm was invited to the 1984 World Cup soccer opening ceremony, held in Swaziland. It was a great privilege jumping in the Royal Kingdom, being part of a twenty-four-way free-fall formation.

In our heyday, after a four-way free-fall, Titch and I would track to each other, and deploy our canopies close to each other and build a two-man compressed stack (sometimes called a bi-plane). Titch would always be on top and then I would pull him down beside me while he maneuvered his canopy, and we would be side by side.

Then, interlocking our legs, the canopies would start to separate. Keeping our legs interlocked, we'd perform a screaming eagle down plane. The crowds would watch us twist and twirl, still locked together as we floated down, and they would gasp and cheer.

The seas became rough and every now and then, a wave lifted us up and as we slid down from its crest, I screamed with excitement, like I used to on the screaming eagle down-plane.

On one occasion a wave lifted us up and then turned IT forty-five degrees in the trough, almost broaching us on the crest of an oncoming wave. At the time, I was at the bow and had to hold on tight while the wave doused me. Until the wave had passed underneath us, the lee rail, ports and jerry cans were all submerged.

The next morning the wind calmed. I sat on the foredeck and marvelled at those forty knot winds that we had gone through the previous day. It had been such a

thrilling sensation…

To assist with covering the long distances between Mussina and the other main centres my dad had acquired a Piper Comanche, 260 aeroplane. I was very keen to fly but knew very well that, as a result of my disability, I wouldn't be able to get a radio licence and thus couldn't even begin to aspire to get a licence to fly.

I understood the reasoning behind this because, other than in sailing, flying a plane without radio contact would turn you into worm food. However, the desire to fly remained and skydiving was my replacement for that.

During the course of my skydiving days, I befriended Johan Dippenaar, whom we called Dippies. He was a police officer by profession, but skydiving was his passion, and the two of us became great buddies, doing plenty of dives together.

Dippies had set his jumping aside for a couple of months to qualify as a pilot, and once he qualified, the two of us often flew together. He wasn't concerned with me being deaf, and taught me how to fly the parachute club's Cessna 210 plane. After a couple of hours, I managed to take off and land without his assistance, he only operated the radio. Every time I flew the plane on my own, the sensation at take-off and landing was so thrilling that it was almost orgasmic.

As a team, Dippies and I flew all over South Africa, logging enough flying hours for him to qualify as a jump pilot. Thereafter, we flew from boogie to boogie, crisscrossing the South African plains in the Cessna. Later, he flew for the Secret Service, and escorted important politicians like PW Botha, Pik Botha, and others.

We once got lost in the mist, and when the wings started to ice-up, we flew very low, following the railway line from Bloemfontein to Stellenbosch. When we landed, we got the fright of our lives, seeing an oil leak and in checking we found the sump was virtually empty. After we had it repaired, Dippies and I sat at the bar with trembling knees. It was a very close call! We were crazy young guns. Nevertheless, I had learned a lot of my navigation skills from Dippies.

He later also qualified as a flight instructor, and I was very sad when I heard the news that his plane went down. He successfully avoided some houses but in the process got killed. However, the student whom he had trained lived and told the story.

And fortunately I, also having been his student, survived to tell my tale. And I saluted Dippies not only for his flying tuition but for ignoring my disability and freeing my soul to fly.

Late afternoon, the winds increased to twenty-five knots, occasionally gusting at twenty-eight, with waves coming from all directions. Willy was working overtime, and I took care not to wear him out. I tried to set a better course and let Andy do the steering. But at that exact moment a cross wave picked us up and hurled us sideways down the slope. The forces on the rudder were so great that the refurbished gears in Andy stripped.

As the damn thing was only two weeks old with less than twenty-four working hours on it, my temper flared up and I swore like a drunken sailor. I had been under the impression that the upgraded model came standard with metal gears.

But assumption is the mother of all F*&^ up's! I knew then that I should have checked them and was angry at myself. The south-west swells made IT unstable, but I managed to take Andy apart and replaced the flimsy plastic ones with some brass gears which I had salvaged from the old belt. After six painstaking hours of sawing and filing, Andy was back in working order.

The next three days were uneventful, but on the fourth day a large school of dolphins made a theatrical appearance by showing off and swimming along both sides of IT. I alternated between port and starboard, happily and intently watching their regal performance.

The dolphins demonstrated their swimming prowess by nobly and majestically sliding carefree in, through and out of the water. Then they were gone. But for a moment or two, the loneliness lessened. The dolphins' magnificent performance reminded me that I had read somewhere that they have a strong connection with French royalty. The King bearing the title of Dauphin and the Queen of Dauphiné.

But then I was suddenly on high alert. I had my first run in with whales. There was a whole pod. They played and splashed, occasionally spouting water out of their blowholes. Their shooting water reminded me of the geysers in Yellowstone Park. I tried to get video footage but they were too far away. From all the stories that had been related to me, whales saw small yachts as a threat and I sailed cautiously past them.

As Friday the 13th descended upon me, I shunned my usual superstition and tried to focus on the tasks at hand. Earlier, in a relaxed the wind, I had put up the spinnaker. I made myself at home in the cockpit and hoped that this time round the 13th wouldn't give me hard time,

playing a prank on me…

I got interested in golf when I was still very young and used to caddy for my dad. Apart from the skydiving, one of the few socialising events I had was visiting the golf club in town, where I played competition golf and eventually reached a four handicap.

One evening there was a boys' night out, which I attended with my brother Christo and a few friends, drinking at the golf club bar. As the evening progressed, the vibrational pattern in the bar changed from low to high, indicating that the music and conversations were getting much louder.

We all knew that we should have gone home long ago, because our families were probably worried sick, with all the landmines that had recently been detonated on the border area.

But I was in a funny mood, the vibrations touching me in an odd way. So, I instructed Christo to go to the pay phone outside the bar and call the bar phone. I had previously arranged with the barman to hand me the phone when it would ring. When it did, he handed it over to me so that I could have an imaginary conversation with the "angry wife" of one of my guilty, not-so-sober friends.

Listening to the one-sided conversation, my friend got so scared that he totally forgot that I was deaf, and did not realise that I was playing a prank on him. He waved his hands madly, signalling non-stop that I should tell his wife he had left hours ago.

After I put the phone down, I told him that I didn't think that she had bought the story, and that I suspected she was on her way to the club. In a flurry, he jumped up and ran for the door, with me trailing behind him. Outside, I reminded him that I was deaf and it was a joke between friends.

He felt like a fool and going back into the bar he was momentarily angry but in realising his folly, he joined in the mocking laughter of the gang. The vibration of the laughter felt good on my skin. He slapped my back and swore that someday he would get even.

But I had to refocus on the job because that evening a Friday-the-13th - curse was playing a prank on me and the hand of Murphy decided to mock me.

The wind increased to thirty-three knots, with the waves knocking hard against the hull. When I tried to run with the wind, I ended up making unexpected jibes. I struggled to keep IT on any kind of course. The next day I triple-reefed the main and rolled out just a small piece of the Obelix's canvass. It made things more comfortable but resulted in a loss in speed.

I spent most of the time on my back in the cabin and only occasionally popped my head out to scan for traffic. While I read Don Pinnock's Natural Selections for the second time, I was touched by the way he described

the magic of Africa…

When I started farming on Overvlakte, the bushveld between the Zoutpansberg and the Limpopo was in a paradisial phase. I was at my innovative prime! From the depths of my soul arose sighs of territorial passion that for me elevated even the craggiest corners of my land to levels of reverence.

The riverine trees along the Limpopo River were enormous, the flood plains lush, fertile, and teeming with a stunning variety of game. The sandy aquifer was wide, deep and held a vast reservoir of subterranean water, ample to bridge any dry year before being replenished by the next flooding. Living there, I felt enfolded in the heart and magic of Africa.

But when the bed-shaker went off, it warned me of an approaching squall, and then the temperature started to plunge. I spent the next two days sailing in miserably cold weather, with a poled-out Obelix and triple-reefed main. The seas were so rough I couldn't sleep, but we covered almost three-hundred miles.

It was impossible to lie on the berth so I built a bed on the cabin sole, using the cockpit cushions. The bed looked almost like a coffin, but it was a comfortable one. It beat being thrown from my bunk onto the floor every half hour. I was dressed in as many clothes as I could manage, and I thought that if I died, at least I would do so dressed, not like when I did my

nudity jump

When one reaches the 100th jump in skydiving it is customary to do a nudity jump. It was quite an experience, with all my private parts flipping and flopping around on the descent. I felt totally vulnerable! All the way down I worried about what my family would say if something went wrong and I would die stark naked. I vowed that the next time I felt like it was the end of me, I would definitely be properly clothed.

And trying to descent back to life, I jumped up to check for a weather fax but couldn't get one from my old source. I changed the channel to Pretoria, in South Africa, and received a clear one. South Africa! I was getting close.

When I stepped on deck for a check, I got a shock. The starboard tang (a stainless steel plate) at the bottom of the spreaders, which held the lower shrouds, had completely snapped off. The mast was normally held in place by shrouds (wires) on all four sides and with one side not supported, the whole rig was in danger of coming down. Those wires, also called standing rigging, designed to keep the mast standing, are amongst the most critical features of a sailboat. I quickly put IT on a port tack to take any strain off the starboard side of the mast.

At that point I was panicked. I was five-hundred miles from Rodrigues, the nearest land. My situation was so grave that I had no option but to stop there for repairs before tackling the boisterous seas of the South African coast.

I immediately e-mailed Dave and Sharon, my mentors and Tartan 37 gurus, inquiring how to reduce the stress on the mast, and to find out whether they knew of somebody who could do welding in Rodrigues (they had stopped there on their circumnavigation).

I had already used the staysail's halyard, fixed to the mast a little above the spreaders, as temporary support, when I received their answering e-mail that I should slow down and take the pressure of the mast.

After various failed attempts, I achieved their suggested method of stabilizing the mast. With Obelix up, the jury-rigged mast was barely holding, but I stuck to a port tack, making speeds between five and six knots. I simply could not, as they suggested, heave-to. It was against my nature not to keep moving.

Suddenly, the wind went calm and most of the day we just drifted in sloppy and confused seas. I contemplated different ways to keep us afloat. As sailors know, a sailboat without a mast loses all stability, and is very likely to turn turtle and sink. Luckily, so far I still had a mast.

But in a panic, walking up and down, I bumped my right foot's little toe. The nail was ripped off completely and I bled profusely, leaving the cabin floor covered with blood. After cleaning the wound, I put a sock on to keep the dressing in place. And it took me a while to clean all the blood from the cabin sole.

For most of the night the throbbing in my toe kept me awake, but it didn't stop me from stressing about the mast and thinking about, at what point should I consider jumping ship, knowing full well that my

safety was on the line…

Titch and I had put our safety on the line when we did an illegal two-way from a bi-plane crop-duster by sitting on the leading edges of the bottom wing, where we strapped ourselves to the struts (they kept the lower and upper wings together).

Then we jumped. Upon landing, I bumped my left foot's tiny toe on a rock in a sweet corn field. The toe bled profusely and the nail had been taken right off. That night I couldn't sleep, the throbbing toe, and the guilt for putting my safety on the line, kept me awake.

The illegal jumping out of crop dusters could have cost us our licenses and my safety was on the line again. The next morning my toe was still throbbing, but that was just too bad because the new day brought old challenges. And I soon had to deal with a series of terrible squalls that were pushing us far south.

Everything was packing up, my laptop wasn't working properly, the mast was bending like hell and the cabin was damp and smelly. I didn't know how much more I could take. What could I do but press on? As the squalls continued to harass us, I kept on a port tack. The jury-rigged shrouds were barely holding and I had to monitor them constantly. But we were moving and by then we were only seventy miles from Rodrigues.

Jimmy Cornell, in World Cruising Handbook, warned that it was extremely dangerous to enter Port Mathurin (Rodriquez) at night. The harbour was surrounded by reefs and the red and green markers, guiding one into the harbour, were reversed. To try to enter in the dark would be foolhardy, no matter how critical my situation, so I waited for dawn.

Although the mast held, it was tricky sailing into the port. At least I had a chance to use my new electronic charts, which were very helpful.

The Tool

The port authorities had been alerted about my predicament and they expected my arrival. At first light, I climbed up the mast to remove the broken tang so that the machine shop would have a pattern to fabricate a new one. I discovered that the screws, which had held the tang in place for more than twenty-five years, were completely corroded and I couldn't remove them. It dawned on me that the mast failure had actually been caused by that stainless steel tang becoming so work-hardened over the many years that it had snapped off at the fabricated bend and it looked as if someone had cut it off with scissors.

Somehow, I had to remove the corroded screws to get the tang off. But it was complicated since I had no foothold and I couldn't get any force behind the screwdriver. I tried various techniques, even hanging upside down with one arm around the mast and my other arm free. Soon a crowd of locals gathered on the pier and, as if I was one of Jane Goodall's chimps, they laughed at my stunts. They got their entertainment but the corroded screws were still solid.

A local machine shop technician heard about my quandary and came over to lend me a special tool. Unfortunately, it started to rain and I had to abandon the project until better weather would arrive.

In pouring rain I received a visit from Paul Draper, ex-Honorary British Consul, who ran the school and training centre for deaf children on Rodrigues. I was extremely flattered to be asked to visit the school and give a motivational talk to the students.

When it was light enough to scale the mast the next morning, I tried the tool, but it didn't work. So I used my grinder to cut off the heads of the stainless steel screws and then hammered the tang loose.

Paul came by and we walked to the school. While Susan Auguste (also British Honorary Consul) translated into French, I gave a speech to the fifteen pupils, ranging in age from six to twelve. I showed them my charts, the route I had sailed, and some video footage of my entry into Port Mathurin. I shared with them that many years ago I had attended a similar school and how it had influenced my life and how it happened that I undertook this journey.

Afterwards, Paul gave me a tour of the workshop where the older students were cutting up coconuts to make souvenirs. Paul told me that he had also started similar workshops in Mauritius and several other countries.

Back at IT, the school, the deaf children and the teachers I had met brought memories flooding back. Invariably, Mary Kihn jumped right back into my head and how

life had taken a weird turn…

In the beginning of my second year farming, I received an invitation from Mary Kihn to attend a school reunion. Due to the painful experience that I had at Mary Kihn, I was initially quite reluctant to go, but later on I was glad that my mom twisted my arm and that I did go.

I flew to Cape Town and met my erstwhile teacher, Beverly Bryant. She was the one whom I remembered wearing very short mini-skirts, and who had also witnessed the thrashing my dad gave me in standard five. During my time at Mary Kihn, she didn't like me much but that was a different time and during that weekend we fell in love.

As a deaf and badly burned person, one wasn't always first on the list of "hunks I'd love to marry," and there was a stage in my life when I had thought feelings of love were exclusively reserved for "normal people." It felt truly special to love and be loved and accepted by a woman.

After that weekend, I went back to the farm and told my parents about her and in time Beverly wrote a letter to them, requesting their permission for us to marry. My parents were thrilled with my choice of a life partner because Beverly understood me very well, lip-read, and could act as an active partner to assist me on the farm.

On December 19, 1984, also my parents' twenty-fifth wedding anniversary, Beverly and I were married in Cape Town. Margie and Rob Johnson hosted our wedding reception in their beautiful garden in Rondebosch and Kate, their hard-of-hearing daughter, and a pupil of Mary Kihn, was our flower girl.

I was twenty-four and Beverly thirty-seven, thirteen years my senior, but the age gap made no difference to our happiness. As newlyweds, we went back to the farm where Beverly got busy with homemaking, assisting me with telephone communications and running errands. Most important, she generally enabled me to farm with renewed vigour. And together we ventured into our African dream.

Come the next day Paul and all the junior deaf students, four at a time, came on board IT. I showed them how my alarm systems worked and demonstrated my mast climbing technique. I presented each one with a "Silent Voyager" T-shirt and we had loads of fun. My departing shot to them was in the form of an encouragement to learn to lip-read, so that they could augment their communication deficit.

Soudine, a local fisherman suggested that the two of us take a bus to the other side of the island where he knew somebody that might be able to help me. I brought the broken tang along with a piece of scrap stainless steel plate. The drive up the mountain provided a breath-taking view of the valleys and of the Indian Ocean.

Soudine introduced me to Nicolas Finniss, an assistant machinist, and I explained my predicament to him. I showed him the broken tang and gave him the details of how to fabricate a new one. He was very kind and told me he would have it completed by the end of the day. He also offered to bring it to me after working hours and we left him to do the job. And this new turn of events restored some hope for me.

At first light I went up the mast, drilled new holes and tapped them. I installed the newly fabricated tang, which Nicolas had indeed delivered to me the previous afternoon, and reconnected the lower shrouds. I tightened the turnbuckles and the mast was as straight as an arrow again.

That evening, sixty-seven-year-old Bill Wilson, on his way to South Africa, came over to greet me. Bill was very anxious to glean more information about South Africa, especially the security situation, but I assured him that there was nothing to worry about, because many years ago we had managed to protect ourselves in the African Bush

without hysteric and dramatics…

Like most other farmers' wives in the district, Beverly had to learn to use a firearm, to shoot accurately, and when driving, to keep a loaded gun beside her. In the event that the "terrorists" launched an attack with a rocket or hand grenades, we had sandbags packed all around our house.

Beverly quickly got pregnant, and on September 26th, 1985, she was transported inside a landmine-proofed army ambulance to Mussina Hospital, where Sharleen was born.

In the early seventies, Beverly's father, Tommy Bryant, had worked for De Beers Diamond Mines, in Namibia, where he met Sam Collins, the Texas mining magnate, who had invited him to America. Sam had offered Tommy a job in Texas, but Beverly's mother didn't want to go and they both agreed to get a divorce.

Tommy flew from Texas to South Africa to attend Sharleen's baptism. There, he met his ex-wife again, who was still living in South Africa. Naturally, Beverly's parents were very worried about their grandchild's safety. However, despite the terrorist threat, we soldiered on without hysterics or drama and accepted it as part of our exciting adventure in the African bush.

I actually didn't know whether this information gave any comfort to Bill Wilson but he thanked me for sharing the story with him.

After checking out with authorities the next day, I went back to the school to bid my new deaf friends farewell. Paul wasn't there but came later that afternoon to wish me a safe journey.

It struck me as quite amazing that in the middle of the Indian Ocean, on a tiny island, Paul was doing such a rare and selfless deed. As a tribute to him and his students at the school, I renewed my vows to successfully complete this crusade.

And within five busy but interesting days the mast got fixed and I was ready to leave.

The Albatross

Sailing out of Port Mathurin, I took it as a good sign when a pod of dolphins accompanied me into the open waters. I was determined to head straight for Cape Town with no stops in between.

In the afternoon, Rodrigues had vanished from the horizon and it was just me and the big blue sea again. A number of times I checked that the shrouds were still tight and the mast was still holding. There was no room for error but it all looked solid.

At first light, I shook the reef out of the mainsail and poled out the modified Obelix. We were riding the swells of the open ocean again. For most of the day, I sat shirtless in the companionway, reminiscing about South Africa, where I was heading and where everything had been

so satisfyingly beautiful…

On the May 7th, 1987, Beverly was again taken by ambulance (landmine-proofed and escorted by the army), to Mussina Hospital where our son, Gideon, was born.

I was overjoyed to have a boy, but mostly, I was extremely grateful that both my children came into the world unharmed and healthy. And I thanked the Lord that they were not disabled.

With the birth of his grandson, Tommy came back to visit us in South Africa. He again met Joy, and realizing that their grandchildren were their common interest, they re-married and Joy went back to Texas with him.

With my wife and our two babies, life on our farm couldn't have been better. Again, even the driest, scrubbiest corners of our farm raised sighs of gratitude from me.

It was all so satisfying and so very beautiful.

And remembering the birth of my son, I knew that I just had to hang in because after a while it would get better. As long as I could keep my mind busy with my flashbacks, the feeling of loneliness was painful but it diverted me from getting enmeshed in a miasma of dark depression.

For the first time in weeks I could sleep on the port aft berth, my favourite place to sleep on IT. And for the first time in weeks I crashed there and was soon dreaming of my other favourite pastime: Organizing mass sky-diving events all over South Africa. For some unknown reason these events were called

boogies

Unlike my parents, Beverly had no qualms with my skydiving and after our wedding I continued with my hobby.

But skydiving is an expensive pastime and I knew that the organizers of skydiving boogies were exploiting the mostly adventurous, but poor young skydivers, and I started doing some calculations. Working out the cost of hiring a plane, fuelling it, paying pilots, insurance and advertising. The break-even point depended on the number of skydives and the cost of a skydive, and playing around with these figures it became clear that there was an optimal combination somewhere. By dropping the going rate by 20% I reckoned we could increase attendance by 50%.

The guys that had trucked my sweetcorn from the farm to the canners were also qualified pilots flying Venda's CASA 212 aeroplane. I hired them and the aeroplane for the first experiment. Beverly made all the arrangements and phoned around on my behalf, soon the word started to spread around the skydiving community. On that first boogie, we did not only break even but made a healthy profit. Thereafter we went bigger, managing to hire various other planes. And "Crispy's (my nickname) Skydiving Boogies" became popular all over. Self-satisfied, I even held a couple of boogies on my farm, where skydivers camped out in their colourful tents under the huge riverine trees on the banks of the Limpopo.

On the 3rd of September the sea became wicked and then very, very big, shit. At first I thought that Willy's rudder shaft broke but the rudder portion had actually come totally loose from the shaft and swivelled into every direction.

I hoved-to, tied a rope around my waist, took a life threatening gamble, got into that rough water and used a hose-clamp to lock the upper collar of the loose rudder to the shaft.

After anxiously working in the water I realised that I had broken every safety rule in the book by putting myself into huge danger. However I justified it by reasoning that something had to be done and that it was a well calculated gamble by taking the necessary precautions.

While manually steering I thought of my family attending the annual Potjiekos Festival (a cooking festival), gathered with many other South Africans living in the United States and my feelings of loneliness intensified. God, I hated every moment of this damn trip. What was I doing? Was this appalling ocean really my fucking burning desire or

just another Jezebel…

The last thing we needed was a long term drought, but when you're vulnerable. And if you are, you'd better not be in Africa.

Apart from running a trading store for the surrounding community, my mother also ran a business on the side, selling donkey carts (the local transportation mode) to the community.

The latter business idea she got from her father, Gerrie van der Merwe, who had managed to survive in the unpredictable, fickle African climate because he applied a very simple philosophy, whenever the game began milling around, it was a clear sign that a drought was looming. He then sold all his cattle and put the money into the bank, keeping busy in the transport sector by building donkey carts for the rural population.

The previous year, the game had started milling around again, and as my grandfather had philosophised, the rains stayed away, the Limpopo river bed turned into a dust bowl, and the underground water turned so brackish that it killed our crops.

Sickeningly, I realised that since we were heavily committed, we were highly vulnerable. That beautiful, alluring valley was just another Jezebel, just a desert in disguise. And our family, like so many Europeans before us, lured into pleasant complacency during the paradisiacal period, was now facing disaster.

I had great admiration for my late grandfather, but never really caught onto the donkey business. I guess the donkeys were far too slow for my taste, and I had to find other ways to survive. I racked my brain for ideas, and as a last resort, I took some of our precious cash and in desperation went to gamble at a casino in Venda. In the midst of that African drought, I managed to actually keep us afloat with my gambling winnings.

In recalling this agonising memory I didn't know whether Willy's broken rudder would be my final annihilation and from here on, emotionally, I barely kept afloat.

And when my satellite phone linked to the laptop started to give problems my panic was indescribable. And the automatic weather fax showed that we were heading straight into a low pressure system and I was badly battered for the better part of the night. As day arrived, the waves crashed over the bow, all the way into the cockpit and the cabin sole was under water.

My mind started to slip again and the huge waves looked like grotesque monsters, trying their best to consume me. Soaking wet, I sat in the cabin with my feet in the water. I felt like a fool and I was sulking, hoping for

a life-line to be thrown at me…

We had been right in the middle of the drought cycle and at that stage the only grazing left was along the banks and inside the sandy riverbed. For three years, the rains stayed away. The grass withered, the crops were recurring disasters and our rain tanks ran empty. The nest egg in the bank was being steadily whittled away and the prospects of recovery diminished month after dry month.

Every week my family and our employees had barely survived. It was deadly serious times and the only income was from the money that I had managed to win from gambling. But the gambling wasn't fun anymore and I was seriously rattled.

But one Friday I took my brother Christo along to gamble and we stayed overnight at the Venda Sun. Christo got a lucky break and won a few bucks. On his way back to the hotel room he bought all kinds of unnecessary stuff like sweets and back in the room he even ordered milkshakes.

I rushed into the room and gave him a tongue-lashing for squandering precious money on nonsense. I ordered him to give me all his winnings. He protested like hell, but had no choice because his big brother was talking. He reluctantly opened his purse and counted out his winnings.

While he remained sulking in the room, I rushed back to the black-jack tables. At two o' clock in the morning, I returned to the room with R15,000. A small fortune to me. When I showed Christo the fat roll of money, his face lit up and he changed his tune about having to hand over the money.

But I knew the gambling money was just a temporary life-line thrown to me.

And once more this was deadly serious stuff and I was again getting utterly depressed. After hand-steering day and night to help with Willy's jury-rigged rudder, I was dog tired. The days flowed one into another, and it felt as if I was flip-flopping in the twilight zone, stripped of any helpful ideas.

When my laptop packed-up, I tried to fix it, but couldn't. My only communication left was to text on the satellite phone. I was so stressed, I started to sob but after I had a good cry I searched deep into my soul for anything that would give me

renewed hope…

The morning after the life-saving winnings Christo and I, headed back to the farm and I stopped over at Louis Trichardt, a town on our way home. There Christo showed me an old second hand Landrover that he had been eying for some time and I bought it for him at the astronomical prize of R2,400.

I also purchased lots of provisions for the farm and went via another clothes store. While Christo was standing at the end of the rail, I reeled all the children's clothes into his open arms. I bought loads of clothes and goodies for the kids.

As we drove back to the farm, with me driving behind Christo in his old Landrover, we were forced to make several stops because the engine of the new acquisition was already overheating. I doubted whether the R2,400 was a worthwhile investment. Nevertheless, that's what my little brother wanted and that's what he got.

Back at the farm we were given a hero's welcome, and I handed the left-over money to Beverly, who carefully stashed it away. The workers were very relieved to receive their long-awaited wages, and in turn, this aided the local economy.

Suddenly, my mother's donkey business flourished. With all the new money floating around, my workers bought donkey carts from Mom and easily slipped through the security fence, to cart much needed food supplies to their families in Zimbabwe.

And with renewed, though fragile hope, we continued our stand against the African climate.

But this memory didn't do much to give me relief, in fact it opened old wounds and when the depression turned into rage, I blamed and cursed my dad for forcing me to take the northerly route. It really sucked, I screamed and shouted, sensing how this trip was slipping through my fingers, and for me too

the writing was on the wall…

During 1985, after Sharleen was born, my brother Gerrie was the first to drive over a landmine in the border territory, and his story made headlines. The fact that he escaped serious injury was seen by our neighbours as a sign of the overwhelming mercy of God. Unfortunately for us, the financial institutions also saw it as a sign - an unambiguous indication to drastically cut back their exposure.

Shortly after Gerrie's landmine incident, a neighbour went bankrupt. Buyers to his dispersal sale had to be trucked in by the South African Army's landmine-proof troop carriers and his farm went for less than half the bank's valuation.

After these two incidents, the banks started to recalculate their exposure and aggressively reeled in their overdrafts. Between the banks and the drought, the writing was on the wall.

And I was sure that the writing was on the wall for me. Again! At that point I gave-up hope and the despair was overwhelming, because the make-shift repairs on Willy's rudder couldn't handle the stress and it came loose again. Eventually, I gathered enough emotional strength to heave-to, and got back into the water to realign the rudder and re-tighten the hose clamps. I deliberately kept our speed low in the high seas and foul weather.

Eventually I had to dive into the water a third time. I drove a hole through the rudder and then forced a wooden wedge tightly into the hole, which compressed the shaft and the rudder together. I didn't care about anything anymore except keeping IT safe. Back inside the cabin I stared into nothingness and prepared myself to face

the wrath of God

The value of our farms had plummeted and three consecutive hailstorms within one financial year selectively wiped out a total of five hundred hectares of our promising irrigated crops.

When the fourth hailstorm struck we sighed with relief because this time around, our crops were fully insured against hail damage. We would have been far less relieved if we had known that our insurance company, AA Mutual, had failed and was sequestered at the very hour the hailstorm had hit us.

We tried every possible avenue for relief, but all the institutions refused to assist us. My dad even flew to Cape Town to personally see the Minister of Agriculture, who just shrugged his shoulders and said, "Sorry."

We were all heavily in debt and after a further year of struggle, Gerrie's and my dad's accounts were foreclosed. They both went bankrupt. I was temporarily spared the humiliation because I had won the cotton ginning company's prize for the highest yielding cotton crop of the previous season. But it was just delaying the inevitable.

After their liquidation, my dad was fortunate to have been offered a good position in his former profession of quantity surveying. Mom, Dad, and Gerrie and his family, moved to Johannesburg.

The result of the auction of their farms was terribly disappointing. The highest bid by the few prospective buyers, who were prepared to risk the land mined roads, didn't even cover the subsidised loans from the Department of Agriculture, and they were not accepted.

Coincidentally, a few months later, the Department sold my dad's farm to someone who had made an offer exactly equalling the outstanding amount. A short while later, that "someone" sold it to De Beers at three times the purchase price. De Beers needed just a small portion to construct a dam, pumping water from the Limpopo River to supply their mine, Venetia, one of the biggest and richest diamond mines ever. They donated the rest of the farm to the government for establishing Mapungubwe National Park, a world heritage site.

In Johannesburg, my mother, wrenched from the area in which she had grown up, and being away from the farm that she loved, missed us terribly. Her beautiful gardens that she had cultivated so carefully were gone. She left behind a whole community who loved her for her fun and smiling fortitude. Without us realizing how serious it was, she slowly drifted into terminal depression.

She was the pillar of my life, but it wasn't enough. Her broken world took her to a very dark place where she couldn't escape. She got stuck at the bottom of a well of despair and saw no way out, except to end her life.

In a frenzy of guilt for not being there for my mother when she needed me most, I was prostrate with grief. I thrashed about, searching for a single reason why I should stay alive.

I held out on the farm for another year, but without heart. And with no working capital, I eventually threw in the towel. The wrath of God and the African climate ultimately took its toll, and the farmer's dream became my nightmare. We were on the street, our dreams in tatters. And two hundred native Africans, who for so many years had willingly given their all, were abandoned to also join the jobless throng.

With our two toddlers, Beverly and I painfully said our goodbyes, and took leave of the farm.

I got a job on the copper mine in Mussina, and we moved to a mine house in town. Then the copper mine closed and laid off all the workers. It was the final blow. We were down and out.

When IT started to roll violently with the boom dipping in the water, I had a nagging feeling that it was time to jump ship. I wanted relief from the seas and the memories.

An Albatross glided around IT. It was a beautiful bird, but the feeling of doom kept pressing on my chest. I watched it masterfully float on a wingspan of eleven feet and wondered whether there was any way in which I could still stay afloat. The waves were enormous and I was in the heart of another gale. I was trying, I had to keep trying and worked constantly to keep everything together. When the waves reached forty feet I could hear the final whistle blowing in my brain. I curled up in my foul weather gear, sick at heart and covered my face with my hands. I knew what was coming. The harshest of the memories flooded in: I had once hung my own

Albatross around my neck…

After I got laid off by the copper mine in Mussina, I was at rock bottom. It was an evil circle because remembering the good times only reminded me of what I had lost.

The mine gave us two months' notice to find alternative accommodations and vacate the house. My dreams were in shatters, and when my dad offered that I assist him with building his retirement house at Morgan Bay, it was a life-line thrown to us.

Beverly and I discussed the offer and accepted the opportunity to get away from the evil miasma that had threatened to overwhelm us, and while I headed for Morgan Bay she remained with the kids at Mussina to organise our move.

On my way to Morgan Bay, I felt a rush of excitement driving through the night with an almost full moon. The adrenaline cheerfully pumped through my veins realising that the next day would be spring low tide, and similar to my Komgha schooldays, I would be just in time to harvest mussels on the exposed rock beds under Keightley's Krans.

For the first time in months I found myself looking forward to something and allowed myself a smile of anticipation.

I passed through Komgha where I had lodged with my grandma and schooled for two happy and wonderful years, slowly driving and criss-crossing the old familiar streets and lingered at those places which I remember so well.

Then I tackled the last sixty kilometres with determination, reliving that deadly serious game that we had played as kids of who could see the sea first, and couldn't wait for my kids and wife to join me.

Nearing Morgan Bay, I knew very well from what point onwards it would be possible to see the sea. As I came over a hill it was WOW and WOW again! This was as good as all those years ago when Morné and I, as eager teenagers thrilled in anticipation of bashing open and slurping down a couple of oysters at Halfway Rocks.

Around eight o'clock that the morning, I knocked on the door of Martie, one of my dad's acquaintances, with whom he had arranged for me to lodge while overseeing the building of his Cape Dutch house. I would stay there until my family would arrive. Martie invited me in and showed me my room, with a beautiful view overlooking the valley. We chatted for a while and then she took me to my dad's building site on top of a grassy, rolling hill behind the village.

Late that afternoon we went to the cliffs to watch the sunset. We sipped red wine while we watched the majestic full moon rise under an emerald sky.

At that time in my life I was very vulnerable; I had lost my mother, our farm and my job. With my wife and kids more than a thousand kilometres away, my heart and soul were crushed. That's my only excuse for what was to come.

I supervised the workers during the day, which was not terribly time consuming, and the two of us had enough time for long walks in the bush. What Morné, my bird-watching friend, had failed to do, Martie succeeded, she taught me to appreciate the bird life in the surrounding area. We stalked the birds for hours, and when tired, flopped onto the grass.

Martie was a free spirit, a woman of nature who was on her own. One day, on one of our walks, she accidentally touched me and the next thing I knew we made love right there in the bush. Our relationship changed from friends to lovers. It was a wonderful experience, but a huge mistake!

When Beverly finally moved from Mussina to Morgan Bay, she soon sensed that something was wrong, confronted me, and our affair came into the open. Beverly threatened to leave me and to take the kids with her to Texas.

After what Beverly had gone through on my behalf, I felt desperately guilty and begged for her forgiveness. She forgave me on condition that we leave as soon as possible, and relocate to Texas where her parents were living, and to never, ever, return to South Africa. I chose my wife and my kids, cut the strings, and left Morgan Bay, never to return until my brother, Gerrie's funeral, in 2003.

The next day the wind started to veer and with no self-steering equipment, I was at its mercy. I hove-to an entire day to ease the battering and drifted along at two knots.

On September the 9th, I received a warning from my dad, via the satellite phone, that yet another storm was on its way. At that point, I just didn't care.

After fourteen vexing days at sea, I slowly crept closer to Durban, and hoped that the 13th would not curse me, again. But it was as if IT smelled the land, hunting it like a hound and I hobbled past the breakwater and into the Durban harbour. The one thing that I was sure of was that the trip was over!

A Mean Team

In that terrible mood with no hope left, I sailed or rather staggered like a zombie into Durban harbour.

I spotted my father standing on the pier, waiting for me. I quickly secured IT, stepped onto the dock and, clinging onto him, I burst into tears. My emotions were raw and I had no control over them. After a sobbing embrace, I looked over his shoulder and there was my brother, Christo, his fiancée, Marie, and my two stepbrothers, Friederich and Ivan. They were all there to welcome me. Later, my other brother Francois, his wife Susan, and their two young children, Annafré and Francois Jr. also joined us. I wasn't the only one crying.

I gave them the details of the nightmarish trip from Rodrigues and told them that I wouldn't be continuing and that Dad should book me a flight back to America. But what a lot of resistance I received? Dad said: "No way, the de Villiers men are not quitters!" I actually laughed when he exclaimed that after all the sleepless nights he had to endure to follow my journey, there was no chance that he would allow me to give up. They all consoled me and assured me that it was definitely not the end of the road. Of course, they were not on IT during the gale!

But safe on dry land and surrounded by loved ones, who made as if the "trip from hell" was actually a brave adventure and I the hero, my resolve to quit the trip dissipated.

My brothers helped me to wash down the salt-soaked sails and we hoisted them up to dry in the breeze. We worked like a mean team to tackle the broken wind-steering unit. Francois and Christo helped while Ivan jumped into the water to scrum with Willy's shaft and rudder and get them out of the water.

Everyone pitched in to help. IT swarmed with people. While Francois Jr. unpacked the soaked ditch and medical bags to dry in the sunny Natal weather, Annafré laid out all my wet books to let them dry, too. Marie and Susan took my clothes to a nearby Laundromat, then worked to clean my messed-up galley and got the IT spotlessly clean.

Seeing all of us together, reminded me of my initial motivation to not only use this trip to honour my late brother Gerrie but also to re-unite our scattered family.

Afterwards, I was briefly interviewed by a journalist from the local newspaper and posed for pictures. The following morning when Dad and I strolled to a nearby restaurant for breakfast, my face featured on the front page of the local newspaper. Leon, a producer and cameraman from M-TV, and his helper, Leslie, arrived. They shot footage upon footage, with numerous interviews to go with it. I was beginning to feel like a celebrity.

I got up early and went to my father's hotel to have a cup of coffee and a quiet moment with him. And new hope surfaced and I knew that I wasn't fighting this battle on my own anymore.

A closer inspection revealed that Willy was in bad shape, the shaft and rudder had completely separated – a result of a bad design and fabrication. We took it to a workshop where Francois, my father, and I tackled Willy. My father is a quantity surveyor, Francois, a mechanical engineer, and I a jack-of-all-trades. Together, we re-designed and beefed-up the wind-steering unit. "'n Boer maak 'n plan!" (A South African saying, meaning a farmer makes a plan). Back on IT, while Francois jumped in the water to reinstall the repaired rudder, I watched from the stern.

There was so much that needed fixing. The autopilot, still under warranty, went to the Ray Marine dealer. The dodger and genoa went to the sail-maker's shop.

Uncle George van der Merwe, seventy years old, came round. Nineteen years ago he had helped me install the irrigation system on Overvlakte. More visitors arrived. Uncle George's twin sister, Aunt Betty, and her husband, Uncle Mannie, brought their daughter, Adele. We had a wonderful reunion and talked about the good old days.

Day after day more people came. And who should show up but Russell Knight? He was the line handler who had, at the start of transiting the Panama Canal, claimed that he didn't know that I was deaf. We met again half-way around the world and he was still telling jokes.

Alan Coetzer, my old Komgha school buddy also popped in. It was as if we had never lost touch. Even Alan's sister, whom I hadn't seen since she was thirteen, brought her daughter Jessica to see me.

Another surprise was Titch Snyman, my old skydiving buddy. He couldn't stay long but it did my heart a world of good to see my old friend again.

I stopped by the yacht club to check the weather forecasts. I got advice from a very experienced yachtsman, that there would be a three-day weather window opening soon and that I should grab the opportunity to make haste to East London, my next port of call.

Vodacom's District Manager, Richard, came round to tell me that Vodacom had decided to sponsor me. I was grateful and very humbled. Money had been one of the greatest challenges on the trip and the sponsorship would help me rest easier about the finances.

Beverly arrived from Texas and Dad returned to his home in East London.

After the nine-day stopover and meeting family and friends, I felt re-inspired and said goodbye to Durban. And I had new hope and knew that I wasn't fighting the battle on my own anymore.

Deaf doesn't equal stupid

On the 23rd of September, I left Durban Harbour. When huge waves began crashing over IT, I struggled to triple-reef the main and for the first time in my life, I saw the notorious freakish waves of the hundred-fathom line.

Following the advice of the sailors in Durban, I headed within one mile off-shore. The land gave me some protection, sailing down the treacherous Wild Coast of Southern Africa.

I spotted two huge whales swimming in our wake, just ten meters away. They kept pace with IT's speed and were getting closer. It baffled me because the engine was running at full speed and I thought the noise would scare them off. They were easily as big as IT. When one of them leapt out of the water in my direction, I threw the camera down, grabbed a jerry can and poured two litres of kerosene alongside the boat. Luckily, the attack never came and a few minutes later they were far behind.

When I passed the mouth of the Kei River old memories rushed back. It was there that my brother Gerrie collapsed and later died.

As I passed the Cape Morgan lighthouse of Morgan Bay, I recalled my fun-filled youth often visiting

this sea-site resort…

Morgan Bay is sixty kilometres from Komgha and I regularly went there with Morné. We would row up the lagoon until we were out of sight of the beach with its holidaymakers. There Morné showed me the magical grass islands where the crowned cranes graciously danced, one leg before the other. He pointed out the grey herons standing like statues in the smooth lagoon waters and the fish eagle staring into the depths of the lagoon, repeatedly throwing back his head, in what he described as a piercing cry.

The whole ambiance is pure Africa, but when Morné said the banshee wail of a trumpeter hornbill gave him goose bumps, we frantically paddled back to the safe haven of the beach.

In the wild beauty of this paradise I fished and bodysurfed. On the rock shelves we fed off the low springtide mussels, gorged on oysters and cockled in the light of the full moon.

From the cliffs one can gaze far out over the ocean to spot the dolphins, whales and thousands of diving seagulls churning up foam during their annual sardine run, feeding frenzy.

During my last visit to Morgan Bay in April 2003, I had strolled along on the beach, seating myself on a rock where Gerrie had loved to sit and re-affirmed that I would pursue our dream to solo circumnavigate.

And I missed him! A lot!

And finally, I saw the pilot lights of East London's harbour beckoning me and I forced myself to concentrate. I followed a freighter into the harbour, the only natural river harbour in South Africa. Arriving at Latimer's Landing, I threw a line to my father, waiting on the pier.

During that night heavy rains started pouring down, so much so that I got worried that the Buffalo River, in which the harbour was situated, would come roaring down and damage IT.

As soon as the rain slightly subsided, Dad and I left for Latimer's Landing to make sure the boat was safe. There I got surprised by a welcoming party. A girl's high school cricket team from the Limpopo Province, touring the Eastern Cape, were at the restaurant. The manager requested me to give them a brief history of my trip. I was bombarded with questions, which I answered in both Afrikaans and English. I received a grand applause after my closing statement: “Deaf doesn’t equal stupid.”

The next morning the sun was out and I rushed down to IT to check that everything was all right and with the better weather, it was time to leave.

Pyrotechnics

I motored out of East London harbour, took a turn and with a fresh northeast wind blowing, I was on my way again. I sailed close to shore to be within cell phone range, so that I could do text messages (the satellite phone had packed up). Soon the wind blew at twenty knots, at times going to thirty and the waves were once again crashing over IT.

During that long stretch across the Indian Ocean, I had done enough risk taking. So after a mere six hours, I decided to head for Port Elizabeth, my city of birth.

On the 28th of September, in a strong South-Westerly, I docked in the Port Elizabeth Marina. Sitting out the storm I didn’t get impatient, instead I used the time to ponder the circle that life had made since my birth on

Guy Fawkes Day…

My late mother used to tell me about that specific Guy Fawkes evening of the 5th of November 1960 in the friendly seaside city of Port Elizabeth where, in the midst of a pyrotechnic display, I was born. My eyes were a combination of my mother’s deep blue and my father’s lighter blue haze.

Every morning from the age of three months my dad took me to the nearby beach where I was seated on a towel while he had practised his skills as a lifeguard. He used to swim far into the sea and back and I inevitably rolled over and ate handfuls of sea sand. According to Mom I not only had the sea in my eyes but also in my mouth.

To this day I relish the feeling of the sea and sand. The people that I meet still comment on the colour of my eyes. And I wondered to what extent the pyrotechnic display during my birth was a coincidence. However, with all the fireworks in my life, it probably had marked the beginning of what would follow in the future.

After a few sheltering and daydreaming hours, the southwest winds abated enough for me to feel safe to leave the city of my birth.

In an attempt to get out of the way of shipping traffic, I headed south. But it didn't help, I couldn't sleep. When it became dark, I switched on all my navigation lights. The radar kept warning of oncoming freighters and tankers but they gave way to me.

The following morning, I was still two-hundred-and-fifty miles from Cape Agulhas, the most southerly point of Africa. The southwest winds were gone. Despite the sleepless night, I felt refreshed and enjoyed the birdlife circling us. A playful seal came alongside IT, I looked into its soulful brown eyes which reminded me of the eyes of the doctor in the hospital who had said that I was in Jesus's hands.

We passed Cape Agulhas lighthouse and I changed bearing, aiming for Cape Point, or as it is more commonly known, the Cape of Good Hope, eighty miles away. It was a big relief to round the southernmost tip of Africa and to begin my journey northwards. I noted that IT had had her best run thus far: A whopping one-hundred-and-seventy miles in twenty four hours. It was high octane sailing!

Early the next morning, I was surrounded by dense fog. My radar outlined land on the monitor but in the fog I couldn't see it. Approaching Cape Point, I cautiously navigated with the main GPS and the C-map on my laptop. It was my first time ever to sail in such dense fog and it was nerve-wrecking. Port Control was made aware of my arrival and with their powerful radar, they guided the freighters and tankers safely around me.

Fortunately, the clouds dispersed and then, as if a giant curtain suddenly opened on the 1st of October, the magnificent Table Mountain and her city, Cape Town, unfolded before my eyes. I was so mesmerised by the splendour in front of me that I didn't pay attention to my surroundings. And all of a sudden a waving movement on my port side caught my attention.

In the dense fog the yacht Thunderchild, had been sailing a mere twenty meters away from me but without me noticing it. A smaller yacht, Endeavour, came alongside IT and guided me to my reserved spot at the Royal Cape Yacht Club.

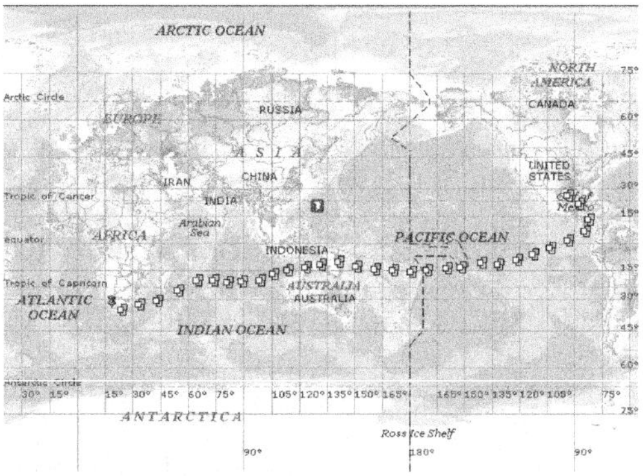

Fair winds and following sea

The reception was overwhelming and with a croak in my throat I struggled to talk. One of the cameramen caught my attention, he just kept on videotaping and when he finally lowered his camera, I recognised him as Oom Pierre Volschenk, an old family friend, with tears streaming down his cheeks. Beverley was standing next to him, also crying.

Nevertheless, as soon as the greetings were out of the way, I got dressed in a Vodacom's T-shirt and cap for a Television interview which took place in both Afrikaans and English.

This was followed by the reporters of the "Argus" and "Die Burger". The one from Die Burger was particularly interested when I told him that many years ago Gerrie and I had delivered their newspapers for pocket money in order to buy our first dabchick.

The manager of the Royal Cape Yacht Club, Trevor Wilkins, introduced himself and heartily welcomed me. I also met the Royal Cape Yacht Club's Commodore, Russell Vollmer, in his wheelchair. Some could perhaps label him a paraplegic but this excellent yachtsman was not in the least disabled and a huge inspiration to me.

For me that memorable day just flew by and after a hearty supper I said good night to everybody. The previous three sleepless nights took its toll and I slept like a baby.

The next morning, sitting at the breakfast table, I read "Die Burger" and "Argus" newspapers, both carried articles and pictures about my solo journey on their front pages.

Vodacom sponsored me to watch the Currie Cup rugby match between Western Province and the Natal Sharks. After the match the news came up on the screen of the corporate suite and there I was on television.

I was invited to a meeting of the members of the Royal Cape Yacht Club where Commodore Russell introduced me as the guest of honour and presented me with the burgee of the Club. Afterwards I took IT out into the Bay, joining forty-five other sailboats for the season's opening ceremony. When the yachts, one by one, passed the anchored boat of the Commodore to receive the traditional sailing salute, a few dolphins could be seen playing in the background.

Cousin Toni came to pick me up and took me around to some yacht stores. While driving I watched his face and couldn't help but wonder where I would have been, had he not thrown the spirits for a second time on the fire. But that's life and there he was helping me to search for critical yacht spares and I was very grateful for his assistance.

We left for Toni's home in Durbanville where we were joined by Deon, my brave little cousin who, by scrumming me down during the burning accident, had saved my life. The wealth of love I received during the course of that day made my crusade worthwhile.

During the burning incident in Durbanville, our neighbours had been Uncle Louw and Auntie Gwen Burger and, after seeing me on television, they came round to IT. We talked about how Auntie Gwen had run red lights, speeding me to the hospital and the finger that she threw at the cop.

Alma Snijder, who had taught me to lip-read in front of a mirror at the Mary Kihn School, spent a great evening with us and we shared lots of memories and also laughed a lot.

The next day Miss Martha Schemper, the erstwhile Principal of Mary Kihn School, came over to IT and we posed for pictures. My previous painful prefect-badge-stripping memories faded away when she said she was so proud of me. It meant more to me than words could ever tell. On her insistence I visited Mary Kihn School where I had spent five painful years, lip-reading and adjusting to being profoundly deaf. Using a map of the world I gave the learners a brief outline of my voyage thus far as well as my reasons for attempting it.

Morné du Plessis, my old standard six and seven school buddy, also came to visit. Zake Pretorius, my old school friend from Mussina, joined the two of us. It was his mother that had been my English teacher and I had always been in trouble with her for rather reading Wilbur Smith than following her lessons. So there I was with two of my erstwhile head boys from different schools that I had attended.

The following day Morné took me to Cape Town University where he was professor in ornithology and showed me around his offices. We reminded ourselves about the dreams we had shared with each other in our youth: He wanting to become a professional bird watcher and I wanting to solo circumnavigate. And there we were, he had already reached his goal and I was still busy with mine.

Nico de Kock, who had studied agricultural management with me at the University of Stellenbosch, came round. We hugged like long lost brothers and after twenty-five years he still proudly carried the pictures of the big game that he had hunted when he visited us on our farm in the Limpopo Valley.

Margie and Rob Johnson who almost twenty years ago had hosted our wedding reception in Rondebosch and Kate, their daughter, had seen me on the news and decided to hunt us down. I couldn't believe how time had flown and yet it was as if it had stood still.

My Skydiving friends presented me with a twenty year old picture of us in a twelve way, free fall, formation over Citrusdal and the Elephant's River. What a moment to remember!

Terryl and I drove to the Skydive drop zone. I twisted Terryl's arm sufficiently for her to organise with Long Pete to pilot the Cessna 210, taking us nine-thousand feet up where we jumped out and turned nine points of doughnut formation in free fall, against a backdrop of the majestic Table Mountain. It didn't even bother me that it was the 13th because it was pure magic and also my first jump for that year.

Beverley and I drove to Gordon's Bay to visit Uncle Pierre and Aunt Marie Volschenk. They organised for their son, an optometrist, to test my eyes. They also introduced me to the famous yachtsman, Bertie Reed, who had single-handedly rescued John Martin in a round a world race. He signed a print of the dramatic event during 1993 and handed it over to me. What an inspiring figure he was.

Francois and Susan flew in from Johannesburg to bid me farewell. We spent most of the morning with IT at the lift-out facilities to replace Willy's temporary rudder with the new stainless steel one which brother Francois had fabricated and brought along.

The next morning family, friends and other well-wishers gathered on the pier to give me the nautical blessing of: "Fair winds and following sea".

And after a wholesome twenty-three day stopover at Cape Town, I hastily cleared the dock lines, not only because I was in a hurry to complete this voyage of discovery, but also because it was hard for me to depart from South Africa.

A WAR OF IDEAS

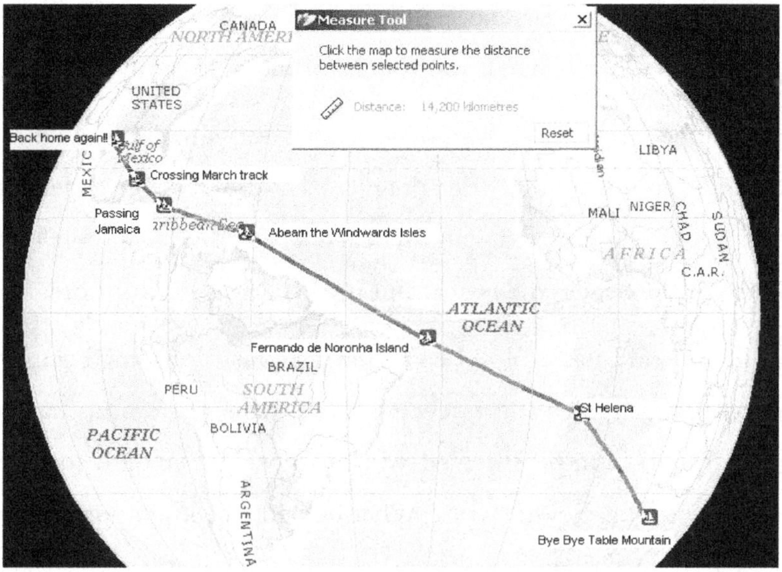

A war of ideas can no more be won without books than a naval war can be won without ships. Books, like ships, have the toughest armour, the longest cruising range, and mount the most powerful guns.

Franklin D. Roosevelt

The Dolphins

Motoring out of the mooring at the Royal Cape Yacht Club, the pier was buzzing with activity. On that perfect Sunday morning, against the backdrop of the majestic Table Mountain, covered with a thin film of haze, I waved to the crowd.

On-board Thunderchild cousins Toni, Deon and their families, Uncle Pierre and Aunt Marie, brother Francois, Susan, as well as many other well-wishing friends, came alongside IT to escort me out of the harbour. They stayed next to me for about an hour, everyone on board busily snapping pictures. Lingering for one last moment, they came close enough for me to lip-read them singing Gavin Sutherland's song, "Sailing" – the one that meant so much to me. They held their arms in the air, swaying from side to side, and tears streamed down their cheeks. When Thunderchild made a smooth turn to head back to Cape Town, it was tough for me to keep my composure.

As I watched them disappear, once again, I was alone. I wanted to turn IT around and stay in South Africa forever. The bow wave tenderly splashed spray on my face and mixed with my tears. The sun glistened off the water, I should have appreciated the beauty but my heart was just too sore.

In a light wind I passed Robben Island, famous for having been the prison of Nelson Mandela for twenty-seven years. Separated from his family and all that was dear to him, he survived with dignity and strength to become the leader of a changing South Africa. What he had to endure pursuing his destiny was far more challenging than what I was going through in attempting mine.

For the rest of the day I watched a cloth of clouds progressively spread itself over the flat top of Table Mountain and then draped itself down the mountain's sides to form a beautiful, wispy white "table cloth." I was under its spell and at sunset, before the beauty of it all dropped out of sight, I threw several kisses to the mountain and to my country.

During the night, I encountered a fishing boat, passing only two-hundred meters away on the starboard side. I quickly adjusted Willy to a new course and, thanks to Francois, the new rudder performed like a star.

As the night rolled into the morning, I sailed northwest, heading for St. Helena. In the morning a solitary Albatross joined me and I recalled the one that I had encountered before I reached Durban. But this time round, whatever its presence meant, if any, it soothed the pain in my lacerated soul and made the loneliness slightly more bearable.

I thanked it for being there for me during the course of that terrible blue Monday, explaining to the Albatross why it was so hard for me to adapt soul-fully to being solo again and the reason why it was painful for me to

depart from South Africa…

After the completion of my father's Cape Dutch house in Morgan Bay and the Martie fiasco, Beverly started to prepare for our imminent move to America.

Our trip was mainly financed by selling a very valuable yellowwood table, and its matching stinkwood chairs. My grandfather, Tony de Villiers, had refurbished it many years ago, and it seemed to me it had been in our family forever. But it had to go. In fact, all of our belongings were sold.

When we left in 1991, there were no friends or family to wish us farewell at the airport in Johannesburg. As I went through the departure gates, a great sadness enveloped me. I was leaving, probably forever, my beloved country.

We took a flight from Johannesburg, via London, to Houston, Texas. Instead of sleeping on the long night flight, I had taken Karin Blixen's book "Out of Africa" along and read it for the second time. Then I gazed through the window at the moonlit magic far below and became overwhelmed with emotion. I was severing my ties with the land that was acknowledged as the cradle of humanity.

I had an intense spiritual connection with Africa, but I promised Beverly that I would never return. For eleven years, until my brother died, I kept that promise and lived in self-imposed exile in America to pay the price for my foolish indiscretion.

But leaving Cape Town this time round, at least, family and friends had been there to wish me well. This time I left as a hero instead of a bum, but both times, I left reluctantly. My feelings overpowered me. I sank to my knees and sobbed. I cried for Africa, my beloved country, and for not knowing when I would see her again. If ever?

While the Albatross was still hovering above me, I got up from my knees, sat back in the cockpit and told it about all the people with whom I had a reunion during my stay in South Africa. All of them had moulded and influenced my life in some profound way, and seeing them again, after so many years, were the soothing balm that contributed to the healing I experienced.

I explained about them, one by one: Cousin Toni, who had thrown the spirits on the fire. Deon, who had saved my life. Auntie Gwen, who had sped with me to the hospital. Alma Snijder, who had taught me to lip-read in front of a mirror. Ms Schemper at Mary Kihn, who had stripped off my prefect badge. Morné, who had realised his dream long before I even attempted mine. Zake, who had dared me to swing the ball at the teacher's head. Smart-ass Alan Coetzer; Uncle George van der Merwe; And so many, many more!

Perhaps I bored it with my litany but the sudden departure of the Albatross brought me back to the present. As it took flight, I consoled myself that I had come so far, I was on the home stretch and the accomplishment of my goal seemed within reach.

And the incessant inner dialogue just wouldn't stop. I tried everything possible to scramble it but nothing seemed to work. It was as if a virus operated on my internal hard-drive, randomly accessing unconnected things in my life and scrambling them into a hotchpotch of total gibberish: If I focused on Willy following the wind it generated thoughts about Overvlakte, the place I had once called "my farm". If I concentrated on the ocean the next thing another thought about droughts, then again Mary Kihn and then back to Mussina again.

There was no control over the hay-wire thinking which had possessed me and it drove me bananas. Finally, I stopped fighting and sat back in the cockpit, and allowed it to go in whatever direction it needed. The flashbacks rolled out of sequence and nothing made sense anymore.

Slowly, the insane thinking began to organise itself sequentially. This time it went from the present to my pyrotechnic past, and then back again, to where everything in some strange way converged during my stop-overs in South Africa.

Throughout this trip my flashbacks had assisted me to vent the painful memories which I had suppressed for so many years. I was returning to America as a totally changed man. Suddenly I snapped out of it and was able to refocus.

I passed the thirty-degree latitude line in strong winds and stayed well clear of the west coast of Africa with its treacherous fog banks. I wanted to save diesel in case I hit the doldrums again, so I went inside the cabin, started the portable generator to charge the batteries and waited, patiently, thinking about

"the moving finger that writes and having writ moves on"

After the night flight from South Africa, we made a four-hour stopover at Heathrow and then flew straight to Houston, where Tommy and Joy welcomed us to America. We moved in with them, but sharing a house with one's parents-in-law isn't always a good idea.

I had great difficulty in adjusting and communication was one of my biggest stumbling blocks. By the time I had arrived in America, I had excellent command of my mother tongue, Afrikaans, but not having been among English-speaking South Africans the previous couple of years in the bushveld, my English got rusty.

From the time that I had gone to school in Komgha, the quasi-English country village, I understood English very well and later read widely, my favourite author being Wilbur Smith. Nevertheless, the American accent gave me stinging headaches, making it hard to lip-read or to understand what was being said.

It was a debilitating struggle and communicating without Beverly's assistance was almost impossible. It also substantially limited my job options. I felt completely isolated and frequently withdrew from conversations or activities that I couldn't understand.

For me, the move to America had turned sour and I longed for my parents, brothers and friends back in South Africa. But there was nothing I could do about it – "the moving finger writes and having writ moves on" - and disillusioned as I had been, I thrashed about, searching for ways to cope. I reached back to my carefree days at Komgha and found encouragement from the example set by my brave ancestors who had refused to be intimidated by society or adversity.

Realising that to work in the exclusively English-speaking America, I had to master the American accent and I became determined to make it a success. I forged ahead with my linguistic education. At the age of thirty-two, aided by television sub-titles and Beverly, I gradually improved my American-English lip-reading and speaking abilities.

I was almost four-hundred nautical miles from Cape Town and all that cogitating was driving me nuts. I searched for anything that would deflect my thinking and suddenly a light went on. There was a library full of books.

I snuggled under warm blankets (it was surprisingly cool) and pushed my nose into Bill Bryson's "A Short History of Almost Everything". The reading worked because the incessant thinking came to a standstill.

I hadn't done so much reading in a while. Finishing the sixth, four-hundred-page book, I contemplated a world without being able to read. Reading, to a very large degree, helped compensate for my disability: Lip reading, reading between the lines, reading the fine print, reading the moods, reading the atmosphere, etcetera. Without being able to read incessantly (the weather was very cooperative), that stretch from Cape Town to St. Helena would have been very emotional for me.

I was reading a Forsyth novel when the sun came out. It lifted my mood sufficiently to take back control of my mind and I decided to stop the reading frenzy for a while.

Strange cross-swells and uneven waves caught me by surprise because the mood of the sea was not what I had expected from the South Atlantic. It kept me busy and when the hull-speed surpassed nine knots, it vibrated tremendously, but I wanted to make the most of it. The gruesome hours working the sails made my body to ache but I persevered. I made myself comfortable in the cabin, staring into the dark, not knowing what the night might hold and whether I would need to do a

nightshift…

Due to my limited English, and strange Afrikaans accent, I started work as a farm labourer and drove tractors at the minimum wage.

After three months, I learned American-English sufficiently well to be employed as a floor sweeper at six dollars an hour. The hours were long, seven days a week, working twelve hours per night. It wasn't that hard but it did nothing for my self-esteem.

In the meanwhile, Beverly worked three jobs. She taught at a private school, where both our children were allowed to attend with her. In the afternoons she started the De Villiers School of Music at our house, giving private lessons in piano, trombone, and clarinet. She also waitressed at night.

I started reading again, Ken Follet's "Fall of Giants" in which the story moves seamlessly from Washington to St. Petersburg, from the dirt and danger to the glittering chandeliers of a palace.

After finishing the book, the "thinking" descended upon me again and I reflected on how I progressed from a farm labourer to a floor sweeper, to a welder's assistant, to a welder and finally to a senior coded welder, by playing my cards right in pursuing my own

American dream…

While sweeping the floors for a dredging company, I was constantly on the look-out for better opportunities. One day the welder's assistant didn't show up and I offered to help out. The welder was so impressed with my work that he informed the boss and insisted that I be employed as his assistant.

Then one day the welder didn't come to work and there was an urgent welding job to be done. The boss asked whether I could help out and I did an excellent piece of welding, so much so that one of the sub-contractors at Formosa Plastic's Point Comfort plant hired me as a welder.

After one year, the sub-contractor was kind enough to put me on evening shift so that I could attend Victoria College in the mornings, where I did a course in AutoCAD.

Things were going well working for the sub-contractor, then one day out of the blue, Formosa offered me a full-time job as a welder-fabricator at the Ethylene Di Chloride plant. Looking at the benefits that they had offered, I felt I had no choice and gave up my job with the subcontractor and also very reluctantly gave up my studies.

Finally, I had a fixed schedule in my life and America became bearable. We were putting away money and were back on track.

And in realising my American dream, my tremendous longing for South Africa had slowly subsided.

When the wind started to increase it blew the flashback right out of my mind and instead of seamlessly sailing in a fixed direction, I sailed in a zigzag pattern.

The radar-controlled vibrator shook me awake very early on the sixth day out of Cape Town. I hopped on deck and saw the Walvis Bay to Rio Express, heading straight for me. At the last moment, I managed to swerve away. When the four-hundred foot freighter passed just two-hundred feet in front of IT, I nearly fainted. The ship left us rolling in its wake, apparently unaware that it almost cut us in half. Obviously, no one was standing watch. Why my radar had let the freighter get so close before warning me, was a mystery.

On Monday, October the 31st, when I crossed the Greenwich meridian, I took video footage of the GPS at a position of S 20 23' 25", W 0 00' 000". I was back in the Western Hemisphere.

For the first time since I had exited the harbour of Cape Town, I started the engine again and let it run for one hour to charge the batteries. But after eight days of feeling no vibration, it felt awkward and

it might sound meaningless but…

I had received information from my cousin, Chris Knott-Craig, a heart specialist who lived in Oklahoma, about a relatively new procedure called a "cochlear implant." It was an electronic device that was surgically implanted, which could return the sense of sound to a person who was profoundly deaf or severely hard of hearing.

Initially, I was sceptical, but as I learned more, I became very excited. Science had developed to the extent that there was a real prospect for me to be miraculously healed, and to be "normal" again. Perhaps to those who had been born deaf and never heard the sounds of birds or their mother's voice or friends talking and laughing, it wouldn't have mattered so much. But to me, who once had been able to hear all those things and took it all for granted, the desire to hear again was overwhelming.

I researched all the available material, and in 1992, to my horror, it was a very expensive operation, - a whopping $45,000. I didn't have the money but I was so desperate to adjust to the hearing world that I continued to explore all possible financial avenues. I didn't qualify for a loan and it looked like those avenues were blocked. When Tommy and Joy offered to take out a second mortgage on their house to finance the operation, I was deeply touched.

At that time, the nearest place where the operation was being performed was in Oklahoma City. Chris offered to let us stay with him and his family, to save on expenses. Unfor-

tunately, my company had no sick leave benefits, and in order for me to take the time for the operation, I was forced to quit my job. That was a blow, especially when money was such a critical factor.

Over a three-day period the doctors did a series of tests to make sure that I qualified for the operation. When I passed all their requirements, my hopes were high, and I finally got the green light for surgery.

In order to further curb expenses, Chris had arranged for me to have the surgery as an outpatient. Afterwards, I stayed behind with Chris and his wife, Danese, who assisted me with the pain management. Beverly had to go back to work because we were entirely dependent on her income.

Later, I went back to Oklahoma to have the implant fine-tuned and reprogrammed according to my personal needs. It was surprisingly jarring to hear sounds again, and the doctors warned me that it would take time to reactivate the atrophied nerves and to grasp the meaning of various sounds.

After being trapped for twenty-three years in my own silent world, it was confusing to hear the meaningless sounds, but it was the only way that I could get back to the world of the hearing and I was bent on getting it right.

In the end the vibration from the engine freaked me out, so much so that I shut down the engine and it was a relief not to feel it.

Getting closer to St Helena I read more about the island which had been discovered by the Portuguese in 1502 and, although I had never been there before, I felt a number of connections to the island:

During the Anglo-Boer War, six-thousand prisoners-of-war from South Africa were imprisoned on St Helena, one of them was my great-great grandfather van der Merwe.

In 1898, fifty-four-year-old Joshua Slocum (born February 20, 1844 – died on or shortly after November 14, 1909), was the first man to sail single-handedly around the world on his yacht, Spray. For me, not overly endowed with patience, a favourite Slocum quote was, "Anyhow, a philosophical turn of thought now was not amiss, else one's patience would have given out almost at the harbour entrance." He stopped over at St Helena and I, being the first deaf single-handed circumnavigator, would follow in his footsteps.

In 1815, Napoleon Bonaparte was sent to St. Helena by the British and spent his last years there. There had been several plots to rescue Napoleon from captivity, including a spectacular one from Texas, where exiled soldiers from the Grande Armée plotted to rescue him and resurrect the Napoleonic Empire in America. And I was on my way back to Texas. I, like Lord Byron, who had viewed Napoleon as the epitome of a romantic hero, a persecuted and flawed genius, was equally fascinated with this character.

One of my favourite Napoleonic quotes is:

"Impossible is a word to be found only in the dictionary of fools"…

After the cochlear implant's fine-tuning, I started to look for a job and got lucky when US Contractors hired me. On my first day at work I was very excited to step into the world of the hearing with my brand new implant, but a few surprises awaited me.

Due to the high noise levels on the plant the implant didn't work on the job. In fact, the noises were so overpowering that I literally got dizzy from the maddening sounds and I had been totally unprepared for it. Beverly phoned the doctor, who advised that I should just persevere.

One day I got so confused that I ripped the external sound enhancer of the cochlear implant right off, and it nearly fell to pieces on the ground. After that I tried it on only at home, but it was not enough to stimulate my residual hearing.

I started to look for a job at a quieter place to enable the implant to work, but couldn't find anything. After all the expenses, I wasn't going to give up that easily and approached the Human Resources Department, explaining my predicament. But my request for an office job was rejected in such a way that I felt like a fool for even asking.

And I, attempting what many believed was an impossible mission, felt like a fool thinking about the conflict between the plant and the implant.

I plotted that the island was twenty-five miles away, but peering into the pitch-black darkness, I couldn't see a thing. The cloudy skies seemed ominous and spooky, but after the clouds dissipated, I could vaguely make out the dark shape of the island. And when a few lights appeared on the cliffs, I knew I was on the right track.

When dawn broke I could see a vast mountainous area which reminded me of the Natal Drakensberg Mountains in South Africa. After non-stop reading and incessant thinking, I entered the mooring area of Jamestown in St Helena.

I searched for the marked mooring buoys which Commodore Russell Vollmer had told me about but couldn't find it, so I dropped anchor near the cliffs to get away from the wind coming down the ravine in which Jamestown was set.

When Harbour Master, Barry Williams, came aboard he told me that he had expected me after watching the documentary on the Super-sport channel. I completed the necessary papers and took the water taxi to the dock, where I had my first shower in eleven days.

I returned to IT to collect my dirty laundry and took it to Ann's Place, overlooking the well cared for botanical garden and a monument for fallen soldiers. Ann told me that stop-over yachties usually gather at her place. There were burgees, flags and T-shirts from all over the world on display. Bertie Reed's and John Martin's were also there. She handed me her scrap-book, signed over the years by visiting sailors, to briefly write about my trip. I gave her a "Silent Voyager" T-shirt which she proudly displayed with the other memorabilia.

Ann served me with a delicious brunch and introduced St Helena's radio broadcasters, Ralph Peters and Gary Walters. They interviewed me and recorded our conversation which they said would be broadcasted over the radio that evening. Of course I wouldn't hear it and when they left, I reflected on the issue of the broadcast which was

interesting but useless information…

Time and again I went back to HR explaining to them how a cochlear implant works but to them it was interesting but useless information. They shrugged their shoulders and said that the situation at the plant made it impossible for them to reconsider my position.

Two years went by without me being able to wear the external enhancer at work, and during my annual check-up the doctors warned that the cochlear implant would soon become useless unless I utilized it.

More determined than ever, I went back and schemed that if I could prove I was a valuable asset, then they might reconsider their hard-ass attitude. I started to formulate an idea to save money for my employer.

I put a lot of thought into a concept I had developed and fabricated a simple system to add strainers to the water chillers. In the process, I proved that I saved them a lot of money. Thinking that money made the world go round, I approached HR again with the results of the savings I had generated, but they adamantly stuck to their guns.

The final blow came when I again approached HR, this time to inquire why they had promoted one of my juniors for a job opening which I had applied for, without considering me. They referred me back to my supervisor.

When I confronted him, he said it was because I was deaf. I couldn't believe it, I had pleaded with them to give me an opportunity to work where I could wear my external enhancer so that I would not be deaf and could participate in the hearing world. I reviewed the job specifications again, I fully complied with all the requirements, and was computer literate. Their discrimination was just beyond me.

I felt so disheartened that I didn't pursue the case with HR any further because by then, I had no trust in them anymore.

And contrary to what I thought, money didn't talk. The employer didn't feel any obligation to create an enabling environment where I could participate among hearing people. It was a bitter blow, how bitter, I could not begin to express.

It was very difficult to make peace with the situation, but with the wisdom of hindsight, I realized that, while they could have done much more to help me, being profoundly deaf for twenty-three years, the neural pathways between the ear and the brain had stopped functioning. Without sound stimuli all those years, they had irreversibly atrophied.

In the end, the implant became useless. It took me ten years to pay back the debt to my in-laws, and once more I had to make peace with the fact that I would remain profoundly deaf, and all the consequences that went along with it.

I snapped out of my daydreaming and feeling emotionally drained, I took the ferry Taxi back to IT for a well-deserved rest.

I utilised the next day to do some sightseeing. Some of the buildings reminded me of the old castle in Cape Town, built with heavy fortress-like walls. I briefly visited the cemetery where it was believed that my van der Merwe, great-great grandfather, as prisoners-of-war, had been buried during the Anglo-Boer War.

The next job was to tackle the extremely steep, Jacob's Ladder, a concrete staircase with one handrail and six-hundred-and-ninety-nine steps, leading to the lookout post on Ladder Hill. During the climb, I realised I was seriously out of shape and stopped three times to catch my breath. Once at the top, I took video footage of the breath-taking scenery below and spotted IT at anchor in the bay. For a moment I had a nagging feeling that she was not in the same spot where I had left her that morning.

Worried about IT, I decided that it was enough sightseeing for the day and hitched a ride back to town. I rushed back to the wharf and crikey IT was a mile out, playing the same old trick as in the Marquesas and Pago Pago. The water taxi took me out and I caught her just in time, dragging her anchor in an attempt to get away. I brought her back and anchored her again, this time closer to the wharf.

November the 5th arrived, my forty-fourth birthday and the first one in twenty years away from my family. I read all the birthday wishes on my website and felt so lonely that I decided on the spot to check out. Although it's a bad omen to leave on a Friday, I didn't want to stay any longer, my feet were itching to get back home.

After clearing customs, I hauled the anchor, double-reefed the main, poled out the headsail and set Willy on a course for the Caribbean.

Go IT, Go!

I spent the rest of Friday being lonely at sea but late afternoon, as a birthday present, a pod of twelve dolphins showed up. They entertained me by swimming side-by-side in front of the bow, all the time frolicking. I was fascinated and they hugely improved my feeling of emptiness. Watching them leap in front of IT's bow triggered memories of sailing in Matagorda Bay and how

the dolphins rescued my soul…

Soon after getting to America, I acquired a seventeen-footer and then two bigger sailboats followed. I used to day-sail from Palacios' Serendipity Marina, out onto the Mata-

gorda Bay Channel and through the Intracoastal Waterway, often being accompanied by dolphins. Those dolphins were lazy creatures, swimming in warm, shallow water with an easy food supply. But every now and then, in deeper water, one would leap and spin, giving me a glimpse of how an open ocean dolphin might behave.

During those difficult days of adjusting in a foreign country, and after the disappointment with the cochlear implant, the dolphins came to my rescue. They didn't physically save me but I was spiritually drowning and they were my life-line.

The disappointments, the depression and the losses could have sent me straight to psychotherapy. But it was not necessary, because I could sail with my soul mates and I had many healing conversations with them.

Over the years, my burning desire to solo circumnavigate faded away in the shadows of all my other responsibilities but decades later, in Matagorda Bay, where I could talk to the dolphins, my dream to be the first deaf person to solo circumnavigate was slowly resurrected.

When I sailed with them, I felt free and unencumbered by my deafness and after each encounter with the playful yet regal creatures, I felt like worthwhile human being.

And having the dolphins as company on my birthday was so special. It was as if they encouraged me to continue, to cast all my demons into the sea until there would be none left to haunt me. After my promise to the tuna in the Pacific, I no longer kept tinned tuna in store and ate beef stew mixed with potatoes for a birthday supper.

The next morning greeted me with strong winds and a whole day of trouble with the sails awaited me. The pole holding the headsail came loose, causing it to tangle around the furling system. There wasn't anything I could do, so I proceeded under a full main.

Later when the weather improved, I untangled the headsail from the furling system, but unrolled it too much and the furling spool became almost empty, with the result that I couldn't furl it up again. Then the seam on the mainsail, just under the top batten, blew out. I took it down, hauled it into the cockpit and it took four hours to stitch it up again.

The next day, I hauled up the asymmetrical spinnaker and tied the clew at the bow, sheeted out the pole to make a broach impossible and we were flying. It wasn't long before the wind strengthened and the cross swells made a huge comeback. The spinnaker was dancing like a madman, and when I tried to get it down, it fell into the water again. It took me a while to fish it out. That spinnaker-fishing business was becoming overmuch for me and I was prepared to trade my kingdom on IT for a dowsing sock, so that I could safely dowse the spinnaker without it always landing in the water. Except for the spinnaker weirdness, the 13th didn't turn out too badly.

I unfurled the genoa, poled it out, and we were running again but I was still seven-hundred-and-fifty miles to the halfway point between Cape Town and Palacios, heading northwest to warmer weather.

The next day the temperature was up to ninety-five degrees, a terribly hot day. When another hotter-than-hell day arrived, I was getting desperate from the heat. I crawled into a spot of shade on the deck and panted like a dog, just thinking about the last time I had felt such

heat…

My in-laws had decided to move to New Mexico for health reasons. Beverly and I remained behind with the kids, staying on Tommy's small holding. Eventually, we managed to buy the property from him but the house was very small so I remodelled and extended it. During November 1992, my dad came to Texas to visit us for the first time. He wanted to check out the problems with my cochlear implant, and while there, he also lent me a hand with the refurbishment of the house. It was one of the hottest winters I had ever experienced in Texas and in that weather the two of us worked non-stop to complete it in time for the spring break.

It was a proud the day when we had a fully-finished four bedroom house with two bathrooms and a wooden porch on the second story. And it was our own little kingdom in America!

I did consider the risk of a rash on my burned skin and a couple of times I scooped up saltwater to douse myself. That night, the cabin was hotter than an oven, so I slept in the cockpit. The stars were brilliant and I wondered why I didn't do it every night.

The following day I used at least twenty gallons of saltwater to stay cool and it was a huge relief when night came. We were moving but the heat was playing on my nerves. I developed an intense longing for a cool breeze. In the end, I had to start the main engine to keep the batteries charged so that I could have cool water in the refrigerator.

Every morning brought more heat. I couldn't cool down enough and, it didn't come as a surprise that all the salt water I had used eventually caused a terrible rash. My transplanted skin became extremely sensitive.

When we were still two-hundred-and twenty miles east of Fernando de Noronha, an archipelago off the coast of Brazil, flying fish and baby squid began littering the deck. This frenzy caught the attention of an errant egret, perhaps migrating from Africa to South America. It made itself at home on the dodger, watching the flying fish and swaying side to side with the motion of the sea.

While watching the egret, I remembered the book on birds that Morné wrote and had given to me while I was in Cape Town, called Penvere (quills). It was the first Afrikaans book I read since I had left South Africa in 1991 and I thoroughly enjoyed it. When the egret took off, nicely rested for his next flight, it left a lot of purple poop behind from feeding on the baby squid and it took a while to clean it up.

We were getting close to the Equator. Since I had encountered the Walvis Bay to Rio Express, I had not seen another freighter. But they started to show up, heading in a northeast direction, which meant I was in the South America to Europe shipping lane. I didn't dare go to sleep and stayed up all night watching the freighters, as they passed us within a two-mile radius. There was no danger this time round but I kept a vigil until the last one was ten miles away.

On November the 17th, I entered the North Atlantic, crossing the Equator at a longitude of 33 58' west. It reminded me of my late mother's birthdate, when I had first crossed the Equator as a novice Slimy Pollywog. I was proud to again nod to Neptune but now as an experienced, Trusty Shellback. I performed the same "crossing of the line ceremony" that I had done in April and remembered what Joshua Slocum had written: "To be taken into account were some years of schooling, where I studied with diligence Neptune's laws, and these laws I tried to obey when I sailed overseas, it was worth the while." This time I didn't solicit Neptune's protection but thanked him for a safe passage through the Southern Hemisphere.

At that exact moment the wind died momentarily and along came a huge squall with two hours of blessed, cool rain. Alas, over the next four days, the wind dwindled to six knots and I sailed an average of three and a half knots. Going zig-zag all the time exhausted me more than storm sailing did and that type of sailing felt more like slow

slope-skiing…

With my dad's next visit to America he flew directly from Johannesburg to Albuquerque where we awaited his arrival and surprised him with some VIP treatment. We collected him with a limousine and drove back to where we had our car parked. We got into our car and drove to a ski resort near Roswell in New Mexico.

During a three day holiday I taught my dad how to ski. Beforehand I had bought him overhauls to ski in because I knew that the usual American sizes would be too small for him. Fortunately the ski resort had stocked a pair of size sixteen ski boots, the only pair available.

Never having done any skiing in his life, as could be expected, he took a few tumbles and got frustrated. So in the end I let him hold onto my waist belt to follow me from behind and slowly dragged him zigzag down the slope. Nevertheless it was great fun and in the end he got the knack of it and could go solo on the easier slopes.

On November 21st, I noticed a dark cloud mass about five miles away. It wasn't long before a funnel shaped cloud, black as Satan, slowly snaked its way down towards the ocean. Then, in a matter of seconds, a perfect water-spout appeared and roiled the ocean as it pulled sea water up into its funnel. It lasted about two minutes, dancing and skipping across the surface. Where it touched down, water flew everywhere. But it soon dissipated and dropped harmlessly into the sea. It was the first waterspout I'd ever seen.

According to Jimmy Cornell's book, the doldrums in the North Atlantic were relatively narrow, but that's not what I experienced. I was already in the hot doldrums for six long days. The northeast trades should have been blowing at five degrees north, but I was almost seven degrees and still there was nothing.

I dug out the small GPS that my father had donated to me in Cape Town. It reminded me that Dad had demanded that I sail the northerly route and that I had acceded to his wishes. It was a decision I had often bitterly regretted. The so-called "safer route" came at a huge price, facing the doldrums, a lot of ocean traffic and the continuous pain-in-the-ass, Pacific line-squalls. I missed my dad and I was glad that I had made peace with him for forcing me not to take the route around Cape Horn. And I guess

"like father, like son"…

After the skiing, just for the kicks and a good night out, I got lucky at the local casino, enough so that my dad and I could fly to Las Vegas. So there we were lightly packed and heading to sin city to hopefully in the process make a bit of money.

After booking in we went our respective ways to go and gamble and each took a responsible amount of $300 for the evening's gambling. After about eighteen rounds of smart and visceral blackjack, I was up to $900. Ok, I thought that's enough gambling for a while and went to check on my dad where I found him fooling around with the slots He was very excited about my winnings and psyched me up to play some more serious blackjack. I returned to the table where I was on a roll, boom, win, split, win, win and win.

The $900 dollars soon doubled and I decided to call it quits. I had made enough money to spoil him with a flight in a Cessna 410, flying low over the Grand Canyon, having an awesome view of this wonder of nature. Dad couldn't stop thanking me for the thrill and the kicks we got out of this excursion. No wonder: "like father, like son".

Dad had spoiled me with the state of the art GPS and as I turned it on, I valued his gesture. I plugged it into the data kit, connected it to my laptop, turned on the C-map software, and in less than two minutes I was able to clearly see my exact location on the world map. I usually plotted my position on paper charts, but playing with the gadgets was a great treat.

I wondered what the reaction of the ancient mariners would have been (men such as Diaz, da Gama, Drake, Van Diemen, Cook and Torres) if they could somehow have known about the modern navigation technology. Perhaps they would have been rolling restlessly in their graves or maybe kicking themselves for missing out.

With this philosophical turn of thought concluded, my impatience (that I thought I'd shed) showed its ugly face again, so I went into competition with the wind and incessantly worked the sails. But when I realized that I would not break my own record of one-thousand-two-hundred-and-fifty miles in seven days, which I had accomplished between Marquesas and Samoa, I just dropped the effort. But in the past there were other

records…

It was only much later, when I started to earn more money, that I could join a drop zone and became an active skydiver again. It gave me the opportunity to make friends all over America.

During 2001, I was part of an all-deaf skydiving team and, together with thirteen others, did a mass parachute jump in free-fall formation. It was the first ever all-deaf skydiving event in Texas. Deaf skydivers from England, Norway, the United States, and several other countries participated.

I had to win at something! So I finished another four-hundred page Colin Forbes novel and seven books in seven days was a record for me.

I took a swim behind IT sailing at three knots and let her pull me on my harness. At the same time, I did an inspection of the hull. The water was crystal clear but too warm and botched my cool-off attempt. The freshwater in my tanks was much colder than the seawater, so I took a freshwater shower in the head, trying to use as little water as possible.

It was Thanksgiving Day back in Texas and I was sure that the family was sitting down for a turkey dinner. On the other hand, in sweltering heat with no clouds and very humid conditions, I crept along aimlessly and felt totally

directionless…

Over long weekends and during holidays we regularly visited Tommy and Joy who lived close to ski slopes. I often took the kids to ski and, despite the disappointments, we had a good life.

One year, after visiting the in-laws for Thanksgiving, we returned to Texas, driving through the night. At midnight I couldn't keep my eyes open anymore, so I asked Beverly to drive and I immediately fell asleep in the back of the car.

After a while I was getting very restless in my sleep and had a nagging feeling that something was very wrong. I woke up with a jerk and immediately told Beverly that we were heading in the wrong direction. Apparently she stopped at the gas station and instead of turning right, she turned left, taking us back to where we came from.

I was brought out of my reverie when yet another pod of dolphins visited and they greatly inspired me with their friendly display. I was in a Thanksgiving frenzy and couldn't stop thanking them, and repeatedly expressed my gratitude for their visit.

I soaked myself with saltwater and flushed it off with freshwater so that the rash wouldn't build up over my legs. However, the freshwater was almost finished and I stopped using it. I was down to the last of my diesel, which meant that I would have to drift the last miles to either Barbados or St Lucia.

At dawn the following morning, I ran into a hell of a lightning storm, which stayed with us for two hours and I watched the fires of God lighting up the sky. It was a spectacular pyrotechnic display and the thunderclaps shook the entire boat, sometimes in a rhythm, like African drums. It was the IPI TOMBI of the seas.

I was still reading obsessively and started my eighth book, another Ken Follet novel. My eyes were burning from all the reading, and rubbing them, I thought about how I felt when Gideon

lost sight…

Gideon, fourteen years old, went to his friend's house where they played paintball. Afterwards, they came into the house for cold drinks. They didn't drop the paintball guns, and while sitting in the kitchen, the two of them continued to mock-shoot at each other, as crazy boys sometimes do.

I wasn't there and only heard about what had happened. Apparently, his friend thought his gun was not loaded and pulled the trigger while pointing the paintball gun to Gideon's left eye. Gideon's eye ball burst and was in shatters. They raced him to the hospital, where emergency surgery was performed, and though the doctors saved his eye, they could not save his eyesight.

We were grateful for the compensation that Gideon had received but it will never bring back his eye and in the process his dream of becoming a pilot was sacrificed.

I was totally devastated. I didn't want any of my children ever to be considered disabled. I knew more than anyone the hard road ahead. And it was agonizing to watch my son in so much pain. For the first time, I knew the torment that my own father must have felt during my trauma, and I understood, at last.

A large squall overtook us about three hundred miles from St. Lucia, where I was heading. When it eventually passed, the much-yearned-for trades arrived. IT smelled land, I didn't have to spur her on, she was giving it her all and I shouted: "Go! IT, Go!"

We passed Barbados at dusk, just twenty miles to the north and I could see the outline of the island with lights twinkling on the hillsides. After twenty-six days at sea, mostly in sweltering heat, I sailed into St Lucia.

Cinderella of the Sea

While I was searching for a berth in the half-empty Castries Marina, IT's old engine came to an abrupt standstill. I managed to throw a line onto the dock, just in time. I crawled on all fours to hastily secure her to the pier post.

I was pleasantly surprised when the Customs and Immigration fellows waived the requirement for a visa, having been alerted beforehand about my journey.

Searching for the reason why the engine suddenly died, I inspected all the filters. Not surprisingly, with only five gallons of diesel left in the tank, the stirred-up sediment blocked the filters. There was also water in the diesel. I took off the congested filters and since I had no spares, I flushed the old ones with stove alcohol and hoped for the best.

I walked to the fuel depot, bought ten gallons of diesel, poured it into the main tank and bled the fuel system. In a matter of minutes, the old 4-108 Perkins diesel engine was purring like a well-fed kitten.

I went to fetch the repaired mainsail, which I had handed in at the sail shop the previous day and after installing the slugs I reassembled it.

Satisfied with my work, I was compelled to go have an English breakfast, because England had beaten the South African Springboks in a rugby match. A Caribbean cruise ship was at anchor and the place was bustling with thousands of people. Mega-sized catamarans were fully booked, offering sunset cruises. There were also afternoon cruises on replicas of Captain Blackbeard's pirate ship.

In that super-rich environment, IT stood out like a sore finger, a Cinderella amongst the fancy, fat cats. Compared to the other ships, she looked like a dinghy toy. The people I met asked me about the size of my boat and my reply that she was a thirty-seven-footer extracted a pitying response: "Oh really, so small!" In my mind I responded: "Up yours".

Late afternoon, I went back to the office, paid the fees and filled up all my water and diesel tanks, as well as other empty containers. The bill amounted to an astounding $100. It was time to go.

And on the 2nd of December at six o' clock in the afternoon, after a sudden downpour, I hauled up anchor to confidently hurry home with IT, my Cinderella of the sea, leaving the fat cats behind to play their millionaire's game.

My own Insular Verdant Tahiti

As the sun set, I departed for the Caribbean Sea. Unlike those huge million dollar yachts left behind in the snobbish harbour, IT was small but she had carried me safely. I held tight onto my Cinderella's steering wheel and assured her that it was only a matter of time before we would attain our goal and she would be crowned my princess for having done the almost impossible.

After only four hours, I passed Martinique on the south side. There was quite a current running between St. Lucia and Martinique. It accelerated us to eight knots, on a bearing towards Jamaica. It also became much cooler, with confused seas and waves breaking into the cockpit.

On the 8th of December the radar shook me awake, I leapt on deck, just in time to see a freighter crossing close in front of the bow, doing about twenty knots. Once again, when I looked at the bridge, there was no one on watch. Close calls like that thoroughly freaked me out. As I sailed through the busy shipping lane, I counted eleven more freighters on their way towards the Windward Passage, between Cuba and Haiti. With all that sea traffic, I was on edge and didn't even catnap.

Moreover, we were in a known piracy hotspot and since leaving St. Lucia, I had withheld my coordinates. But on December the 9th, I felt safe enough to reveal my position.

Things calmed down and before dark, I took a bath in the cockpit and it was finally cool enough to put on

my Kwagga rugby Jersey…

I have fond rugby memories. Growing up we used to watch tons of rugby. It was still played with a leather ball and was not as a professional sport as nowadays. Players would play for their country but still have to work to pay the mortgage.

When I moved to Texas, I was afraid there'd be no rugby but was pleasantly surprised to find how many clubs existed. In trying to find a niche for myself, I joined the Victoria Rugby Club and soon found myself in a position of not only playing but also coaching and refereeing.

As a referee, I had been sent all over Texas. I had met a few South African expatriates, passionately playing blood-and-guts rugby. One of them and I discussed the idea of forming our own team and to market it with other ex-pats, we would use zebra-striped rugby jerseys. Immediately, many home-sick South Africans caught on to the idea and wanted to identify with the zebra which they all knew very well. We called our team the Texas Kwaggas because a Kwagga, or Quagga, had been a sub-species of the zebra family that had become extinct.

We all had full-time jobs and self-sponsored our activities. But once a year, it was show time. That's when the Kwaggas gathered to play in the Austin Rugby Tournament with our rugby jerseys proudly displaying the black-and-white zebra stripes.

When the South Africans and their families gathered in Austin we would barbeque boerewors and drink Castle beer, which I had specially flown in from the African Hut in California. We reminisced about the old days back in South Africa and sunk into nostalgia. During those annual tournaments, it was almost like being home again in South Africa.

After four years of losses in the finals, the Kwaggas gathered once more in 2001 and this time we were in full strength. My dad and Maria flew over and brought my sixteen-year-old stepbrother, Ivan, who in family solidarity played flank for the Kwaggas.

From the word go we smashed and bashed the other teams. They were bigger and faster than us but they lacked the inbred rugby instincts and desire that form part of the DNA of a South African male.

We managed to pass through to the finals where we met the Austin Huns, one of the most feared teams in Texas, consisting of New Zealanders. It was an enormous physical confrontation with players on both sides giving their all. In the end we were too much for the Huns and we won the game, though by a narrow margin.

I felt so proud that day for having brought together a bunch of home boys and their families and having had, at the age of forty, played flank alongside my sixteen-year-old stepbrother.

My weepy Dad watched as I was called by my captain to receive the winning trophy. It was a proud victory and a monumental memory. The Kwaggas went on to win the tournament several more times.

And my Kwagga buddies were following my solo journey closely and I knew that they were cheering me on.

I was getting closer to home, only 1,174 miles to Port O'Conner (the entrance to Matagorda Bay) and it was hard to control my excitement. I was thirty miles south of Cabo Cruz, the southernmost point of Cuba and could clearly see the mountain range.

Not far from the Cayman Islands my weather fax indicated a northerly front was approaching. Since it was late autumn in the Northern Hemisphere, it would bring cold north winds.

The batteries were low and the diesel limited. I knew that soon I would have to decide whether or not to switch on the engine, one of my toughest judgement calls…

As a referee I often had to make tough judgement calls. One such game was refereeing the headline match between the U.S Navy and U.S Army in San Antonio. That day the stands were jam-packed with the two teams' supporters and the mood palpable. One would have thought it was two different countries playing against each other and not just the US forces.

From the onset a nagging feeling plagued me that the game could any moment turn into a battlefield and I realised that I had to take strict control. I called both teams and explained to them that I was deaf but they better watch out because I can see everything. I inspected their boots and everything seemed to be fine. But when I blew the whistle for the game to start, it was foul play from the beginning.

I strictly applied the rules and on a number of occasions, I called the captains to discipline their guys. Then, I lip-read one of the players from the US Army swearing at me, without hesitation I sent him straight to the dog box. From that point onwards the guys realised that they shouldn't mess with me and started to toe the line.

After ten minutes, I called the swearing guy back onto the field but it wasn't long before he made another big mistake, climbing into the scrum with his boots. He was like a loose cannon and after his third foul play transgression, I gave him a red card and sent him off the field. He actually caused the US Army to lose the game.

And I decided to start the engine to charge the batteries and knew that it had been the right choice because, at the next moment, I was hit by a squall with strong winds and rain.

I entered the Yucatan Channel on December 12th, at nine o' clock at night. At last, I was returning to the Gulf of Mexico. The sea traffic increased and I watched a super-tanker approach, passing IT three miles away. It was so gigantic that it seemed to be much closer. Two Caribbean cruise liners were obviously headed to the Cayman Islands and one of them was on a collision course with IT. I repeatedly signalled with my powerful spotlight and it turned to pass a half-a-mile away. That night, I counted fourteen ships with their decks decorated by Christmas lights.

With all the traffic I felt as if I was "squeezing" through the Yucatan Channel. In the morning a pod of twenty dolphins welcomed me back into the Gulf of Mexico.

It wasn't long before a fresh northeast breeze came up and we were gliding over the rolling Gulf swells. With the wind coming from the northerly quadrant, we were suddenly sailing straight west. Not good, I knew that another cold front was on its way and I needed to gain as much latitude as possible. Before the seas became too rough, I quickly wrote and sent e-mails.

As the seas grew IT crashed hard and the lee rail was constantly submerged. I felt a different vibration on the hull and I saw that the spinnaker pole had come loose. It was banging on the mid-stay with the other end dragging in the water. I tried to grab it through the forward hatch, so I wouldn't have to go on deck. The moment I opened the hatch, we went down into a huge trough. IT's bow submarined and I took the full brunt of the hundred or so gallons of seawater, right on my upper torso.

I ended up flat on my back on the cabin sole and my head missed the starboard bunk by inches. It took a couple of seconds to get my wits back and I jumped up to secure the hatch. The cabin sole was covered in several inches of water, so I switched on the main bilge pump.

I went outside, clipped myself onto the safety rail and crawled on all fours towards the bow where I secured the spinnaker pole. In doing so, I was drenched by three more breakers.

I estimated the seas were between twelve and twenty feet. The twenty-footers came in series of three with very deep troughs behind their crests. The weather warning report had predicted twenty to thirty knots, so I expected bad weather but not winds above forty knots. On December 15th, I encountered a gale with winds gusting to forty-eight knots. I could have (should have) hove-to but I was too close to home to stop.

Suddenly, we hit the bottom of a trough with such a force that I went flying to end up in an awkward position on the port aft quarter berth. In the process, I hit my head against the port-side locker and both my left elbow and right leg hit something hard. I writhed around, gripping my elbow and my leg and cursed the sea-gods in every language that I could think of (Xhosa, Zulu, Venda, English, Afrikaans and American).

I saw that everything on the starboard upper bunk had made itself at home on the port side settee, on top of my toolboxes. The dishes in the galley sink, including a pot with my leftover food, had nestled themselves on the navigation table.

They were the worst seas I had ever encountered. The forty-footers-plus that I had encountered off the South African coast was a much easier ride. I requested another weather-fax and damn, we were caught on the east side of a full gale. My yearning for home was such that I pressed on.

Water came in everywhere, through the main companionway, the front and aft starboard vents and through the mast-step. Everything inside was once again a soggy mess.

We took a gale force beating for nineteen hours. Every time IT went free-falling into those deep holes, I gritted on my teeth and wondered how much more she could take. Was this the ultimate test for her or a kind of warning to me? Was I just another lunatic?

At that point I was grateful that I had no crew on board because I was sure that any other person would have jumped ship or turned on the EPIRB a long time ago.

I shuddered when I received a message from Norris Johnson: "At almost midnight last night, an earthquake was recorded at the exact position that you had been last Friday." And in trying to stay focussed, I wondered whether this was my

last match…

Rugby is not just fun-play, and like American football its mock war for territory and a release valve for aggression. Moreover, it contains and engenders all the emotional ingredients of a real war, but without actually killing anyone.

April 2002, I played my last match for the Kwaggas. We played in the finals, again in Austin. The roar of the crowd buffeted, palpably on the skin of my back and I was overcome with emotion. I silently thanked my mother for supporting me through those difficult years and encouraging me to live a normal life.

Overcame with intense emotion, I momentarily wept. Then I grasped for air and almost stumbled. During the match, I experienced a thrill made in heaven, the "thrill" of being on a battlefield and, while not ever having had to run onto a real battlefield, that feeling was sufficient to emulate it.

It was the last War with a capital "W" that I fought for the Kwaggas, the expat team of South Africans that I had put together in 1996 and, seeing where we came from to where we were on that day, it was almost as real as the war whereby you put your life on the line for your battalion.

To be invincible you must believe you are and we did believe and we were triumphant. After that experience, I imagined that running onto a real battlefield without that feeling of invincibility must scare the shit out of you.

I took on the circumnavigation not knowing whether I was going to win but I tried to believe that I would and shouldered the opposing sea. All my muscles were hurting from the terrible

free-falling

During 2003 three deaf skydivers, namely David Armstrong, John Woo and I, participated in the Pops in a big way in Rosharon and we broke the old record to form a new Texas POPS State Record of 62 skydivers linked up and it was the very first state record where three deaf skydivers had participated.

With 1,700 skydiving jumps under my belt the one thing that I don't fear are heights.

But what I feared was that the continuous free-falling against the berth boards, will give me brain damaged. It knocked the senses out of me and at that stage I was hugely distressed. I held tight and counted seven more freighters and tankers passing close-by. I sailed into a large oil field and steered between two oil platforms. Night time revealed more platforms but some of them were not lit so I kept a careful watch.

And the anxiety gave me heartburn feeling totally burned out. It felt like I was on fire from the inside for the second time in my life but then it hit me that actually this would be the third time because there had already been a second time that everything around me had

burned out…

During 2003, one evening after returning from work, it was cool and we shut down the air conditioners to let the house breath in some fresh air. Beverly lit some candles near the windows on the outside upper deck of our house and I prepared the fire to barbeque.

Suddenly a gust of wind blew the curtain over the candle and they caught fire. As I ran inside to get a blanket to douse the flames, I relived the same nightmare all over again. When I got back the flames were already licking on the deck wood and when I threw the blanket over the flames they shot out from under it. I felt the flames burning my skin and yelled at Beverly and the kids to get out of the house.

At the last minute Beverly grabbed the parakeet cage and ran outside with it. When she and the children got out of the kitchen door the house exploded in flames. I was stuck on the porch and the flames kept rolling towards me. It happened so fast and there was no way to get past the flames, so I jumped off the porch, four meters down and my experience as a skydiver saved me because I knew how to roll-jump.

Within minutes the fire brigade was there but they were not able to save anything. The house was gone, my kingdom in America, burned like a matchbox and we lost everything. My family was safe but it was a devastating blow.

That fire was a turning point for me, and having lost everything for a second time, having to start all over again, was very painful. The final blow came when the insurance only paid out a third of the value of the house, claiming that we were underinsured.

Recalling the second fire and its consequences made me cringe and I wished that I would be able to prevent such incidents in the future. But when dawn broke with one more day to go, I was exhausted and very relieved. On a close-reach, starboard tack, I was ninety-five miles from the Matagorda Ship Channel's entrance which the locals call the Port O'Connor jetties.

I was very moved when a pod of thirty-six dolphins joined me for my last miles of ocean.

My thoughts circled around my late brother and how his untimely death had re-ignited my desire to do the trip and I remembered his

half-lived-life…

During December 2002 Gerrie took a well-earned break. Almost thirty years after he and I bought our first Dabchick, "The Char-Ger", he together with his stepson Lionel visited my father at Morgan Bay for the Christmas holidays.

The day after Christmas, while my dad and Christo watched them from the bank, Gerrie together with Lionel went sailing with the two-man Dart on the Great Kei River.

While sailing on a broad-reach in near gale force winds Gerrie collapsed and Lionel, only twelve years old, not knowing what was happening, tried to bring his stepfather around and hysterically called for help. My dad and Christo saw that something was wrong and asked one of the other yachts to race to Lionel's assistance.

But Lionel, well trained by Gerrie, managed to get the catamaran to the riverbank where Christo with the assistance of some bystanders got the unconscious Gerrie off the catamaran and managed to revive him. There was no doctor around and my dad sped with Gerrie the eighty kilometres on a bad dirt road to the nearest hospital in East London.

During the trip to East London Gerrie was vomiting all the time and arriving at the hospital he underwent a series of tests to determine the reason for his unexpected collapse.

Late that same Sunday afternoon, when the results eventually came out, it came as a huge shock. The neurologist on duty found that, unbeknown to Gerrie and us, a silent aneurism (a weakness in the wall of a brain artery and which had been lurking there for years) ballooned out and burst during the sailing effort. And that was what caused him to black-out.

However, there was still hope and Gerrie waited for five days for the swelling to subside before the doctors could attempt surgery. For those days prior to the operation we were on pins and needles but remained positive.

And after the six hour operation the neurosurgeon cautiously approached my dad to break the devastating news that during surgery another aneurism exploded and that Gerrie was in a critical condition, kept alive only by means of a respirator in the Intensive Care Unit. After saying his goodbyes, three days later, my dad consented that they could switch off the life support and Gerrie, at the mere age of forty, passed away.

In the knowledge that from here on I needn't face the horrors of a life halve-lived, I felt very close to Gerrie. I could step ashore with courage after experiencing my own insular verdant Tahiti and start to live life to the full.

After dodging more oil platforms and a tanker, lying at anchor, I was welcomed by the U.S. Coast Guard, who escorted me through the Matagorda Ship Channel. In fact, the Coast Guard stayed with me all the way through the inter-coastal waterway and then through the Palacios Shipping Channel.

Soon "Clueless Waters" with Randy (who I had taught to sail) and friends approached and, after hailing them, they followed IT. Not long afterwards "Mariposa" with Norris at the helm and "Heart and Soul" with Tommy skippering, joined us too. All of them were members of the Palacios Yacht Club and they waved to congratulate me.

A large powerboat soon joined the flotilla as well as two large gulf shrimpboats with their outriggers fully extended to celebrate my return. As we approached the harbour entrance I could see the marina was stacked with people.

Crossing the finishing line and wanting to give them a good show, I shot a parachute signal flare off from IT's bow. I then took two handheld bright red flares and ignited them walking alongside IT's port-side rail, holding the flares triumphantly above my head. When I passed the crowd who cheered and clapped, holding up banners with "welcome home" slogans, I became very emotional.

I passed the crowd and motored to the end of the harbour. There, I turned around, lit more flares and headed back to triumphantly sail to a dock reserved for IT beside the Serendipity Marina's, "Blue House," where the crowd of almost three-hundred people had congregated.

FULL CIRCLE

As I docked, assisted by Gideon and friends tying up the lines, I jumped off and held my family close. Looking up I couldn't believe it, my dad was also there, all the way from South Africa. Pastor Ron then came forward to say a prayer of thanks.

My fellow Kwagga rugby players, Philip, Jaco and Hugo, proudly wearing their Kwagga jerseys, squirted and soaked me with champagne. And they picked me up and held me triumphantly on their shoulders.

After posing for pictures and a brief interview with the television and newspaper reporters it was time to greet all my friends, supporters and well-wishers.

I took my time chatting with each one who came to encourage me. All the other fans that couldn't be there, but had followed my daily travails on the internet, were thanked for watching, caring and praying for me.

I was presented with a proclamation from Palacios' Mayor, John Connor, who designating December the 19th 2004 as Charl de Villiers Day for: "He has shown great courage, vision and tenacity to bring a positive image of deaf and disabled to all people of the world, promoting the cause of the hearing impaired by demonstrating that a perceived handicap does not stop a person from fulfilling his or her dreams."

A Commendation issued by the Texas Governor, Rick Perry, stated that my journey of inspiration demonstrated that even the most ambitious goals can be made a reality. In addition, a presentation was made by a representative of the Port Lavaca Chamber of Commerce and I was given a collection of drawings made by Palacios elementary school children, commemorating my crusade.

I returned to IT and hung a special wreath from the mast winch, acknowledging that she was my silent partner in materialising my dream.

From the outset I had anticipated that it would take nine to ten months to accomplish my solo circumnavigation. I had aspired to be back in Palacios on time for Christmas and I accomplished it.

I returned to the marina from which I had set sail two-hundred-and-eighty-eight days earlier and I became the first deaf person to have sailed around the globe, completely alone.

In mastering the command of my own little ship to conquer the world's vast seas and their moods I have learned that one should respect the seas or it will wreak havoc upon you.

And as a totally changed man I accomplished my burning desire.

However, I could face whatever lies ahead in the future with fresh but hard-earned, confidence and courage.

ACKNOWLEDGEMENTS

The mother of my children, Beverly, and my late parents-in law for their support.

My children Sharleen and Gideon for making life an exciting experience.

My dad, Johan de Villiers, for always being there for me.

Gerrie who had inspired me to solo-circumnavigate.

Brother Francois and his wife Susan and their children Boeta and Annefré.

My brother Christo de Villiers who made several contributions to my stories.

All of my de Villiers and van der Merwe families.

David Clark my second cousin who had in 2003 sponsored our flight to South Africa to attend Gerrie's funeral.

Vodacom for their sponsorship.

Mr Pearce from Dixie Computers for his kind donations.

Mike Mondrik who had helped me to overhaul IT's engine.

Ivan Herselman for proof-reading numerous versions.

Dave and Sharon Ragle for their mentoring.

Dennis and Truda Ward, managers of Serendipity Marina. Their hard work had made my return to the marina a success.

Matt and Kyalla Riccio: Matt took the pictures of my return to Matagorda Bay. Kyalla had contacted Rick Perry for a proclamation and later the President of the US, George Bush, also sent a proclamation from him and his wife, Laura.

All my good friends Norris Johnson, Randy Waters, Gary Woodring and his family, Tommy Gustaveson. Robert and Cynthia Garrett: (At the time of my voyage Robert had been the Commodore of the club).

Eric Boyd for his permission to use the photo he had taken of the 62-free-fall formation.

But, most importantly, my wife Wanda, for her inspiration to complete the book and after eight years to tell my tales, even though I agonised to talk about it.

PEOPLE WHO REGULARLY SENT EMAILS

Tannie Andy, Oom Alan, Alan jr, Oom George vd Merwe, Toni, Daleen en Gideon, Donnie en Noeline Botha, Eric, Charmaine, from Messina, Nico and Morné. Oom Piere Volschenk en Tannie Marie, the Moll's in Paarl, Karel Koster and his paragliding mates Clive Ridley ex-golf partner, Michael Dovey, the Boyes family, Doug and Lucile and Grant Brook, Chris Ross, André Pretorius, Ari and Marietjie Badenhorst, Colleen Coetzee.

To my friends and co-workers at Formosa Plastics: Mark Barefoot, David Stanley, Ken and Ofie, Jimmy Wilson, thanks buddy, Richard Langston my co-welder, Jen and Mike. Ex-Formosa workers: Andy Bednarz and Scott Pena. Jeff my ex-helper at Formosa Plastics.

Chris, Danese, Chris jr and Mary-Ann Knott-Craig. David, June, Robynne and James Clark.

The Victoria Rugby Club: Tom and Judy Murrah, P-Nut, Jeff, Bob and April, the O'Neil's, Rob Pupi and family and Canadian Neil Redfern.

My skydiving friends: Phil and Deb from San Marcos, Texas, Billy and Flo from Alabama, Marc Rubin, from San Marcos and Titch in South Africa.

Co-referees from Texas: Chris Callan and Nora and James Wolfinger.

The Serendipity and Palacios Yacht Club members: Tommy, Ray, Norris, Mike, John and Darlene, Dennis, Truda, Dub, Donna, the Mutaseks, Hartwell, Robert , Cynthia , Richard, Teresa, George.

Kwagga players inTexas: Swazi, Reka, Dini, Hugo, Heidi, Jessica, Luke, Gert, Maryke and girls, Mark, Tania, Emma.

Friends in Port Lavaca, Olivia, Lolita, Edna and the whole Texas area: Ron and Kathleen Shott, Sue, Dick and Tres Traylor, the Toombs, the Larkins, Dan and Jackie, Carl and Debra Critendon, Cyril, the Weavers, John, Joan, Holly and Brooke Behrens, Will, Linda Johnson, Mike Mondrik, the Benavides family, Vernon and Joyce Ruddick , Fred and Cathy, Wanda and Wyle Harris, Jerry Lawrence from Fuzzy's.

The surveyor of IT, Mike Firestone.

Gary Woodring and his parents, Ken and Betty.

The Waters clan: Randy, Cella, Cory and Hank.

The other Tartan 37 owners: Jennifer Dark, Anne Sieling, Tom and Sandy Wells.

People around the States: Frankie Watson, Arnold Barrera, Doris and Lucian Russel, Juan Cobos, Judy Zwahr, FW Sellers, Dale Pigot, Bonnie Kimball, Ronnie Shea, Linda Rizpah, Carlynn Huffer, Kelly Diole, David Adriaan, Adeline and Sara Casper, Frank Tilley, Andy McComas, Doug Hillyer, Courtney of Palacios, Youngbuck, Alan Albrecht, Randy Hamilton, Cyrill, Linda Johnson, Melanie Gage, Jamie Jones, Shawn, the Haydens, Randall Stolze, Robert Steed and Ann Hynes, Griff Griffin, JV Helms, Danny, the Wright family.

Dave and Eileen Elley and kids.

Clive, ex Navy SEAL, and his wife Angelia.

PEOPLE WHO MADE A LASTING IMPRESSION ON ME

Panama

Jerry Logan, from Georgia, on a three year circumnavigation on their luxury 55 foot ketch

Reidar Lohne, a Norwegian, also on a solo circumnavigation.

Americo on his yacht called "Buzz" had docked right across from me and helped me when I had difficulty understanding people.

Kevin Worthington and his crew mates, Becky Low and Russ Evans, all from the UK. Americo, Kevin, Becky, Russ and I became close friends hanging out at the club and had many suppers together.

Later, our gang was joined by Paulie from Florida, living in Cairo, Egypt. He spoke fluent Greek, Spanish, Arabic and English and did most of the talking. He was sailing across the Pacific, through Suez to the Nile, in a 32 footer, called the Marvos.

Dracula, the taxi driver, his wife and daughter. Dracula carried my sail on his shoulders.

Peter, Roger and Carlos, transitting agents. The admeasurer, also a Carlos, who was very patient and to speed up the transfer.

Doug and Kyle Hopkins with their young girls, Eliza and Abigail, sailing into the south Pacific on "Estrela".

Frenchman, André Driollet and his son Chris with crewman Greg Lipman from Boston, USA who was on a 2 year circumnavigation on "Olive Oyl".

The then 43 year old Morgan Castle, from Durban SA, who had invited me onto his yacht, a Du Bois design by builder Pirini Navi, called the SQUALL.

Morgan's crew: Nathalie, the stewardess, from France; Kate, crew chef from UK; Craig, engineer from Australia; Charles, 1st mate from UK and deckhands, Holly and Nat from the USA. Then, all of them were in their 20's.

The Yacht club's boss, an elderly lady with a very bad temper, who chased me away from the office computer.

Des and Alison Des and Alison's on the Alii Nui.

Ron and Suzanne on Tapasya from South Carolina, USA.

Doug and Kyle Hopkins with their young daughters.

Russel Knight, whom I had met while transiting through the Panama Canal. Russell.

Two plastic thru-hull fittings that had been donated to me by Desmond during my stopover in Panama.

Pago Pago

Nicole Carbone who made sure that my family didn't panic when there was the burglary in American Samoa.

Fili Sagapolutele Samoa News Correspondent

Karyn Owebridge from Australia and Cliff Cummings from Texas onboard Odyssey.

Eric and Ann Nesbitt from Michigan onboard Temerarius.

Josh and Suzy onboard Suela. Cruising with them were Hank and Nicole. All of them from California. Hank and Nicole have since immigrated to New Zealand.

Ana, the Samoan woman who mended my sail and Richard her husband and their teenage daughters Lisa and Diane.

Mr. Lauli and Mrs. Wanda Alofa and their daughter Aitulagi of Malaeimi who made a generous donation which enabled me to continue my trip.

Forty two year old Marine patrol officer Michael Nix who acted as my translator.

Monica Miller News Director of 93 KHJ Radio in American Samoa.

The First Lady and the Chief of Police who hosted a dinner in my honour.

The Marine Police and the detectives who investigated the burglary.

Tiss and Candyman, the owners of Tisa's Barefoot Bar who presented me with a nice T-shirt, card and a donation.

Wolf Muller-Fabian and Barbara Miroslaw onboard CHINTA 2.

Duncan, Anita and their friends Michael and Bird who showed me the Island and went surfing with me.

Diane and Frank McCann. Frank took me to the fuel depot.

Marquesas

The man (whom I can not name because he requested to remain anonymous) who helped me to obtain diesel when nobody else wanted to sell any to me.

Thursday Island

Immigration officer Saliman Bin Juda who was very helpful with the paperwork and granted me a thirty day visa.

Andrea from Germany and Natalie from UK on a coastal cruise around Australia on a 60 footer whom I met at the Laundromat.

Dave Donnan, supervisor of customs operations, Torres Strait, at Thurday Island and the rest of the staff for their very professional manner and kind help whilst I was there. Thank you mates!!

Darwin

Sue and Kevin who arranged a berth for me at Tipperary Waters Marina.

Hans Kokholm who skippered Joy, a 10 meter yacht on a solo circumnavigation from Denmark.

Soren Andersen (a friend of Hans who studied in Australia.

Marine officer Diane who came aboard and we set out on the 2 miles through the shallow waters to the marina.

Peter and his wife Sylvia on their motor cruiser.

Steve and Jackie on Harlequin 2, Australians who were on a coastal cruise.

Store owners George and Carol who were kind enough to help me find a suite for my visiting family.

Tony, the welder who welded my bow light back onto a new location.

Peter the lockmaster (supervisor of the marina) who gave me a lift to the the alternator shop.

Dietmar Froboese on Anke 2 from Germany who did a quick dive down to retrieve the windpilot's stainless rod. Unlike me, Crocky the croc didn't never brothered him!

Tony's whose bicycle I borrowed to peddle over the hill to Fannie Bay and then followed the shoreline to Cullen Bay Marina.

Dan and Yolanda Hellier on circumnavigation via the Suez, onboard Jakana, who came over to help me download the electronic charts onto my spare laptop.

Officer Geoffrey who tracked my package to the airport.

Tony, Steve, Jackie and Canadians, David and Linda regularly visiting at the Dinah Beach Yacht Club.

German Andrea and her Swiss boyfriend who came to meet me on IT.

Peter and Sylvia at Tipperary Marina for their generosity and assistance during my stay.

David and Linda from Canada onboard Nimbus.

Sue Paulucci and the rest of the staff at customs for their kindness and assistance.

Single-handers: Leo Nigg from Switzerland on Moonlight. Jack Oldenburg (72 years old) from Sweden on his 31 footer Vindela. Steve from Minnesota on Hana and my new good old buddy Hans from Denmark on Joy.

Cruising couples: Steve and Jackie from OZ on Harlequin on a coastal cruise. Henry and Mattie from Hudson, Florida on 2 Extreme. Gunmar Erikson and Eva Troost from Sweden on Kahiba. David and Linda Seller from Canada on Nimbus. Anthony (Gatesy) and Ali Gates from OZ on Legs Eleven. Yolanda and Dan from OZ on Jakana. Frazer and German gal, Linda on a coastal cruise.

Friends made: German gal Andrea on a her way to Cairns for a month of diving and her Swiss boyfriend Beat on his way to Bali. Store owners George and Carol.

Lockmaster Peter and his very friendly wife, Sylvia, live-onboarders Tony the welder and Ana on her ferro-cement boat.

From customs: Sue, Diane, Geoffrey, Anthony and Bill. I will cherish fond memories, Always!

Rodriquez

The big game fisherman, Soudine, on board SEALINE.

Bill from Alaska on his second circumnavigation on Privateer and crew member Gilles from France.

Paul Draper, ex-Honorary British Consul, who runs the school and training centre for the deaf in Rodrigues.

The machine shop technicians who lend me a "tool" (combined screwdriver connected to a homemade adaptor to a socket set wrench or "spanner").

German, Derick Krehl, owner of Sealine and his girlfriend Birgit Rudolph.

Mrs. Susan Auguste (also British Honorary Consul) who translated my talk to the deaf kids into French.

Nicolas Finniss, an assistant to mechanics at the training centre.

The Frenchman, Guy Capon, Dominique Chatain and Jean- aques Guyon on board Utopia.

Dirk at the Chinese bar.

Durban

My late Mother's cousin, Uncle George van der Merwe, his twin sister, Betty, her husband Mannie and their daughter Pastor Adéle.

Kobus and Gavin, Dell computer technicians.

Aaron who did a magnificent cleaning job on IT.

Workshop owner Johan who drilled a new hole through the Willy's lever arm and the shaft.

Leon, producer and cameraman, from M-TV and his helper Leslie.

Alan Coetzer, his wife Zelda and their 17 year old son.

Vodacom's district manager and local Public Relations Manager, Richard and Michelle.

Titch Snyman my old skydiving buddy and very good friend.

East London

My niece Monique de Villiers and cousin Gillian Morris.

Lew Elias journalist from the Daily Dispatch.

Jack and Amy both are 100 ton certified skippers.

Cape Town

Ccousins Toni, Deon and Susandra.

Oom Pierre Volschenk and his wife Marie

Manager of the Royal Cape Yacht Club Trevor Wilkins.

Jane and Steve Theron.

Vodacom's representative, Michelle.

The Royal Cape Yacht Club's Commodore, Russel Vollmer.

Dad's long time friend, Charl van Rensburg.

Nico de Kock and his wife Jeanne and children Nico jr, Riana and Annette.

Steve.

Nephew Matthew Knott-Craig.

Miss Martha Schemper, principal and teacher at the Mary Kihn School.

Margie and Rob Johnson and their daughter Kate.

Jane and Steve Theron.

Cherry and Peter, Mike Young and his wife

Bertie Reed

Johan Meyer my dentist from Messina days

Zak Pretorius, my old school friend from Messina High School.

My Skydiving friends Langes, Anton, Terryl, Jeffrey and Ronel.

Susan Staak and Mrs Louw.

Douglas and Jennifer, two deaf friends at the RCYC.

Jack and Amy on Lady K.

Marjolyn and HB from Mary Kihn.

Eric and Alma Snijder.

An old friend, Thys Liebenberg

Long time neighbours Louw and Gwen Burger as well as their son, Boetie.

Morné du Plessis, my old std 6 and 7 school buddyand and his wife Lindy.

Jaco from in Waller Texas.

Long Pete the pilot

Thomas Boecker on his 30 foot sailboat

Jack from Australia.

Pieter and Leonie van der Merwe, my late Mother's brother and their friends Willem and Louina Malherbe. Nephews Helen, Bez, Jan and Piet van der Merwe.

Deafie friend Kobus van der Merwe and his girlfriend, Angel.

Jennifer, her son Paul and Douglas.

Rod Alexander.

St Helena

Skipper Conor Fogerty, his wife Kamelia, and crew member Jonathan Couture.

Customs agent Pamela Francis and harbour master, Barry Williams.

St Helena's radiomen, Ralph Peters and Gary Walters.

Ann from Ann's Place.

THE WHITE HOUSE

WASHINGTON

March 14, 2005

Mr. Charl de Villiers
Post Office Box 43
Point Comfort, Texas 77978

Dear Charl:

Congratulations on circumnavigating the globe.

You have led a remarkable journey that is great in accomplishments. I join your family and friends on commending you on your successful endeavor. Your strength and determination are an inspiration.

Laura and I send our best wishes to you and your family.

Sincerely,

George W. Bush

Office of the MAYOR

CITY OF PALACIOS

Proclamation

Whereas: Charl de Villiers is a member of the extended community of Palacios, Texas, and holds his Tartan 37, *Island Time* at Serendipity Resort and Marina.

WHEREAS, de Villiers has sailed around the world, solo, putting himself and his yacht against the vast oceans and their moods.

WHEREAS, he has set a world record by becoming the first deaf person in history to solo circumnavigate.

WHEREAS, he has shown great courage, vision, and tenacity, bringing a positive image of deaf and disabled to all people around the world.

WHEREAS, de Villiers has furthered the cause of the hearing impaired by demonstrating that a perceived handicap does not stop a person from fulfilling a dream.

WHEREAS, Palacios, Texas has been placed in a spotlight on the world stage as a result of this record setting voyage.

THEREFORE, by the power vested in me as Mayor of the City of Palacios, Texas, I hereby proclaim December 19, 2004, as Charl de Villiers Day and urge citizens of Palacios, Texas and the surrounding communities to reflect upon the incredible world record Charl de Villiers has set and to strive to bring their own dreams to fruition. Further, to support efforts of the deaf and disabled to be productive and respected members of our country.

John O. Connor, Mayor

Congressman Ron Paul
U.S. House of Representatives
Washington, D.C.

□ District Political Office:
837 West Plantation Dr.
Clute, TX 77531
(979) 265-1996

□ Capitol Political Office:
P.O. Box 3372
Falls Church, VA 22043

February 9, 2005

Mr. Charl De Villiers
C/o Palacios Chamber of Commerce
420 Main St.
Palacios, TX 77465

Dear Charl:

Congratulations on achieving the historic and record-setting circumnavigation of the world. What a wonderful and exciting trip that must have been!

It takes such an incredible person to do what you have done. I would like you to know that your bravery and strength are very inspiring to everyone around you.

I wish you and your family much happiness and many more adventures.

Again, Congratulations!

Sincerely,

Ron Paul

Ron Paul
U.S. House of Representatives
District 14, TX

THE STATE OF TEXAS

GOVERNOR

To all to whom these presents shall come, Greetings: Know ye, that this certificate is presented to:

Charl de Villiers

As Governor of Texas, I am honored to extend a Texas-sized welcome home as you complete your journey around the world.

Your inspirational voyage has been an adventure of which few can even conceive. Your tenacity and fortitude demonstrate that even the most ambitious goals can be made a reality. The path to success is paved with determination and diligence, and I have every expectation that you will continue to add to your legacy of excellence.

Anita joins me in sending best wishes for continued success.

THE STATE OF TEXAS

In testimony whereof, I have signed my name and caused the Seal of the State of Texas to be affixed at the City of Austin, this the 17th day of December, 2004.

Rick Perry

Rick Perry
Governor of Texas

NOTE FROM AUTHOR

After sustaining 80 percent burns in a freak braaivleis (barbeque) accident Charl's uncomplicated life took a dramatic turn and he had to face a new reality. Tackling the long road to recovery took him and his family into unchartered waters. But born out of this tragedy was his passion for sailing which, in turn, spawned his dream to one day sail solo around the world. However, it was only many years later that he had found the courage to pursue his goal.

Once his mind was made up, it took him six months to complete the necessary preparations and then he ventured onto the big and unknown blue.

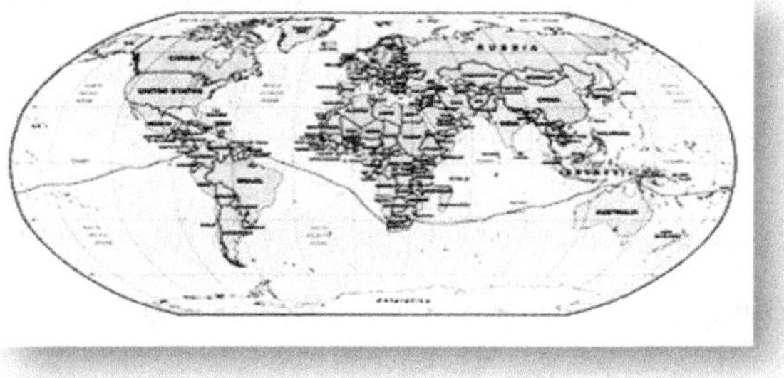

On the 6th of March 2004 he departed from Palacios, on the southern coast of Texas, on the first leg through the Gulf of Mexico and Caribbean seas to Cristóbal in Panama. From here he transitted the Canal and briefly anchored at Balboa.

On his second leg he had hoped to sail non-stop from Balboa to Australia's Thursday Island but on the way a few reality checks knocked on his door, forcing him to make two stopovers: Marquesas and American Samoa's Pago Pago Harbour. Regaining some lost hope he set out with renewed vigour, heading straight for Darwin.

The many trials and tribulations he had to face made him to tackle the third leg from Darwin to Cape Town with much more circumspection but, yet again en route, he had to make critical repairs at Rodriquez and Durban.

Departing from Durban he made a courtesy call at the Port of East London. Heading for Cape Town typical South African wild coast weather dowsed his over-optimism and he had to sit out a storm in Port Elizabeth. From here on he sailed around the Cape of Good Hope into the Atlantic Ocean and Table Bay.

On the fourth leg, heading back to Texas, he dashed in and out of St Helena and made a swift call to repair a mainsail at St Lucia. Sure that it was just a question of devouring the last sea miles, he headed north and west but, in the face of a bone-crashing storm, he almost didn't make it. Once out of the gale he traversed the oilrig-infested waters of the Gulf of Mexico to sail back to his original starting point in Palacios.

From departure on the 6th of March 2004 to return on the 19th of December 2004, his four legged epic journey took him two-hundred-and-eighty-eight days of which one-hundred-and-ninety-six were spent on the open seas and ninety-two on stopovers.

At the time many people around the world followed his daily progress and, as he transformed from novice to experienced sailor, they had encouraged him to hold on.

During the journey, the various experiences he had to endure, triggered *flashbacks* about his life. The trip around the world significantly changed his life. It was not only a brave adventure, a journey of discovery of the first deaf person to have done a solo circumnavigation but of a man living an action packed life while silently navigating the treacherous waters of a hearing society.

Nine years after the completion of his crusade another person claimed to be the first deaf person to have sailed solo around the world. This prompted Charl to finally pluck up enough courage to tell me his story and to set the record straight.

Maria de Villiers

Made in the USA
Middletown, DE
01 July 2025

77730050R00146